BOW AND ARROW

BOW AND ARROW

The Comprehensive Guide to Equipment, Technique, and Competition

Larry Wise

Illustrations by Jon Wert

STACKPOLE
BOOKS

Published by
STACKPOLE BOOKS
Cameron and Kelker Streets
P.O. Box 1831
Harrisburg, PA 17105

Printed in the United States of America

10 9 8 7 6 5 4 3 2 1

First edition

Cover illustration and design by Mark B. Olszewski

Library of Congress Cataloging-in-Publication Data

Wise, Larry.
    Bow and arrow : the complete guide to equipment,
technique, and competition / Larry Wise. — 1st ed.
          p.   cm.
    Includes bibliographical references and index.
    ISBN 0-8117-2411-5
    1. Archery.   2. Archery—Equipment and supplies.
I. Title.
GV1185.W57   1992
799.3′2—dc20   91-34325
                                                         CIP

CONTENTS

1

Choosing a Bow

THE BOW AND arrow changed the course of human existence. It provided a safer method of putting food on the table, and it swung the outcome of many wars.

Early man had to get his meat at close range, attacking with spears and knives. The bow and arrow enabled him to remain at a distance from his quarry so that he was less likely to become the hunted and more likely to return to his family with meat.

During the past four thousand years the bow and arrow has been used as a weapon of war by many nations to defend against invaders and to defeat other armies on their own soil. It has helped small armies defeat forces three to four times as big.

Today, about fifty thousand years after its invention, it is used by more than a million hunters annually to harvest game animals across the United States. About a tenth of that number participate in one of the many forms of tournament archery, including the Olympic archery events.

The bow and arrow started as a simple tool—a stick and a piece of vine were used to launch a smaller twig—but today it is very sophisticated. Bows and arrows have undergone more changes in the last fifty years than in their entire previous history. Today's bows and arrows involve high-tech design and materials; no wood is required.

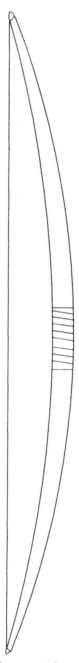

The longbow, the simplest of all bows, consists of a single piece of wood and a string. The ends of the wooden stave are shaved to form bending limbs, and a cloth or leather wrap is applied to the grip.

There are four basic types of bows: the longbow, the recurve bow, the compound bow, and the crossbow. You need to understand their designs and uses in order to decide which you want to use and how you want to shoot.

LONGBOWS

As a nine-year-old watching the adventures of Robin Hood on television, I was very impressed by his feats with a longbow. Several of my neighbors hunted deer with longbows and this, too, interested me. I had to have a bow — any bow — so I could shoot like they did.

My parents gave me a simple, straight, one-piece fiberglass bow with a plastic grip that was built so the bow could be shot from either side of the handle. Three wooden arrows made the set complete, and I was now an archer.

I stuffed a detergent box with cardboard to serve as a target and backstop. Close shots were easy to make, so I gradually moved farther away. As I launched the longer shots, I became fascinated by the flight of the arrow. Sometimes I would actually hit the box from the end of the driveway. That felt good; I was just like Robin Hood!

The longbow of Robin Hood was a good bit different from my first bow, however. The English longbow was 5 to 6 feet in length and had a draw weight of 80 to 90 pounds when pulled to a draw length of 30 inches. These were powerful bows that required great strength to use, and they could cast an arrow more than 250 yards.

In order for you to understand the next few chapters, here are a few terms you should know:

Traditional draw length is the distance at full draw from the back of the bow — the side away from you — to the end of the arrow that fits against the string, called the nock end.

Draw weight is the number of pounds of force required to pull the bowstring a given number of inches of draw length.

The *anchor point* is that location under the chin, on the jaw, or on the side of the face to which you draw the bowstring while aiming.

The Single-Piece Longbow

The English longbow was constructed of a single stave of yew wood. The leather-covered grip was narrower than the limbs and did not have a shelf on which to rest the arrow; instead the arrow was rested on the first knuckle of the bow hand. The tips of the limbs were sometimes made of horn or bone to add strength to that vulnerable area.

To ensure that the arrow would fly straight, the limbs of the bow were tillered. In this process the thicker limb would be shaved on its front or belly side to make it weaker so that it would bend the same amount as the other limb. Then the two limbs would perform nearly equally and wouldn't impart any strange flight characteristics to the arrow.

The bowyer would tiller the limbs as he built a bow. The best time to tiller was during the seasoning or drying of the limbs. Sometimes these bows would have to be seasoned for several years before they could be drawn and the final testing done. A well-made single-piece longbow could last a lifetime if cared for properly.

Longbows with an Arrow Shelf

Most newer longbows have a small shelf that takes the place of the knuckle as a resting spot for the arrow. Since the shelf is fixed on the bow, it adds a degree of accuracy because the arrow will remain in the same position throughout the shot.

Archers often cover the shelf area to make it soft and quiet. Some use leather; others use small pieces of feather to support the arrow. Frequently the side of the bow just above the arrow shelf is also covered with leather, felt, or some other material to soften and silence the arrow on its departure. This also aids in making small adjustments to the center-shot location of the arrow as it passes the bow handle (see chapter 7). Remember

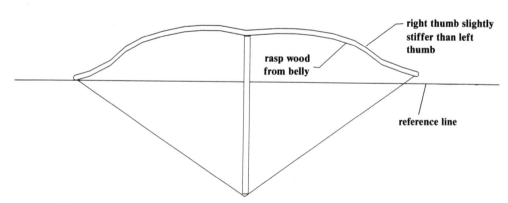

Tillering a bow is done with the bow drawn and held by a stick or board. Using a reference line perpendicular to the stick, wood is rasped from the stiffer limb until the desired balance is attained. Most longbows are tillered so the lower limb is slightly stiffer than the upper.

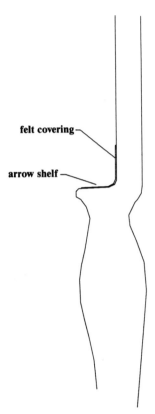

felt covering

arrow shelf

When the longbow has an arrow shelf, felt or leather is used to cover and quiet the shelf area.

that if you add layers of material to the side of the bow, this moves the arrow farther to the left and can affect its flight and your shooting accuracy.

Laminated Longbows

Most of today's longbow manufacturers use several layers of wood laminates backed with fiberglass, which greatly increases the strength and longevity of the bow.

The Longbow Force-Draw Curve

The force-draw curve of a bow is the visible record of the pounds of force that are exerted on the bowstring as the bow is being drawn. To make such

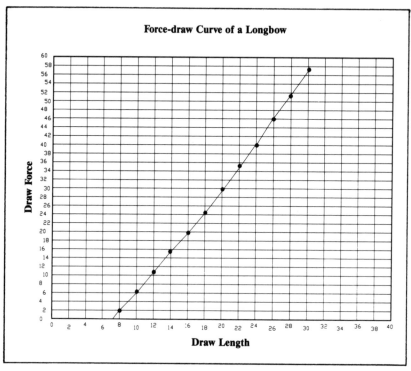

The force-draw curve of the longbow is usually a smooth, slightly concave-upward curve.

a record, all you need is a scale that can accommodate at least 60 pounds, a yardstick, a piece of quarter-inch graph paper, and a pencil.

Attach the yardstick to the bowstring with tape so that you'll be able to take a weight measurement at each inch throughout the draw stroke. A boat winch device works wonders in drawing the bow, but you can also do it by hand. The draw weight will start to register on the scale when the bow is drawn to about 9 inches. As you draw the bow in one-inch increments, record the increasing weight in two columns, with the draw weight beside each draw length. Once you've recorded these pairs of measurements for each inch from 9 up to 30, you can plot a graph.

Label the horizontal axis in inches of draw length, using a scale of one inch of draw per square on the graph paper. Label the vertical axis so that each square represents one pound of draw weight. Once you've plotted your pairs of measurements, you'll have an easy-to-read picture.

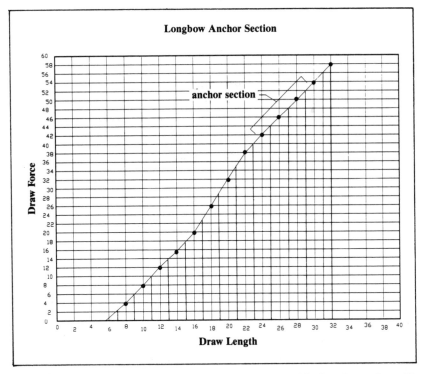

Your plot of the curve may look more like this one. It is difficult to be perfect with equipment bought at the hardware store. Counting the squares under the curve will give you the number of inch-pounds of energy stored in the bow. From 0.8 squares in the column between 6 and 7 inches of draw to 24.5 squares between 27 and 28 inches of draw the total number of squares is approximately 269. In this graph each square represents 2 inch-pounds, or 538 total inch-pounds. Five hundred thirty-eight divided by 12 inches per foot is 44.8 foot-pounds of energy stored by drawing the bow to its optimum 28 inches.

In the case of the longbow, your results will be very close to a straight line with just a slight curve upward like the right half of a smile. A better-designed longbow may have a force-draw curve that turns slightly downward at the ends, showing that a little more energy has been stored.

The feel of the longbow during the draw cycle is one of almost constant increase. The farther the bow is drawn, the more weight is needed to draw the bowstring. The increase in weight is fairly steady until the end of the draw cycle (28 to 30 inches) is reached. Here the weight increases at a higher rate and the bow begins to feel extremely stiff. This higher rate of increase is called *stacking*. If you are lucky, your draw length will allow you to reach your anchor point before this stacking takes place.

The Stored Energy of a Longbow

Stored energy is the amount of energy contained in the limbs when they're at full draw. When the string is released, some of this energy is passed on to the arrow and some of it is used to move the parts of the bow and to overcome friction. The energy required to draw the bow is slightly more than what is stored by the limbs since friction and vibrations occur during the draw stroke and energy is needed to overcome these forces.

The stored energy of the bow is represented by the area between the force-draw curve and the horizontal axis. To determine the area under the curve, count the squares on the graph paper between the curve and the horizontal axis, estimating the total of the partial squares. Your result is the approximate total number of inch-pounds of energy stored in the limbs of the bow. Dividing the number of inch-pounds by twelve will give you the stored energy in foot-pounds.

You can compare the stored-energy value only between bows with the same draw length and peak weight; if those measurements aren't the same, a comparison would not be valid. What remains to be calculated is the efficiency with which the longbow transfers its stored energy to the arrow. This subject, termed *bow efficiency*, is discussed later in the chapter.

How to Order a Longbow

The first item of business before you order any type of bow is to measure your draw length. If you don't have a bow of your own yet, try a friend's or one from a pro shop. Have a friend watch as you draw an arrow. When you feel comfortable at full draw, your friend should mark your arrow at the arrow-rest mounting hole (directly above the point where your bow hand presses against the grip) and at a point even with the back of the bow (the edge of the bow farthest from you). The distance from the inset of the nock to the mark at the arrow rest is your true draw length and to the mark for the back of the bow is your traditional draw length.

Some knowledge of the force-draw curve of a bow you plan to buy is helpful. If the bow has any stacking in its draw stroke, make sure it occurs at a point beyond your anchor position. If you have a traditional draw length of 28 inches and the stacking begins to take place at 29 inches, you will enjoy shooting the bow more than if the reverse were true.

If you buy a custom-made longbow, you may not have the opportunity of testing before buying. If such is the case, you should still plot the force-draw curve so that you might make adjustments in your anchor or some other part of your form to better take advantage of the bow's characteristics. Your bowyer should be able to build your bow with the proper draw-stroke characteristics, however. Ask about this important point before agreeing to have a bow custom built.

It's always best to test before buying. This is especially true for the beginner purchasing his or her first longbow. Find a dealer or another archer who is willing to let you test-shoot several bows before you buy one. There are always people at local clubs and archery shops who are willing to help. That's one of the best things about archery!

When you find a draw length and draw weight that feel good to you, buy that bow or order one with those same specifications. If you want to shoot accurately and consistently, it's very important to be comfortable while you're shooting.

RECURVE BOWS

Only in the last fifty years have bows been developed that exceed the shooting capabilities of the Turkish bows of the fifteenth and sixteenth centuries. The Turks shot composite bows built of sinew, horn, wood, and tendon glue. These bows had great strength and durability and could shoot arrows more than 700 yards.

The Turkish bow was short limbed and reflexed. The reflex was so great that the limbs were bent as much backward before the string was attached as they were bent forward after the bow was strung. These short, highly stressed limbs could shoot lightweight arrows long distances time and time again and not break because of the superior design and materials.

As the gun became the predominant weapon of war in the sixteenth century, these bows and the art of building them began to decline. Although archery remained a Turkish sport for many years, fewer and fewer armies needed bows and arrows and the number of bowyers gradually decreased. A short revival took place in the mid-nineteenth century, and this supplied us with much of our knowledge about the earlier Turkish composite reflex bow.

About a hundred years later, in the 1950s, a bow of a similar design — the recurve bow — grew in popularity. Improved materials and laminating techniques made it possible for bowyers to build a recurve bow for the

average archer. The recurve remains popular today and serves as an intro-
duction for most newcomers to the great sport of archery.

Modern Recurves

My second bow was a recurve that my dad brought home in 1958 from a
local hardware store. He bought two of them—one for me and one for
himself—and we were suddenly into bowhunting. Both were one-piece
fiberglass bows with molded plastic grips. This bow, like my other one,
could be shot from either side of the handle. I was really excited, especially
since Dad was going to shoot too.

The single-piece fiberglass was really tough and not very expensive,
and it wasn't long before other kids in the neighborhood had bows like it. I
think we invented bowfishing all on our own that next summer, and if the
farmer next door ever reads this book, he'll know who knocked down
about two hundred corn stalks while playing war games. That bow lasted
a long time and eventually got passed along to another member of the
family. It may still be in use today.

Not many years passed before Dad bought himself a new bow. This
one was a wood-laminated bow with fiberglass layers on the front and
back. The handle blank was cut from walnut, and the interior layers of the
limbs were laminations of rock maple. Fiberglass was then laminated to
the maple layers to form the strong outside surfaces.

This layered type of bow was strong and lightweight. The limbs were
able to bend and unbend more quickly than heavier materials, and less of
the bow's stored energy was required to move them. This enabled more
energy to go toward propelling the arrow, which is the main advantage of
the laminated bow over the thicker- and heavier-limbed fiberglass bow of
the fifties.

The Three-Piece Takedown Bow

In the 1950s, Bear Archery Company founder Fred Bear developed the
takedown bow—a new type of recurve hunting bow that continues to be a
preferred design to this day. It was developed to make the hunting bow
easier to transport when not being used. The wooden handle was fitted
with metal mounting brackets to hold the laminated recurve limbs securely. You could remove the limbs by releasing the brackets and store the
bow in a small carrying case.

The takedown bow appealed to a large number of hunters and to
tournament archers. This appeal has resulted in many improvements,

Parts of a Recurve Bow

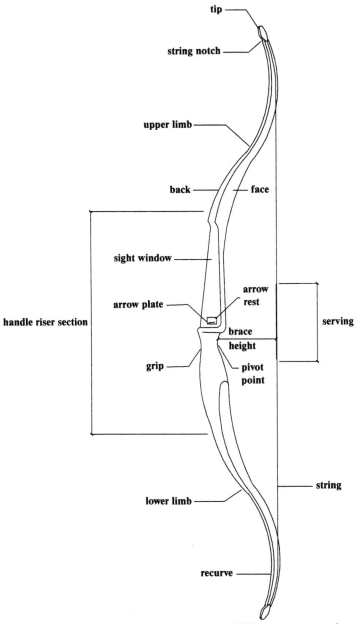

The modern wood-handled recurve bow stores a little more energy than most longbows and is slightly easier to hold and aim at full draw.

Takedown Recurve Bow

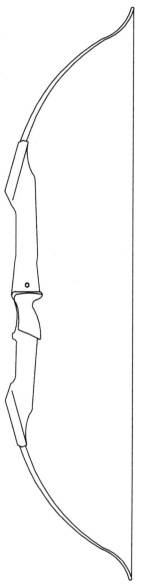

The present-day version of the three-piece takedown recurve bow has a metal handle riser and two limbs that can be easily mounted to the riser when the bow is not strung.

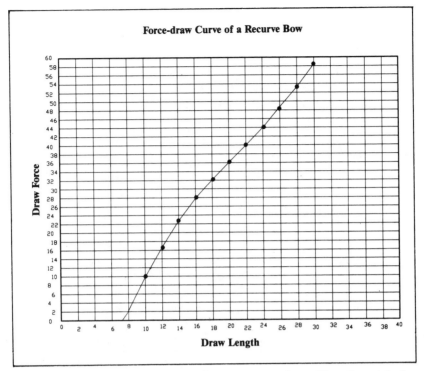

Recurve bows have force-draw curves that are concave down (like a frown) during the first half of the draw. The remainder of the draw curve is concave up and creates a sweet spot for anchoring, aiming, and releasing.

including a change to metal handles in the sixties and seventies, which has led almost all recurve-bow manufacturers to produce takedown bows.

Another big advantage of the takedown design is the ease with which you can test many different limb combinations. By simply replacing one or both limbs, you can test a completely different bow. Sometimes this can help you find a great shooting combination, and in tournament archery that is the ultimate goal.

The Force-Draw Curve of the Recurve Bow
The force-draw curve of the longbow, discussed earlier, depicts a draw weight that increases at a faster and faster rate. In other words, the curve was slightly concave upward throughout. The force-draw curve of the

recurve bow is not concave upward everywhere; the bow stores a little more energy and is smoother to draw at the end of the draw stroke.

The limb tips of the recurve are usually designed so that near the middle of the draw cycle they begin to unbend. This causes the rate of increase in the holding weight on the string to lessen, so the draw weight increases faster than that of a longbow during the first half of the draw cycle and then lessens slightly to match the force-draw curve of the longbow.

The advantage of the recurve bow is a slight increase in the amount of stored energy and a more pronounced sweet spot at the full-draw position. More stored energy gives the recurve a potential for more arrow speed. The lessening of the rate of increase in draw weight at full draw makes the

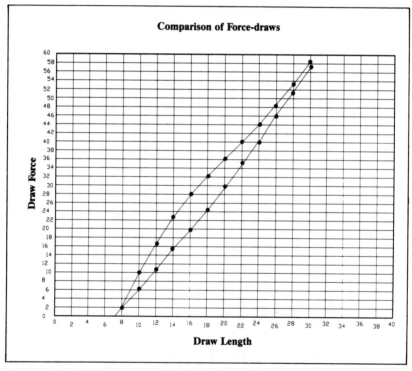

A comparison of the recurve with the longbow shows a slight increase in stored energy because of the steeper increase in weight at the beginning of the draw stroke.

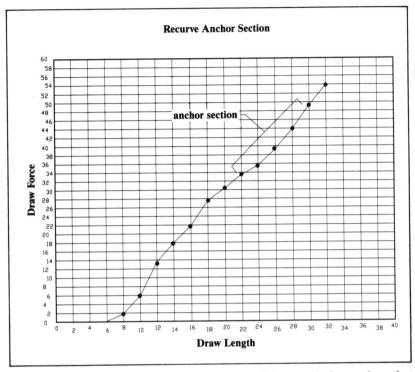

Recurve Anchor Section

Your graph may look like this one—not perfect. This curve is from a bow that should be shot with an anchor point that is 26 to 28 inches from the bow handle.

recurve easier to hold and aim than the longbow. Both explain the popularity of the recurve bow.

How to Order a Recurve

Recurves, like most other bows, should be ordered according to your traditional draw length. A recurve's draw weight usually appears on the bow; for example, a single line of print might read 50# at 28″ or 60# at 30″. The weight needed to draw the bow to a given distance is written so that you can determine which bow is closest to what you need. Very seldom will you draw exactly the distance stated on a bow. Therefore, you must draw and shoot the bow to test its feel and draw weight at your anchor. Most dealers will let you test-shoot their bows; after all, satisfied customers return with friends to do more business.

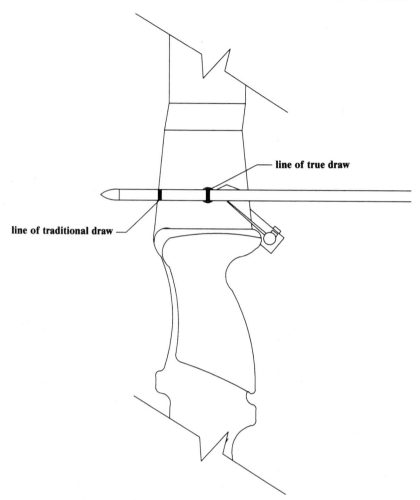

line of true draw

line of traditional draw

Measure draw length while you are at full draw. From the nock to the arrow rest is true draw, while the distance to the back of the bow is traditional draw.

To be sure of the draw weight of a bow, you can test it by hooking the string to a scale and pulling the bow to your full-draw position. The weight recorded on the scale when the bow reaches your draw length is the weight you feel on the string at your anchor point. Be sure of what you are getting when you order a recurve bow because there is very little you can do to change its draw weight.

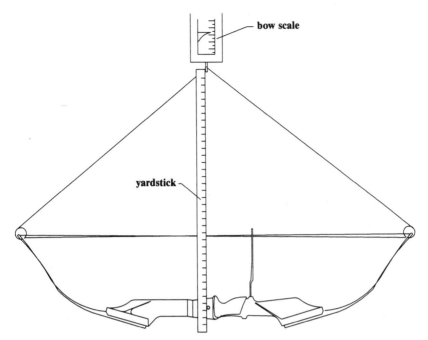

Use a yardstick attached to the bowstring and a weight scale to determine the draw weight of any bow at any draw length.

COMPOUND BOWS
General Construction

Since its development in the midsixties, the compound bow has used a higher technology than any previous bow design. The bow's eccentric wheel system, round or cam shaped, requires highly accurate machine work as well as the engineering to make it function properly. Because this system bends the limbs far less than those of the recurve or the longbow, they must be shorter, stiffer, and more durable.

The Handle Riser

A handle with superior strength is needed to hold the stiff limbs and eccentric system together. The best material for this job is some kind of metal. Magnesium and aluminum are both ideal. Properly designed, a magnesium handle riser is strong enough to withstand the torque generated by the compound system and also light enough to be carried without

Parts of a Compound Bow

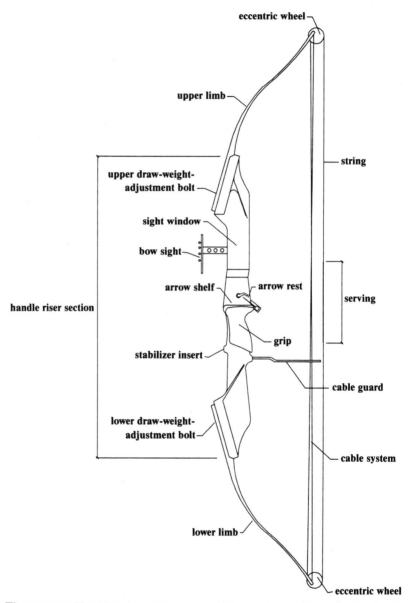

The most notable difference of the compound bow is the eccentric wheel and cable system. The off-center wheel axles allow weight to shift from the bowstring to the cables halfway through the draw stroke so that you can hold less weight on the string at full draw.

much effort. Aluminum is stronger than magnesium but heavier. Either material, however, gives excellent shooting results.

Other design features that are distinct advantages are also possible with these metal handles. Because of the limited strength of wood, the sight window and arrow shelf of a wooden handle can't be cut near its center line. Consequently, the arrow has to bend around the handle. A

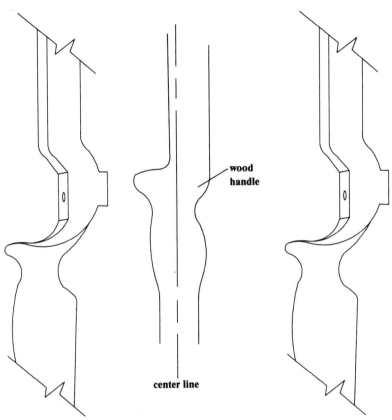

wood handle

center line

Aluminum or magnesium has enough strength to allow the arrow shelf area of the handle to be cut away through the center line as shown in this tunnel design.

The wooden riser must not be cut away through the center line since it does not have the strength to withstand the force exerted by the compound wheel/cable system.

Most compound bows have the arrow rest area cut away through the center line of the handle. The arrow can be placed in this line and shot through the center of the handle.

metal handle, however, has enough strength to allow complete center-line cutaway so that the arrow can be launched through the exact center of the handle. The center-shot, or tunnel, handle enables archers to achieve good arrow flight with less work, obtaining relatively high accuracy without a lot of high-tech training.

Other materials are being developed for bow handles. The new high-tech composite materials, some containing carbon, are stronger than magnesium and have the same density. Future materials will be lighter and stronger and will do an even better job than magnesium.

Most metal handles are molded. The process is rather expensive, costing nearly one hundred thousand dollars for each mold. The new composite materials are also molded and cost about the same to make. The only alternative to molding is to machine a handle from a piece of metal. This is time-consuming and therefore more expensive per handle.

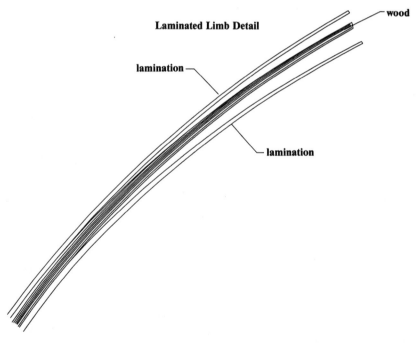

Laminated Limb Detail

wood

lamination

lamination

Many compound limbs are made by gluing three layers of wood and fiberglass together.

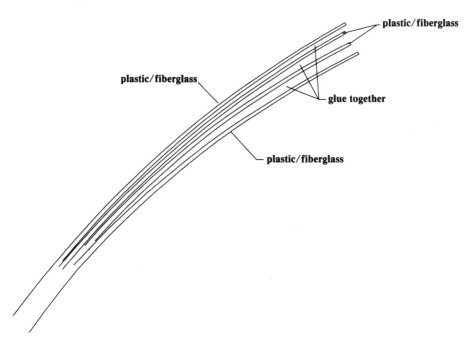

plastic/fiberglass

plastic/fiberglass

glue together

plastic/fiberglass

More and more compound bow limbs are being built using four or five layers of fiberglass-reinforced plastic.

Some bow manufacturers make machined handles as a specialty item for those who are willing to pay a little more for their equipment.

The Limbs

While the handle provides the skeleton for the compound bow, the limbs provide the muscle. Bow limbs store energy when they are bent as the bowstring is pulled. The energy is transferred to the arrow upon the string's release. Compound bow limbs are most commonly made of layers of wood laminations and plastic with fiberglass reinforcement. These materials have strength and elasticity and store and release energy with relatively high efficiency.

How well the limb does its job depends not only on what materials are used but also on how those materials are put together. Several thin layers of fiberglass laminated around a layer of wood creates a strong, flexible, and resilient limb. Some manufacturers laminate three, four, or five layers of fiberglass together to make high-strength limbs.

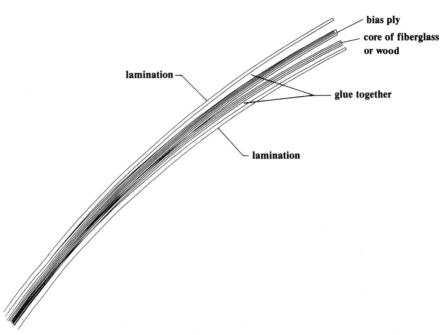

While most layers of limb laminates have the fiberglass running one direction, some have one layer of bias fiberglass, which has a crossing pattern to add resistance to torque.

What the future holds in the area of limb materials is almost unlimited. As new resins and fibers are invented, new combinations for bow limbs will be molded, laminated, and tested. Carbon fibers are used to add flex strength to limbs, while bias ply layers of glass and carbon are used to decrease limb splitting. Combinations that shoot better and don't break will be used and the others will be discarded.

I recommend that a beginner stick with materials that have proven their durability. Most beginners do not have the skill level to see the improved grouping characteristics of some of the new and expensive materials. Buy a bow that performs well for you, is not too expensive, and can easily be resold to another beginner.

There are two basic shapes of compound limbs. The straight limb has been used the longest, dating back to the late 1960s. The recurve compound limb, first seen in the 1970s, did not become widely used until the

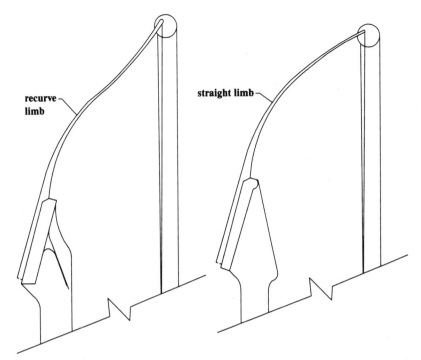

Two basic designs are used to make limbs: the recurve on the left and the straight on the right. Both work well on the compound bow.

mid-1980s. Most compound-bow manufacturers today produce both styles of limbs.

Recurve and straight limbs function a little differently depending on how the limb tip is constructed. If a thick wedge of limb material is laminated into the recurve limb tip, the tip will bend little or not at all. If the tip does not bend, then the working area of the limb is reduced to the short straight section between the wedge in the limb tip and the fade-out wedge in the butt end of the limb. In other words, the recurve design is for looks only.

Other recurve limbs on compound bows are wedged only in the axle area and not through the recurve bend of the limb. In these cases the recurve of the limb unbends as the bow is drawn to full draw. This unbending adds some smoothness to the draw cycle but also adds another factor that can have an effect on the tuning process of the bow. If the tips unbend differently, the bow may not shoot accurately or consistently. With today's technology, however, recurve limbs are made with great consistency and only a very few highly skilled archers would be able to discern any differences between limbs.

The straight limb may also be designed in one of two ways. The tip of the limb will have either a long, thick wedge or a short, thin wedge through which the axle is mounted. The longer wedge reduces the working area of the limb to four or five inches, while the shorter wedge provides a longer working area. The longer working area should make a smoother-drawing and more efficient bow, but regardless of this, most top-of-the-line compound bows perform well.

The key to building a good limb is that the tip area must not be overloaded with a lot of bulk and weight. A large tip wedge may add strength, but the extra weight decreases efficiency and, ultimately, arrow speed. A balance must be maintained to ensure both strength and efficiency.

Since about 1979 the compound limb has been designed to allow the axle to run through the ends of the limb tip so that the wheel could be mounted in a cutout slot in the end of the limb. This split-limb design did not require the use of a hanger bracket to hold the axle on to the limb and

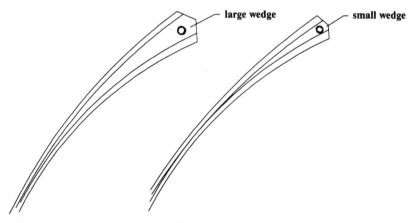

Some compounds have hanger-bracket axle mounts attached to the limb tips, while others have wedges laminated in the limb tips that can be drilled to receive the axles.

thereby decreased the weight on the limb tip. The end result is enhanced arrow speed.

The down side of this design feature was the weakening of the end of the limb and the need to protect against lateral split. To prevent limb split, stress-distributing washers or buttons have been placed in the V of the limb so that the two tip ends will not bend differently. The yoke harness cable system also prevents the tip ends from bending differently.

The limb's butt end is designed to prevent bending so that the limb can be mounted to the bow handle by a single bolt. A limb pivot-rocker is placed between the limb and the handle to fix the position of the limb so that it does not move left or right as it bends. The limb bolt can then be

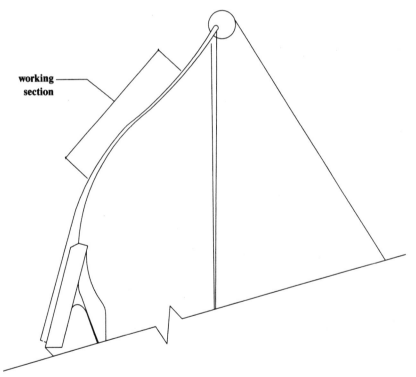

Not all of the limb bends during the draw stroke of the compound bow. Wedges in either end of the limb reduce the working area of the limb.

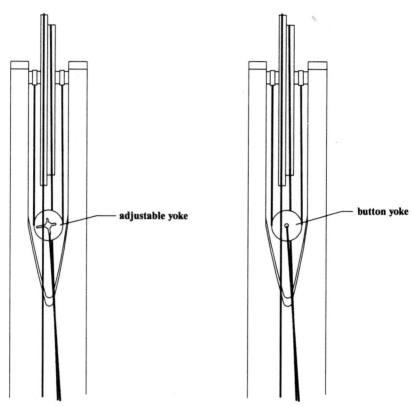

To prevent the limb tips from twisting, a yoke system is added to some compound bows. The yoke divides the force on the power cable so that equal amounts of pull are hooked to either side of the wheel.

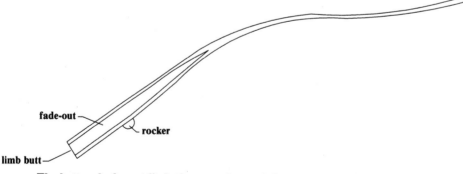

The butt end of most limbs has a wedge or fade-out to strengthen the end that attaches to the bow handle. A rocker is mounted under the butt of the limb to provide a fulcrum and to prevent the limb from pulling out of the handle.

tighten bolt for more weight   **loosen bolt for less weight**

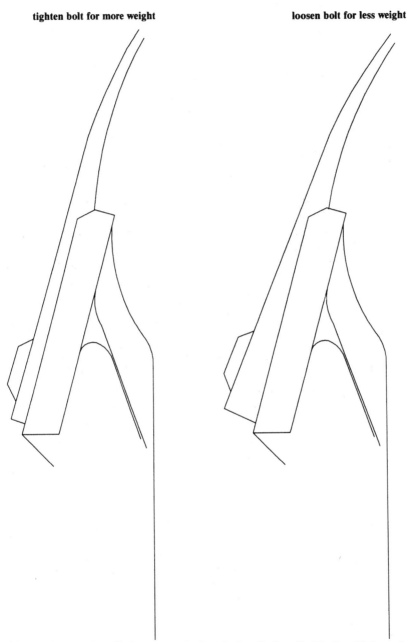

Most compound bow limbs are attached to the handle by a limb bolt, which can be used to adjust the peak weight of the bow. Turning the bolt inward will cause the draw weight to increase.

adjusted to increase or decrease the amount the limb bends during the draw stroke, which in turn changes the maximum or peak weight of the compound bow. As will be mentioned in the tuning section for compounds, this weight-adjustment feature greatly increases one's ability to achieve good arrow flight with a given size arrow.

The Eccentric Wheel

The function of an eccentric wheel is to provide a means of transferring holding force from the string of the compound to the power cables. Since a great amount of torque and force are involved, the wheel must be made of a material that will withstand the punishment. Most are machined from round stock aluminum alloy, although a few are molded. Many of the less expensive bows on the market use molded plastic wheels, which offer enough strength but at low cost. Of course, the best material is aluminum.

There are almost as many wheel designs as there are compound bows. The variations of diameter, shape, step-down, and let-off give an unlimited number of combinations. I will begin with two categories of shape: round and nonround. The round eccentric wheel creates a smoother draw stroke than nonround shapes do. The round wheel causes a gradual increase in peak weight, then a gradual drop-off to the holding weight. This feature lends itself nicely to tournament archery, where consistent comfort over a long period is necessary.

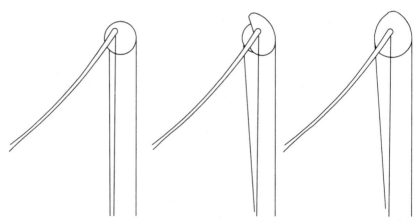

Eccentric wheels come in many diameters ranging from one to three inches. Their shapes vary from round to exaggerated cams.

Nonround shapes cause the draw weight to increase rapidly to peak weight, stay there for two to six inches, and then quickly drop off to the holding weight. The jerky motion that results is at first unsettling, but the archer can still become quite comfortable with a nonround, or cam-shaped, wheel. Usually the novice starts with the round wheel and later, after developing good shooting form, may switch to a cam.

A prominent feature of the eccentric wheel is step-down — the reduced diameter of the side of the wheel that the power cable wraps around while the bow is drawn to full draw. With the smaller diameter of the working side of the wheel, the bow limb bends less than it would otherwise. Less bend during the draw stroke translates to more efficiency and ultimately more arrow speed.

The amount of step-down determines how much the limb bends during the draw stroke. The smaller the diameter of the cable side of the wheel, the less the limb bends and the more efficient the bow becomes since the limb does not move as far on the power stroke after the bowstring is released. If the limb bends very little, however, it will have to be thicker to provide the desired draw weight, and when a limb gets too thick it becomes slower. A balance must be maintained to have the best of both sides of this design feature.

Let-off refers to the difference in pounds of draw weight between peak weight and the lower holding weight. This is expressed as a percent of the peak weight. For example, a bow that has a peak weight of 60 pounds and drops 36 pounds to a holding weight of 24 pounds has a let-off of 60 percent.

The amount of let-off is determined by two design features of the eccentric wheel. The more obvious is the location of the axle hole relative to the center of the wheel: The farther the axle is from the center, the greater the let-off. The distance between the track of the power cable and the axle hole also affects let-off.

Since eccentric wheels must accommodate some kind of cable, a method of attachment must be designed into the wheel. When steel cables are used on a bow, they are most often run through a hole drilled laterally through the wheel and are locked in place by a setscrew. Some steel cables are held in place by a swage placed in a recessed groove in the wheel. Other times a post is machined into the cable side of the wheel and either steel cables or Fast Flight string cables can be attached by loops on the ends of the cables. This makes changing cables quite easy.

If the steel cable is held in place by a setscrew, the end of the cable that wraps around the string side of the wheel must have an anchor molded

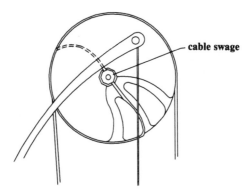

cable swage

Some eccentric wheels fasten the cable by using a setscrew to lock it in place or a swage to hold it in the wheel.

on its end to receive the bowstring. This anchor is usually made of a zinc alloy. The end loop of the bowstring is attached to a small hook on the anchor and can be changed with ease using any kind of bow press.

If the post concept is used on both the string side and the cable side of the wheel, the string anchor can be eliminated. The bowstring must have an end loop served with Fast Flight serving thread, which can be attached to the post. The serving will enable the string to withstand the wrapping and unwrapping that takes place as the eccentric wheel rotates while the bow is drawn and released.

The Bowstring

The most popular material for bowstrings over the last forty years has been Dacron. With its strength and durability, it can well withstand the punishment dished out by the flexing limbs of a compound. The string market has greatly changed, however, with the recent development of Fast Flight bowstring material because of its strength and damping properties. Fast Flight, although smaller in diameter, is rated at 80 pounds test per strand, while Dacron B-50 is rated at only 50 pounds test.

Fast Flight is made from high-performance polyethylene through a process that arranges the molecules in a parallel alignment. This gives it great ability to dampen the vibrations of the limb after the bowstring is released, thereby increasing bow efficiency and adding speed to the arrow.

With its great strength, Fast Flight can also be used to replace the steel wire power cables; it has no problem handling the forces applied to it

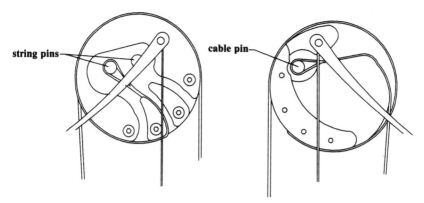

Many eccentric wheels are designed to receive the Fast Flight String material as cables by having an anchor pin near the center on both sides of the wheel.

on the power side of the wheel, which can be three to four times as high as those on the bowstring. Fast Flight is highly resistant to abrasion and cutting, so string and cables made of the material can be used on hunting bows with little risk of being sliced with a broadhead. It also frays very little through normal use, so it keeps a good appearance for a long time.

The only disadvantage of the material when used for cables on a compound is that the two Fast Flight cables used on any given bow will not be exactly the same length. This is true of steel wire cables to a lesser degree. If the two cables are simply twisted twenty to thirty times before installation, however, they can be made the same length. One cable may need to be twisted more times than the other and a bow-press device will have to be used, but it can be done without much time or difficulty.

The Two-Wheel Design

The most prominent compound design on the market today is the two-wheel variety. The two-wheel compound, introduced in the early seventies, has taken over the market because it is simple both to build and to use and is highly efficient. With one wheel mounted on the end of each bow limb, it has a smooth, streamlined look and little bulk to carry around on the target range or in the woods. The power cable attaches one wheel directly to the axle of the other to complete a closed-circuit system. As long as both cables have been made the same length, the wheels will always be synchronized when they roll over.

The two wheels can be round or cam shaped. With the round wheel, the bow draws and shoots very smoothly. Cam-shaped wheels on the limb tips will yield more stored energy and hence greater arrow speed when the bow is drawn to full draw, but that energy comes at a price: It takes more effort to draw the bow.

Before the advent of the two-wheel compound, four wheels were used to store the energy in the limbs of the compound bow. Two eccentric wheels were mounted on the limb tips and two idler pulleys near the middle of the limbs. Sometimes a second pair of idler pulleys would be mounted near the ends of the handle riser.

With the idler pulleys, more energy was stored in the bow limbs and the user could make fine adjustments to the draw length of the bow and to eccentric-wheel synchronization. The ends of the cable system were not attached to the axle of the opposite wheel but to an adjustment device on the handle; thus the cable length could be changed by the simple turning of an adjustment screw or bolt. By turning just one adjustment screw, the archer could make one wheel roll over differently than the other and the bow could thus be tuned.

The four-wheel compound was great to tune if you were technical minded, but most archers didn't like the idea of all the extra parts and adjusting involved. The two-wheel compound offered a means of escaping the high-tech world: There was no need to adjust eccentric synchronization since that was already set by the factory.

Several bows on the market today use a slight variation on the four-wheel design: The eccentric cam is mounted on the handle riser instead of the limb tips. The results are a handle that vibrates very little when the compound is shot and a bow that has a bit more stored energy and shoots slightly faster than the two-wheel compound. The bow tends to look more high tech with the wheels mounted on the handle. Its only drawback is the extra weight added to the handle.

Force-Draw Curves of Compounds

The force-draw curve of the compound bow shows three phases in the draw cycle. First, the draw weight increases rapidly until peak weight is reached. Next, the eccentric wheel causes a shift in weight from the string side of the wheel to the cable side, and you feel a reduction in weight on the bowstring. This let-off, or downward slope in the curve, continues until the lowest holding weight is reached. This low-weight section of the curve is called the valley. It is in this valley section that you need to anchor and release the bowstring. You can anchor anywhere within the valley, which is

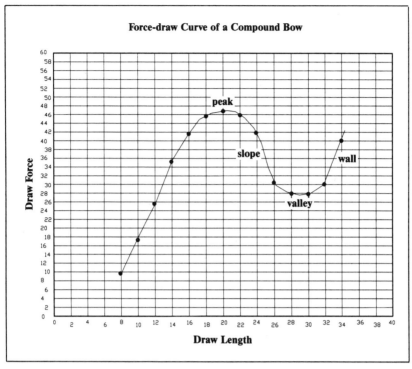

Force-draw Curve of a Compound Bow

Draw Force

Draw Length

Because the axle of the eccentric wheel is not in the center, the force-draw curve of the compound moves through three phases. The sharp increase in weight at the beginning leads to a peak weight, which is followed by a slope or let-off into the lowest weight, called the "valley." Beyond this area the weight increases very quickly to form the "wall."

usually one-half to one inch long, and feel confident that the arrow will get a smooth start at the same weight. If you shoot out of the valley, any change in your anchor will result in a different-weighted start for your arrow.

The diameter of the eccentric wheel determines the length of the draw stroke of the bow — larger wheels have longer draw strokes — and once the effective length of the draw stroke has been used and the end of the valley has been reached, the weight on the bowstring begins to increase again. Now the third and final phase of the draw cycle has been reached. It is called "the wall" because it seems as though something is keeping you from drawing any farther. When the bow is drawn 2 or 3 inches past the valley, the weight increases 20 to 40 pounds in one inch. Such a rapid increase makes it feel as if the bow is simply stopping at the end of the valley.

Because of this third phase of the draw stroke, you must know and understand the force-draw curve of the compound. Without some knowledge of the phases of the curve, you will not know how to order a bow that fits your draw length or how to adjust and tune a bow to fit you better and to shoot tighter groups of arrows. Nothing is more frustrating than to aim and release a good shot and have it hit somewhere other than where it was aimed.

The Round-Wheel Force-Draw Curve

The force-draw curve of the round eccentric wheel is the smoothest of all compound bows in production. It begins with an increase to peak weight that is spread over the first 8 to 10 inches of the draw stroke—the first half of the distance to the valley. Once peak weight is reached, the curve begins to drop off toward the lower holding weight in the middle of the valley. This drop takes another 8 to 10 inches, depending on how the draw length of the bow is set. The valley is usually reached between 24 and 32 inches of draw.

The round eccentric in most cases has the longest valley of any compound. A long valley makes the bow easier to shoot and to tune because less consistency is required on the part of the shooter. You can anchor and release within a region as long as one inch of draw stroke and still make accurate shots with good arrow flight. The length of the valley depends on the diameter of the wheel: The larger wheels (2.5 to 3 inches) have longer draw strokes and valleys.

If the round-wheel compound is drawn beyond the valley, the weight on the string begins to increase because the wheel is no longer transferring weight from the string to the cables. Once the effective length of the draw stroke has been used, the compound bow becomes a very short-limbed longbow and all the work required to draw it farther must be done by the archer.

Drawing the compound bow beyond the valley is uncomfortable and produces poor shooting results, so you must make sure you have the correct size eccentric so that you reach the valley when you are at full draw. If not, you will not be able to perform at your best and the bow will not perform at its best. The correction for this situation is a draw-length adjustment, which is covered in chapter 7.

The Half-Cam Force-Draw Curve

The half-cam eccentric wheel is designed so that the string side of the wheel is round but the cable side is slightly cam shaped. The result is a wheel that still feels relatively smooth but stores slightly more energy than a purely round one. The increase in stored energy usually produces an increase in arrow speed.

The force-draw curve generated by the half-cam does not look much different from that of the round wheel except for the width of the curve on either side of peak weight. The cam shape on the cable side of the wheel causes the draw weight on the string to increase more rapidly than it would with a round wheel. The weight also stays near peak longer. The net result is a broader curve around peak weight and more stored energy.

The Full-Cam Force-Draw Curve

Both sides of the full-cam eccentric wheel are nonround, so more energy is stored in the limbs as the bow is drawn. The end result may be a faster arrow, but the bow does not feel as smooth as one with a round wheel and the archer has to put more energy into the draw stroke.

The force-draw curve of the full-cam is significantly different from that of a round wheel in that the draw weight increases much more rapidly to peak weight, stays at peak longer, and drops into a shorter valley much later in the draw stroke.

The sharp increases and decreases in draw weight generated by the full-cam require that you be more particular about setting the draw length and about your shooting form. If the draw length is not set within one-fourth inch of your true draw length, you will not get the best shooting results nor will you feel comfortable. The narrow valley of the cam bow will lead most inexperienced shooters to anchor where it is set rather than where they should be anchoring to feel comfortable.

Stored Energy of the Compound Bow

As mentioned before, stored energy is the amount of energy contained in the limbs when they are at full draw. When the string is released, some of this energy is passed on to the arrow and some of it is used to move the parts of the bow and to overcome friction. The energy required to draw the bow is slightly more than what is stored by the limbs, since friction must also be overcome in the draw stroke.

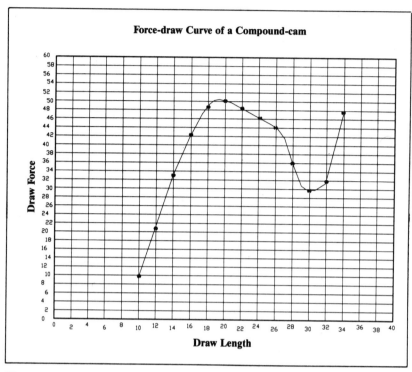

The cam-shaped wheel is designed to increase the amount of energy stored in the limbs by keeping the bow near peak weight for a longer duration through the draw cycle.

You can determine the stored energy of a compound by graphing its force-draw curve as outlined earlier. The number of squares in the area under the curve gives the approximate amount. Compare stored-energy values only between bows with the same draw length and peak weight. Any good round-wheel compound should be storing energy at a level that slightly exceeds the value of its peak weight. A cam bow should store more energy than a round-wheel bow, and a compound will store more energy than a longbow or a recurve of equal draw length and peak weight.

A typical round-wheel compound bow with a peak weight of 60 pounds will store about 63 or 64 foot-pounds of energy. The same bow with half-cam eccentric wheels will store about 67 or 68 foot-pounds, and with full-cam wheels, about 71 or 72 foot-pounds.

The only question that remains is whether the compound really delivers more energy to the arrow or whether its machinery takes so much energy to operate that the arrow receives less and is actually slower than one shot from a longbow or recurve. This will be discussed later in the chapter, under bow efficiency.

How to Order a Compound Bow

Compound manufacturers usually take orders based on traditional draw length, so you will need to be fitted while actually drawing the bow. A dealer should be able to help you do this using an arrow that is labeled with an inch scale. Once you draw a bow to full draw, the dealer can read the scale and determine the traditional draw length that best fits you.

If there is no dealer in your area that can do this for you, use the following procedure. First, find someone who is about your height and test draw his or her bow. If it feels comfortable, have someone stand beside you as you draw an arrow. While you are at full draw, this person should place a mark on the arrow at the arrow-rest mounting hole in the center of the handle just above the grip. Now measure the distance from the mark to the nock of the arrow. This measurement is your *true* draw length. To obtain your *traditional* draw length, add 1¾ inches. The Archery Manufacturers Organization has set this standard to give consumers a consistent method of ordering bows.

Most compound bows have eccentric wheels that can be adjusted to fit draw lengths across a three-inch range. Order the draw length that will enable you to shoot the bow set in the shorter half of this range; that way the cables and string will have more tension on them and usually the bow will sound and shoot better. If you can't do this, have no fear: The bow will still perform well for you. By doing so, however, you'll also have enough adjustability in draw length that you'll be able to make a change after you start shooting, if necessary. It is more difficult and less desirable to adjust draw length so that it is longer than the advertised maximum of the bow. Adjusting it shorter than the minimum can be done with far fewer problems.

CROSSBOWS

The crossbow has a long history dating back to 500 B.C., when it was used as a very effective weapon of war. It also was and still is used for hunting, and many target archers use it for tournament archery. Most major tour-

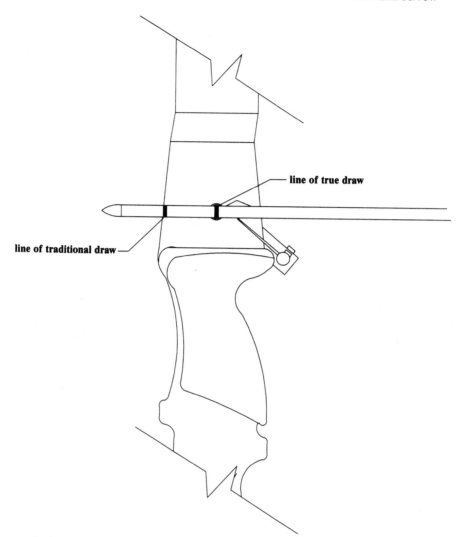

line of true draw

line of traditional draw

At full draw have someone mark your arrow at the arrow-rest mounting hole to measure true draw or at the back of the bow to measure traditional draw.

naments now have a special class for crossbow archers. In some states the crossbow is not considered a primitive weapon and is not allowed to be used for hunting. It is nevertheless available through any archery dealer in any state.

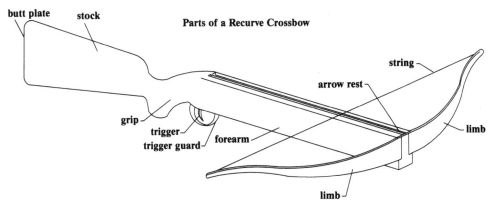

Parts of a Recurve Crossbow

The crossbow can be handled with ease since it is not long or heavy. Crossbows can be aimed and shot like a gun using a short, lightweight arrow called a bolt.

The Recurve Crossbow

The recurve crossbow is the type that most often comes to mind. The original crossbow was developed to provide foot soldiers with highly effective weapons. Any soldier could pick up a crossbow and become adept at using it with very little instruction, and because of its short design it was easy to transport. Its biggest advantage was that with its high draw weight it could propel a shorter arrow at a higher velocity, while at the same time it was still relatively easy to load because this could be done using both hands. The archer did not have to be strong and long in the arms to use this more powerful weapon.

The disadvantage of the crossbow compared with the longbow or recurve was the time needed to load an arrow. The longbow could be shot repeatedly in only a few seconds with great accuracy, but the crossbow needed to be lowered to the ground, its string pulled and set into the trigger mechanism, the arrow or bolt placed into the bow, and the bow brought back to the aiming position. All of this took valuable seconds during the heat of battle, so crossbow soldiers were usually accompanied by other legions with longbows.

The original crossbows had the same basic design as the longbow and recurve. The first limbs were one piece, and the wood was seasoned for several years before being prepared for placement on the stock. The chief difference between hand-held bow and crossbow limbs is in the length. The crossbow limb is shorter, and the shorter the limb the stiffer it is (as long as it is not made thinner).

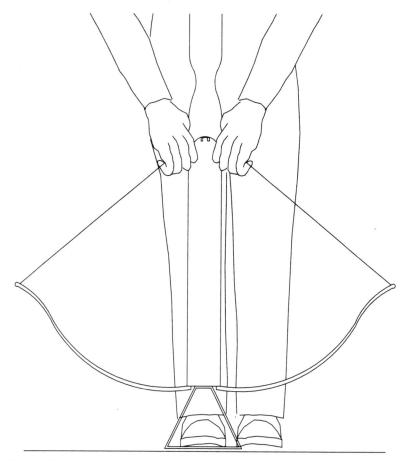

The crossbow is drawn by using both hands on the string while a foot holds the forearm to the ground. Never place the bolt in the crossbow until after the bow has been pointed in the direction of the target.

Modern technology in the form of the laminated limb did not change the basic design of the crossbow, but it increased strength, speed, and efficiency. This type of limb also is less affected by change in weather conditions and has a longer life.

Because the years of seasoning are unnecessary for the laminated limb, it can be built in just a few days. Modern limb-building techniques also enable manufacturers to mass-produce bow limbs, which makes the crossbow affordable for the average archer.

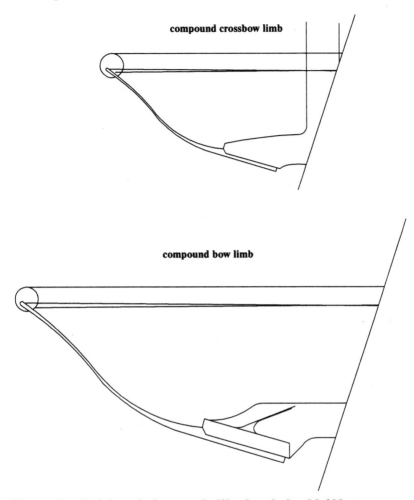

compound crossbow limb

compound bow limb

The crossbow limb is much shorter and stiffer than the hand-held bow.

The Compound Crossbow

The development of the compound bow from the late sixties through the seventies had its effects on the crossbow. During the eighties, bow manufacturers applied the features of the compound bow to the crossbow. The short, stiff limbs of the hand-held compound can be adapted to the crossbow, as can the eccentric wheel system.

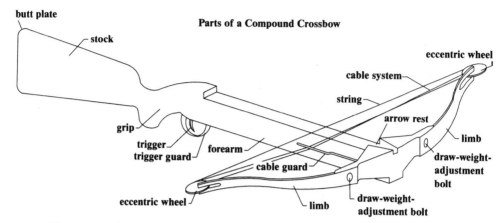

Parts of a Compound Crossbow

butt plate

stock

eccentric wheel

cable system

string

grip

arrow rest

limb

trigger
trigger guard

forearm

cable guard

draw-weight-adjustment bolt

eccentric wheel

limb

draw-weight-adjustment bolt

The compound wheel/cable system adds more speed to the crossbow.

When the compound eccentric system has the correct length cables attached, it can be made to fit almost any bow. The only factor that may not work well is the draw length created by a given size wheel. But with a crossbow, one bow basically fits all shooters; a person's draw length or arm length is not a variable in the bow-building or bow-tuning process.

Because a crossbow can be drawn with both hands, it is possible to shoot one that has about twice the draw weight of the conventional bow you shoot. In the case of the compound crossbow, that would be 100 to 140 pounds. That much peak weight will result in a significantly greater amount of stored energy than with a noncompound crossbow. The end result is a very fast arrow when the bowstring is released.

The most important aspect of the crossbow eccentric system is the timing of the wheel rollover. If one wheel is not synchronized with the other, then the grouping ability of the bow will be adversely affected. You must adjust the eccentric system to correct the synchronization just as you would with a conventional compound bow. Fast arrows are worthless if they don't hit what you aim at, and nonsynchronized wheels will cause a lot of missing. (This subject is covered in detail in chapter 7.)

The Force-Draw Curve of the Crossbow

The draw stroke of the crossbow is significantly shorter than that of a conventional bow. Instead of beginning at 9 inches of brace height and ending near 30 inches, the crossbow's begins at about 6 inches and extends only to 18 or 20 inches. Thus the force-draw curve of the crossbow is

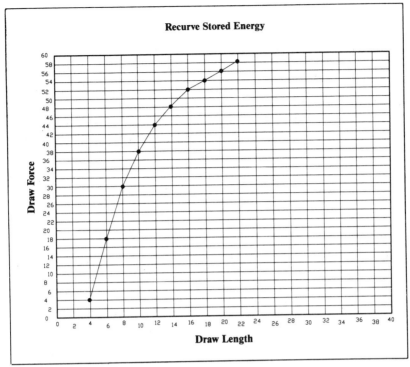

Recurve Stored Energy

Draw Force vs. Draw Length

The force-draw curve of the crossbow is similar to the hand-held bow except that it is shorter. The maximum draw length of this example is 22 inches.

shorter than its conventional counterpart, although it is otherwise the same shape, and it rises at a much faster rate because of the heavier peak weight occurring over a shorter draw stroke.

The compound crossbow force-draw curve has the basic characteristics of the compound force-draw curve. The force required to draw the string increases so rapidly that the curve has an almost vertical beginning. After reaching peak weight, the force on the string drops toward the valley weight very quickly. Once through the valley, the weight on the string increases rapidly again.

The valley should occur at the point at which the string is locked into place in the trigger mechanism. The valley's location is not as critical as it is with a conventional hand-held bow, however, since the trigger always holds the string at the same position in the draw stroke. Nevertheless, always check valley placement to be sure it is close to correct.

How to Order a Crossbow

The crossbow is the easiest to order. You just need to decide what draw weight you wish to shoot and how much you want to pay. The draw length does not need to be adjusted for different people — one size fits all — and everything is preset at the factory.

THE STORED ENERGY OF BOWS

The bow is a simple machine with a simple job to do: transfer the energy in the limbs to the arrow. Like any machine, it uses some energy to operate, and only the energy remaining can be transferred to the arrow. And also like other machines, some bows perform their jobs better than others.

The efficiency of a bow is measured as a percent that is the ratio of the amount of energy the bow gives the arrow to the amount of energy stored by the limbs. It will always be less than 100 percent, since the arrow cannot receive more energy than is stored.

The bows on the market today have efficiencies that fall between 50 and 85 percent. In other words, today's bows give between 50 and 85 percent of the energy that is stored in their limbs to the arrows. In general, the better the design of the bow, the higher its efficiency.

The longbow and recurve bow need resilient woods and fiberglass laminations in order to be highly efficient. The compound needs these same things, and in addition, all of its moving parts must be lightweight and have little friction. The right combinations get close to 80 percent efficiency, but poorer combinations get much less.

Stored-Energy Calculation

The stored energy of a bow can be calculated by measuring the area under the force-draw curve and the arrow's speed and weight. With these measurements you can determine both how much energy is stored in the bow after it's drawn and how much energy the arrow has after it has been shot. Dividing the second amount by the first will give you the percent efficiency for that bow shooting that specific arrow.

When you make your bow's force-draw curve, as detailed earlier in the chapter, you should record the weights at each inch of draw length. To obtain the stored energy, add these weight amounts together. A sample of the weights from 9 to 28 inches might be 8, 11, 16, 23, 32, 38, 45, 49, 51, 53, 52, 49, 43, 37, 32, 28, 26, 24, 23, and 22. The twenty weight measurements total 662. If each rectangular column represents one inch of draw length, then you have stored 662 inch-pounds of energy in the limbs of this bow. To convert this to foot-pounds, just divide the total by twelve; in this case there are 55.16 foot-pounds of stored energy.

You can calculate the energy of the arrow using the following formula for kinetic energy:

$$\text{kinetic energy} = \frac{\text{arrow weight} \times \text{velocity} \times \text{velocity}}{450{,}240}$$

According to this formula, a 400-grain arrow that is shot from this bow at 225 feet per second will have 44.98 foot-pounds of energy.

You can then determine the bow's efficiency by dividing the amount of energy of the arrow by the amount of stored energy of the bow. This bow stores 55.16 foot-pounds of energy and gives an arrow 44.98 foot-pounds of energy, so it is 81.5 percent efficient ($44.98 \div 55.16 = .815$). That is extremely good and is a rarity in bows.

Comparison of Bow Efficiency

Most recurves and longbows on the market today have efficiencies from 60 to 85 percent, while the compound bow ranges from 50 to 85 percent. This might lead you to think that the recurve should be faster than the compound bow, but that is not necessarily the case. The compound stores a significantly greater amount of energy, so even if it is less efficient, more energy still gets to the arrow and propels it at a faster velocity.

To give you a better picture of how the different types of bows work, here's a comparison of three bows that all have the same peak weight. A longbow with a peak weight of 40 pounds at 30 inches of draw length will store about 34 foot-pounds of energy. If the longbow is 80 percent efficient, this amount of energy will propel a 400-grain arrow at about 175 feet per second.

A recurve that peaks 40 pounds at 30 inches of draw and operates at 80 percent efficiency will be slightly faster. It will store about 37 foot-pounds of energy and propel the same 400-grain arrow at about 182.5 feet per second.

A compound that peaks 40 pounds at 30 inches of draw and operates at 75 percent efficiency is even faster, however. It stores 44 foot-pounds of energy and the 400-grain arrow will leave this compound at about 192 feet per second. The advantage in stored energy makes the compound bow faster. In fact, even if it were only 68 percent efficient, it would still be faster.

If only 75 percent of the stored energy is getting to the arrow, what is happening to the other 25 percent? The answer was given earlier when I mentioned that the parts of the bow must be moved along with the arrow. Although these parts don't move far in the case of the compound bow, they are heavier. The wheels, cables, and bowstring also rub against one another at various places and some energy is lost to friction. Still more energy is lost to vibrations in the limbs, cables, and string. With all these factors, it is difficult to build a compound that is 80 percent efficient.

You should follow one caution here: When comparing bows, be sure to compare them at equal draw weights and draw lengths and shooting the same arrow. Otherwise it would be like comparing apples with oranges.

2

Selecting and Assembling Arrows

BASICS OF THE ARROW AND ITS FLIGHT

EVERY ARCHER SHOULD know what happens to an arrow as the bowstring pushes it forward upon release. If you know what motions an arrow makes during its first thirty inches of flight, you will be better able to attain your goal of hitting a distant target with that arrow. The parts of some common arrows on the market today are illustrated below.

Arrow flight begins when the bowstring is released. This process applies a great amount of energy to the nock end, and the arrow begins to move. The point, however, usually the heaviest part, will try to remain at rest. The rear of the arrow, since it is lighter, will move forward immediately and as a result the arrow shaft will bend. Because of this, arrow shafts must be flexible. You need to understand this flexing motion in order to achieve good arrow flight and accuracy.

The bending of the arrow shaft in three-dimensional space is the answer to the age-old paradox that wood-handled bows have presented since their invention. With these bows the arrow must be shot around the handle and not through its center. The puzzling event that takes place has

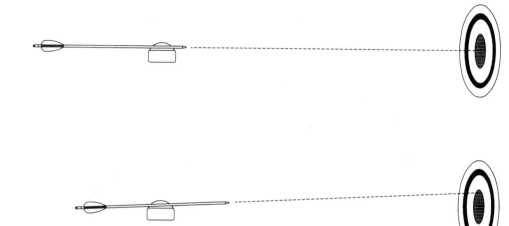

Archer's paradox exists for noncenter-cut bow handles. For these handles, the arrow can be aimed at the target at full draw, but as the string comes forward on the center line, the arrow points to the left and can only hit the target if it bends around the handle when shot.

to do with where the arrow is pointed at full draw and then at brace position. When you draw the wood-handled bow, you can aim the arrow at the target. If you let down the bowstring and arrow to the relaxed brace position without moving the bow handle, the string and nock end of the arrow travel toward their normal positions in line with the center of the handle. The point of the arrow, however, is now aiming to the left of the target; it cannot remain in line with the nock unless the bow handle has a cutout center.

How then does the arrow hit the target if the string drives toward the center of the bow and causes the arrow to point to the left of the target's center? The answer lies in the fact that the arrow does not remain straight during the power stroke of the string.

This "archer's paradox" was described by Paul Klopsteg in his 1947 book, *Archery: The Technical Side*. His work has guided modern archers to better methods of dealing with the bending motion of the arrow shaft during the power stroke of the string and beyond. Through Klopsteg's work it became evident that this bending motion was critical to shooting accuracy. If an arrow bent so that the nock end hit the side of the bow handle as the arrow passed, then poor flight and inaccuracy would result. If the arrow bent wildly and too often as it was being driven by the string, it would also fly poorly and miss the target. To have the best chance of striking the target, an arrow should bend with some degree of consistency and cleanly pass the handle.

There are three phases to the typical bending motion of an arrow before it completely passes the handle. First, the nock end bends left as it moves before the point does. Next, there is a reverse motion as the elasticity of the arrow causes a straightening of the shaft but the momentum carries the flexing beyond straight. Third, the shaft again bends the way it originally did, as the shaft goes back to straight and beyond in the first direction. This oscillation continues for some distance after the arrow has

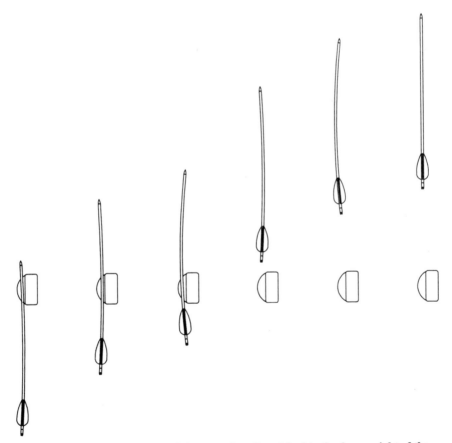

When the stiffness, or spine, of the arrow is well matched to the draw weight of the bow, its center bends first inward, then outward as the string propels it past the bow handle.

passed the bow handle. With the newer metal handles that are cut beyond the center line, the arrow remains pointed at the target throughout the entire draw, aim, and release sequence of the shot. Even so, the arrow still bends when the string applies force to the nock end.

To get an idea of how much an arrow bends, pick up a shaft by its ends and flex it between your fingers and thumbs. It will bend in an arch. If you bend it too far it will break, but it can be flexed several inches thousands of times with no effect, which is exactly what happens during the power stroke of the bow and the launch of the arrow. How much an arrow bends and how long it continues to bend depend on what it's made of and the strength of that material.

Arrow Spine and Point Weight

After a few days of shooting, the first archer in history learned that if he or she wanted arrows to withstand the impact of hitting solid objects, something would have to be added to the front end of the shaft to prevent damage. That's when the weighted point was invented. Well, maybe it didn't happen that quickly, but it wasn't long before archers learned to use points other than the sharpened end of the arrow. After all, stone tips could do far more damage than sharp sticks, and besides, they caused something good to happen to the arrow flight.

When weight is added to the point, the dynamic forces applied to the arrow by the string have different effects than when no weight is added: The heavier point will remain at rest and the lighter end moves ahead first as the arrow bends.

The arrow shaft continues to bend and unbend for some distance: It will oscillate for 40 or 50 yards on its downrange flight, unless it hits the target before that. With the oscillation of the arrow, the most important thing is the timing: If the timing of the first, second, and third bends of the arrow is correct, the arrow will bend around the wooden bow handle and fly accurately to the target. If the timing is not correct, then the arrow will fly to the left or right of the target; it may even strike the side of the bow handle and fly erratically.

The oscillations of the shaft are determined by several factors, the two most important being the spine of the arrow and the weight of the point. The spine value of an arrow shaft is a direct indication of how much the shaft bends. To determine the standardized spine measurement, an arrow is supported one inch from either end and a two-pound weight hung from its center. The number of inches that it bends at its center is the spine value

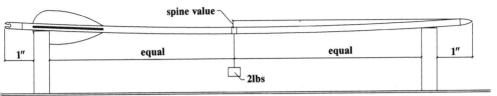

Hanging a two-pound weight at the middle of the shaft will cause a bend that can be measured in inches for stiffness, or spine, value.

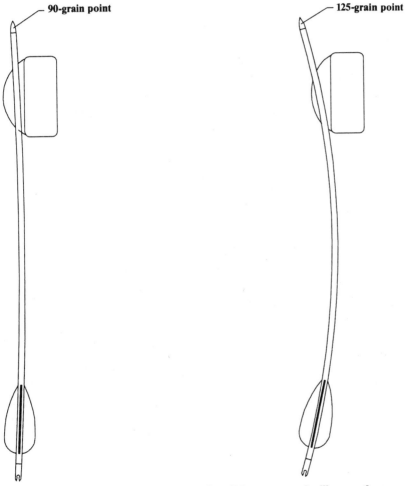

Heavier points will remain at rest longer than lighter ones and will cause the arrow to bend more as the string pushes the back end.

for that shaft. Weaker shafts bend more than stiffer shafts, and thinner shafts usually bend more than thicker ones. Recent developments in shaft materials have created some exceptions to this rule. Most notably, a carbon shaft of even a small diameter is often extremely stiff.

The point that is placed on the arrow shaft has a direct relationship to the spine: The heavier the point, the more the arrow will bend when a force is applied to the nock end. A lighter-weight point will not remain at rest as long as a heavier one, so the arrow will bend less and seem stiffer.

Long-range Arrow Flight

The point weight cannot only be used to control how the arrow acts during the initial stages of flight, but it can also determine long-range flight. After an arrow has been launched, its oscillations eventually subside and it flies steadily under its own guidance. Sometimes this guidance is stable and sometimes it is not. You can vary the point weight and fletching size to help create the proper balance for accuracy at distances from 50 to 100 yards.

There are two basic characteristics to look for in long-range flight: arrow instability or extreme arrow drop beyond 60 yards. Arrow instability is caused by a point that is too light or by too much fletching. After a long distance has been covered, the arrow will begin to float erratically. Your arrows may impact all over the target in a random fashion instead of in a tight group about the size of a paper plate.

An arrow may seem to fly well for a long distance and then suddenly drop from the sky like a rock. This is usually caused by a point that is too heavy. If you are not shooting more than 60 yards, you may find that your arrow groups are exceptionally small with the heavy points; to improve long-range performance, however, you will need slightly lighter points.

Selecting the Proper Shaft Size

Spine and point weight are extremely important when choosing arrows. So important, in fact, that the major manufacturers of arrow shafts have gone to great lengths to provide arrow spine charts to aid consumers in the selection process. These charts allow you to match arrow spine, peak weight of the bow, arrow length, percent let-off, and arrow weight.

Using the charts can save you a lot of time and money. They are accurate enough that you can narrow your choice of shaft sizes down to two or three. At that point you need to do some test-shooting to determine which will shoot best with your specific bow setup. If you can, borrow these sizes of shafts and test them. This can be done at a local pro shop or from friends at an archery club. If neither is available to you, then I suggest you pick the heavier of the shaft sizes that seem appropriate. The heavier will tend to be easier to work with in the tuning process and have more stable flight characteristics. The lighter shafts are more easily affected by flaws in your form.

In the following sections of this chapter are two arrow spine charts. The first one is from Easton Aluminum and will assist you in selecting aluminum arrows. The second is from AFC Corporation and will help you select those carbon shafts that will shoot the best from your bow.

WOODEN ARROWS

Archery is more than sight, touch, and sound to me; it is also many different smells. No matter where I am, when a box of cedar arrow shafts is opened, I am once again twelve years old and my dad and I are building arrows in our basement. That smell will never have another meaning for me. Cedar shafts are linked to my early days of archery and bring a lot of magic moments to mind.

Wood has been the material of choice for arrows since the bow was first invented. It was handy, easy to work with, and durable. Cultures the world over have used wood for arrow making, and many archers in this country still use it today. Bamboo and reed are related materials and share properties that make great shooting arrows. Only in the last fifty years have other materials been developed that will outperform these shafts.

A good shaft must be flexible as well as strong, of a material pliable enough to be straightened but tough enough to withstand the punishment of many shots. The outside needs to be smooth so that it will pass the arrow rest cleanly. The material used for arrows should be uniform in diameter and density so that all of an archer's arrows will fly the same and hit the target. The wooden, bamboo, and reed shafts have these necessary properties and have made good arrows for thousands of years.

The Modern Cedar Shaft

The wooden shafts that are commercially available today are made of cedar, which lends itself well to shaping, sizing, and hardening. It has a straight grain that allows the arrow to bend while passing the sight window of the bow. Its elasticity permits the shaft to recover from the bending and remain straight. It is also relatively inexpensive compared with the other, more exotic, materials available today.

When selecting cedar shafts for arrow building, follow two simple guidelines. First, make sure that the shafts are not cut so short that the tips of the arrows will be drawn onto the arrow shelf: The tips should always extend beyond the shelf of the bow. Second, the shafts should all be spined for the peak draw weight of the bow you intend to shoot. Shafts are usually sorted by spine value and marked according to the range of draw weight that would be appropriate for that shaft. For example, a spine value might be stated as being suitable for a 40–50 pound range of draw weight. Others might be 50–60 pounds, 60–70 pounds, and 70–80 pounds.

If you intend to shoot a 60-pound bow, you can use either the 50–60 or the 60–70 spine. If you are not sure which value to choose, I would recommend the heavier spine. It will be easier to tune, as long as it is not too stiff. The heavier shaft will recover more quickly in flight and will be less subject to erratic flight because of bad releases by the archer.

Assembling a Wooden Arrow

Wooden shafts are available either assembled or unassembled. If you elect to assemble your own shafts, purchase the full-length raw shafts, feathers, nocks, points, and glue from an archery dealer and follow the instructions below. You will also need to borrow or buy a fletching jig to hold the arrow and feather while you glue them together.

Shaft Preparation

Once you have chosen the wooden shafts, you need to first prepare them for fletching and then fletch them. The process is not simple or quick, but it's very gratifying to be able to shoot arrows you've built to your own specifications. If you are a tournament archer, you'll know that all of your arrows have been built the same and will not fall apart.

You begin by cutting the shafts to the proper length. You can determine the arrow length you need by drawing any arrow. When you are comfortable at full draw, have someone place a mark on the shaft about one inch beyond the back of the bow. Measure the arrow to this mark and cut all your arrows to that length. You can use a common miter saw. Try to do this without splitting the ends. Some people recommend rolling the shaft so that the entire circumference is cut before you slice through the middle.

Now the ends of the shafts need to be shaped to receive the nocks and points. You can do this with a taper tool, which is nothing more than a

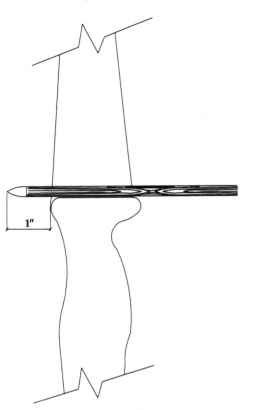

1"

To reduce chances of the arrow falling from the arrow shelf and injuring your hand during the shot, cut your wooden arrows so that about one inch extends beyond the back of the bow.

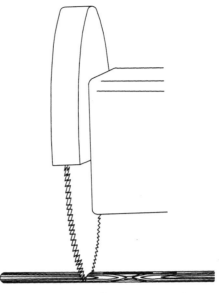

For best results, be sure to cut wooden arrows with a fine-tooth, high-speed saw.

pencil sharpener angled to match the inside of the nocks and points. This and other devices you will need for building arrows are available from most archery shops and mail-order magazines.

Use light sandpaper to smooth the tapered ends and the lengths of the shafts, then wipe clean with a dry cloth. Twist the nocks onto the shafts but do not glue them yet.

Staining and painting wooden shafts is a long-standing tradition. You can rub ordinary wood stain onto the shaft with a cloth or apply paint by aerosol spray or by dipping the shafts into a paint tube. Be sure to allow

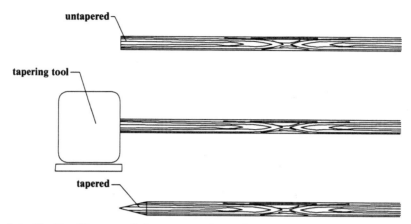

A tool looking like a pencil sharpener can be used to put a taper on each end of the shaft so that points and nocks can be attached.

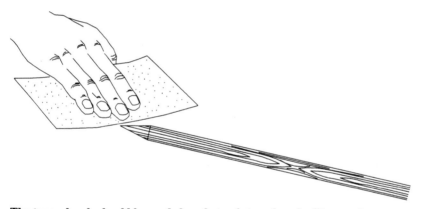

The tapered ends should be sanded so that points and nocks fit properly.

plenty of time for the stain or paint to dry before beginning the cresting process.

Cresting, or painting rings and bands on the fletched ends of the shafts, has been done for centuries so that one's arrows are marked uniquely and thus are distinguishable from arrows of other archers. You can use a cresting jig to hold the arrow (which includes a motor to turn it) while you hold a brush dipped in colored lacquer against the arrow to make the rings and wider bands forming the crest. Nothing looks better than a back quiver full of a dozen beautifully crested wooden arrows!

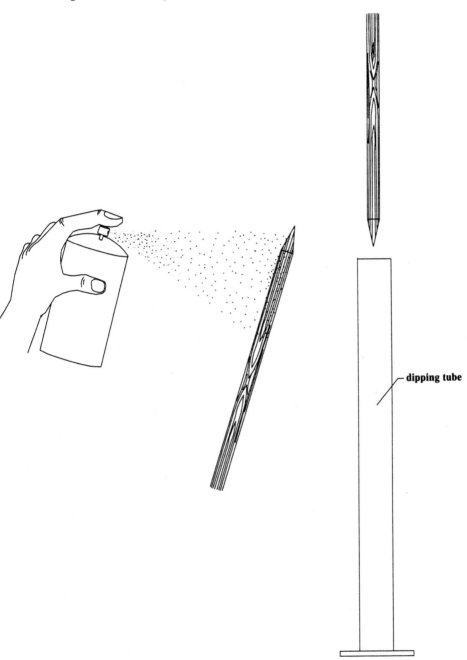

dipping tube

Stain or paint can be applied by aerosol or by dipping the shaft into a tube of finish.

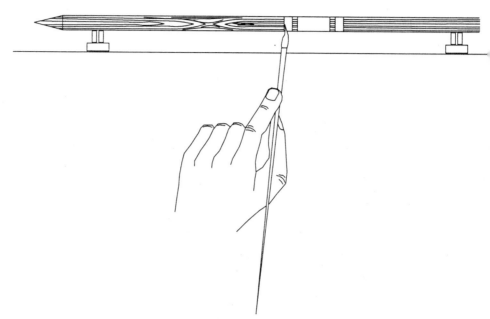

Colored rings of different widths can be painted on the shaft when the shaft is held and rotated by a cresting tool.

Point and Nock Installation

Now the nocks and the points are glued in place. Apply hot-melt glue, which is available at most hardware stores and archery shops, on the tapered end of the shaft and then push the point on in the proper position. Rotate the nock so that the tighter grain of the wood shaft is on the side that will be next to the bow. Use fletching cement, airplane glue, or hot-melt glue to affix the nock.

Fletch Preparation

Wooden arrows are usually fletched with feathers rather than plastic vanes. Tradition, I suppose. Whichever kind of fletch you use, you will need a fletching jig to hold the arrow while you glue the fletch onto the shaft. Single-fletch and multifletch jigs are available at archery shops. They may seem expensive, but if you intend to make several dozen arrows, the jig will more than pay for itself.

For wooden arrows I recommend using a single-fletch jig and three feathers that are four or five inches long. The longer feathers will help the arrow stabilize more quickly in flight.

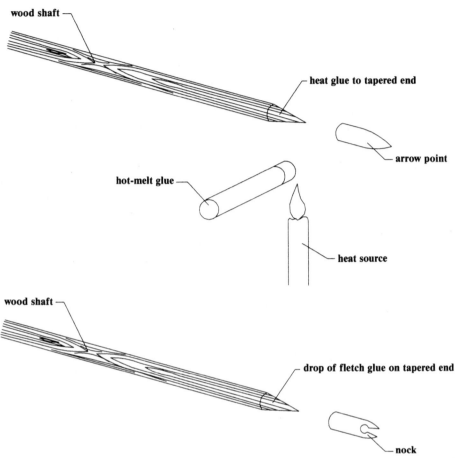

Points for wooden arrows should be installed using hot-melt glue applied to the end of the shaft. The nock can be mounted using a drop of fletching cement.

Place one feather in the jig's holding clamp and set it on the jig next to the arrow shaft. Adjust the angle of the clamp so that the entire base of the feather is touching the shaft. Do not place the feather in line with the shaft; having the feathers at a slight angle will help stabilize the flight of the arrow. Most feathers available are from the left wing, so you should angle the clamp two or three degrees to the left as it runs down the shaft.

Run a bead of fletching cement along the base of the feather. Next, place the clamp on the magnet of the jig so that the base of the feather is close to but not touching the arrow shaft. After you position the feather in the desired location near the shaft, slide the clamp closer to the shaft until

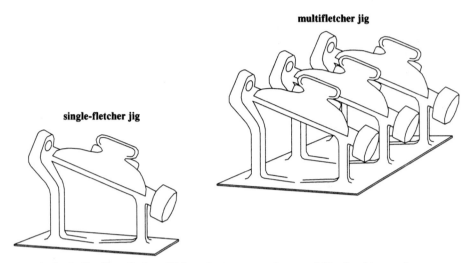

A single fletching jig is sufficient, but many prefer a multijig fletching tool to get the job done faster.

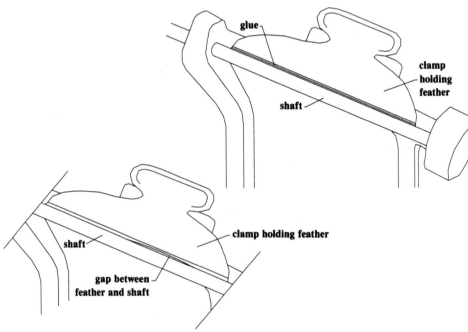

After a bead of glue has been placed on the base of the fletch, place the clamp on the jig so that no gaps appear between the fletch and the shaft.

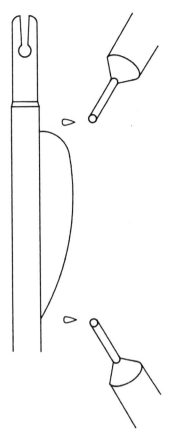

Complete the fletching process by placing one drop of cement at each end of each fletch.

the base of the feather is against it. Be sure the base is touching at all points along the shaft so that no gaps are present.

Allow the glue for each feather to dry for about fifteen minutes. I usually work on other projects while I'm fletching arrows, and every ten or fifteen minutes I return to the jig to install another fletch. I can't stand to sit and watch glue dry!

Once the three feathers or vanes have been installed on a shaft, your last step is to place a spot of fletching cement at the ends of each one. This helps prevent the fletching from coming loose when the arrow passes through a target. Allow the completed arrows to set for a day before you shoot them.

Maintenance Tips

When cared for properly, wooden arrows can provide hundreds of shots over a period of several years. I still have some of the first arrows I made thirty years ago.

Store your arrows in a dry place. Dampness can make wooden arrows warp slightly, which may affect how they shoot. Check your shafts periodically for cracks and splinters. Small splinters can sometimes be repaired with glue and sandpaper, but cracked arrows should not be shot again; discard them.

After you have used your arrows awhile or if they have gotten wet in the rain, you can place the feathers over the steam of a tea kettle for a few seconds to help them regain their shape. If the feathers become too badly damaged, you will have to peel them from the shafts and fletch the arrows all over again.

Feathers can usually be returned to normal shape by placing them in steam for several seconds.

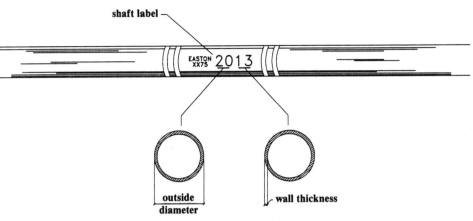

Aluminum arrow sizes are printed on the shaft as four-digit numerals. This arrow has a diameter of $^{20}/_{64}$ inch and a wall thickness of $^{13}/_{1000}$ inch.

ALUMINUM ARROWS

The aluminum arrow shaft has been around since the early 1940s, when James D. Easton developed the first trademarked aluminum shaft, ushering in an era of increased arrow durability and consistency. Since then aluminum arrows have been responsible for more national and international records than one can imagine and have given thousands of backyard archers many hours of shooting enjoyment.

According to Easton Aluminum, four aluminum alloys are currently being used for arrow manufacturing. There are about thirty different sizes of aluminum arrows available, with the variables being the diameter of the shaft and the thickness of the tubing wall. The size is printed on the shaft near the nock end of the arrow.

A four-digit number is used to indicate both the outside diameter and the wall thickness. The first two digits indicate the outside diameter in sixty-fourths of an inch, and the other two give the wall thickness of the tubing in one-thousandths of an inch. For example, the diameter of a 2213 shaft is $^{22}/_{64}$ of an inch and the wall is $^{13}/_{1000}$ inch thick. Thus a 2213 arrow shaft has a wider diameter but a thinner wall than an 1816 shaft.

With the different shaft sizes, it is very easy to match an arrow to the draw weight of the bow. If one size seems to be a little weak, try a bigger size; if one size is too stiff, try a smaller size. Most archery dealers have a variety of arrows for you to try so that you can decide which size you need before you buy.

All arrow manufacturers make selection charts that give the final cut lengths of various sizes of shafts and recommendations for different draw weights. These charts are designed to help you determine the shaft sizes that will work well with your bow. Do not look for one specific size that

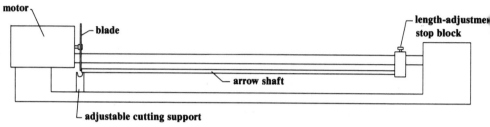

When cutting aluminum arrows to length, use only a high-speed abrasive cutting tool. Other types of cutting tools will damage the end of the shaft.

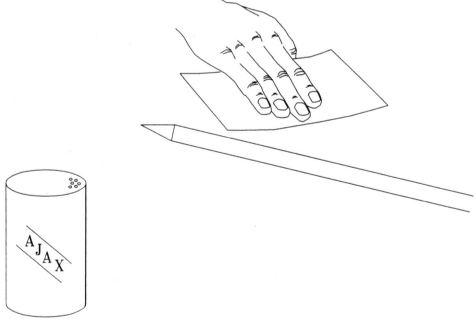

Scrubbing aluminum shafts with Ajax and rinsing with clean water will provide a clean surface for fletching.

will be "magic." Find three that are suggested and then test-shoot them. You can do this at your local archery shop. Testing is the only way to be sure which size will work the best for your bow with you shooting it. Following is a sample selection chart, from Easton Aluminum.

Fletching Aluminum Arrows

The fletching procedure for aluminum is similar to that for wooden arrows: The shafts have to be cleaned, the nocks installed temporarily, and the fletching cleaned and then affixed to the shafts. Then the points and the nocks can be glued onto the shafts.

Shaft Preparation

If your archery dealer did not cut your arrows to the desired length, you need to do that first. The only device that should be used for this job is a high-speed cutoff tool. It is motor driven and uses an abrasive disk to cut the shaft cleanly. Other devices, such as tubing cutters or a hacksaw, will alter the shape of the end of the shaft. After cutting, remove any burrs from the ends of the shafts with a small file.

The arrow shaft must be clean in order for the glue to be effective. Dirt, resins, and oils from the manufacturing process may remain on the shaft if you wash them with water alone. Use an abrasive cleanser like Ajax to remove these materials and create a good bonding surface for the fletching cement. You can also use acetone to clean the shaft.

After washing, rinse each shaft in warm water and dry with a paper towel. At this point, do not handle the area of the arrow that is to be fletched in order to keep it dry and free from any oil or dirt from your hands.

The cement you choose can be any of half a dozen found at your local archery shop or sporting goods store. Get the store owner's or clerk's recommendation. Any of the fletching cements and glues will work well on clean aluminum shafts.

Nock Preparation

After the arrows are cleaned, twist the nocks onto the ends of the shafts. Do not use glue at this point; after fletching you will remove and glue the nocks in the proper position, which is determined by the arrow rest you plan to use and how the fletching passes around or through that rest. (Chapter 3 gives details of this important concept.)

Bow and Arrow

EASTON HUNTING

RECURVE BOW — Actual or Calculated Bow Weight (Pounds) — Broadhead or Field Point Weight Only					COMPOUND BOW — Actual or Calculated Peak Bow Weight (Pounds) — Broadhead or Field Point Weight Only				
75 (65-85)	100 (90-110)	125 (115-135)	150 (140-160)	175 (165-185)	75 (65-85)	100 (90-110)	125 (115-135)	150 (140-160)	175 (165-185)

Shaft columns (Shaft Size / Shaft Model / Shaft Weight):
- **22"** (21½"–22½")
- **23"** (22½"–23½")
- **24"** (23½"–24½")
- **25"** (24½"–25½")

This shaft selection chart was set up using Fast Flite® String, finger release and modern, efficient recurve and compound bows. The shaft size recommendations for compound bows were determined using 40-65% let-off and round wheels. If your equipment varies from the above, see the EASTON BOWHUNTING brochure to determine your Calculated Bow Weight or Calculated Peak Bow Weight before using this chart.

Recurve 75	100	125	150	175	Compound 75	100	125	150	175	22"	23"	24"	25"
30-34	27-31	24-28	21-25	18-22	35-40	32-37	29-34	26-31	23-28				1813 X/75 197 A
35-39	32-36	29-33	26-30	23-27	41-46	38-43	35-40	32-37	29-34			1813 XX75 189 A	1913 XX75 209 A; 1816 XX75,E 232 A; 3L-04 A/C/C 173
40-44	37-41	34-38	31-35	28-32	47-52	44-49	41-46	38-43	35-40		1813 XX75 181 A	1913 XX75 200 A; 1816 XX75,E 223 A; 3L-04 A/C/C 167	1913 XX75 209 B; 1816 XX75,E 232 B; 1818 XX75 268 A; 3-04 A/C/C 180
45-49	42-46	39-43	36-40	33-37	53-58	50-55	47-52	44-49	41-46	1813 XX75 173 A	1913 XX75 192 A; 3L-04 A/C/C 160	1816 XX75,E 213 A; 1818 XX75 257 A; 3-04 A/C/C 173	2013 XX75 225 A; 1916 XX75,E 251 B; 1818 XX75 268 B; 3L-18 A/C/C 186
50-54	47-51	44-48	41-45	38-42	59-64	56-61	53-58	50-55	47-52	1913 XX75 184 A; 1816 XX75,E 204 A; 3L-04 A/C/C 153	1913 XX75 182 B; 1816 XX75,E 213 B; 1818 XX75 246 A; 3-04 A/C/C 166	2013 XX75 216 A; 1916 XX75,E 241 A; 1818 XX75 257 B; 3L-18 A/C/C 179	2013 XX75 225 B; 1916 XX75,E 251 B; 1918 XX75 290 A; 3L-18 A/C/C 186; 3-18 A/C/C 195
55-59	52-56	49-53	46-50	43-47	65-70	62-67	59-64	56-61	53-58	1913 XX75 184 B; 1816 XX75,E 204 B; 1818 XX75 235 A; 3-04 A/C/C 154	2013 XX75 207 A; 1916 XX75,E 231 A; 1818 XX75 246 B; 3L-18 A/C/C 172	2013 XX75 214 B; 1916 XX75,E 241 B; 1918 XX75 278 A; 3L-18 A/C/C 179; 3-18 A/C/C 187	2013 XX75 225 B; 2016 XX75 264 A; 1918 XX75 290 B; 3-18 A/C/C 195
60-64	57-61	54-58	51-55	48-52	71-76	68-73	65-70	62-67	59-64	2013 XX75 198 A; 1916 XX75,E 221 A; 1818 XX75 235 B; 3L-18 A/C/C 164	2013 XX75 207 B; 1916 XX75,E 231 B; 1918 XX75 266 A; 3L-18 A/C/C 172; 3-18 A/C/C 180	2113 XX75 223 A; 2016 XX75 253 A; 1918 XX75 278 B; 3-18 A/C/C 187	2113 XX75 232 C; 2114 XX75 247 B; 2115 XX75 264 C; 2115 XX75 269 A; 2018 XX75,E 307 A; 3-30 A/C/H 202
65-69	62-66	59-63	56-60	53-57	77-82	74-79	71-76	68-73	65-70	2013 XX75 198 B; 1916 XX75,E 221 B; 1918 XX75 255 A; 3L-18 A/C/C 164; 3-18 A/C/C 172	2013 XX75 214 A; 2016 XX75 243 A; 1918 XX75 266 B; 3-18 A/C/C 180	2113 XX75 223 B; 2016 XX75 253 C; 2115 XX75 259 A; 2018 XX75,E 295 A; 3-30 A/C/H 194	2113 XX75 232 C; 2114 XX75 247 C; 2115 XX75 269 B; 2018 XX75,E 307 B; 2020 XX75 337 A; 3-30 A/C/H 202
70-74	67-71	64-68	61-65	58-62	83-88	80-85	77-82	74-79	71-76	2113 XX75 205 C; 2016 XX75 232 A; 1918 XX75 255 B; 3-18 A/C/C 172	2113 XX75 214 C; 2016 XX75 243 C; 2016 XX75 248 A; 2018 XX75,E 282 A; 3-30 A/C/H 186	2312 XX75 223 C; 2115 XX75 259 B; 2018 XX75,E 295 B; 2020 XX75 324 A; 3-30 A/C/H 194	2312 XX75 229 A; 2313 XX75 246 B; 2215 XX75 267 A; 2117 XX75 301 A; 2020 XX75 337 B; 3-39 A/C/H 210; 4-18 A/C/H 226
75-79	72-76	69-73	66-70	63-67	89-94	86-91	83-88	80-85	77-82	2113 XX75 205 C; 2114 XX75 217 B; 2016 XX75 232 C; 2115 XX75 237 A; 2018 XX75,E 270 A; 3-30 A/C/H 178	2213 XX75 226 A; 2115 XX75 248 B; 2018 XX75,E 282 B; 2020 XX75 310 A; 3-30 A/C/H 186	2312 XX75 229 B; 2313 XX75 235 B; 2215 XX75 256 A; 2117 XX75 289 A; 2020 XX75 324 A; 3-39 A/C/C 202; 4-18 A/C/H 217	2312 XX75 229 B; 2314 XX75 235 B; 2215 XX75 267 B; 2117 XX75 301 A; 2216 XX75 301 A; 3-49 A/C/C 216; 4-28 A/C/H 232
80-84	77-81	74-78	71-75	68-72	95-100	92-97	89-94	86-91	83-88	2213 XX75 216 A; 2214 XX75 217 C; 2115 XX75 237 B; 2018 XX75,E 279 A; 2020 XX75 297 A; 3-30 A/C/H 178	2312 XX75 216 A; 2215 XX75 245 A; 2117 XX75 277 A; 2020 XX75 310 B; 3-39 A/C/H 193; 4-18 A/C/H 208	2312 XX75 216 B; 2215 XX75 256 B; 2117 XX75 289 B; 2216 XX75 289 A; 3-49 A/C/C 206; 4-28 A/C/H 223	2315 XX75 292 A; 2216 XX75 301 B; 2219 XX75,E 344 A; 3-49 A/C/C 216; 4-28 A/C/H 232

The chart indicates that more than one shaft size may shoot well from your bow. **Shaft sizes in bold type are the most widely used**, but you may decide to shoot a lighter shaft for speed, or a heavier shaft for greater penetration and durability. Also, large variations in bow efficiency, type of wheels or cams, bow length, string material and release type may require special bow tuning or a shaft size change to accommodate these variations.

The "Shaft Weight" column—indicates shaft weight only. To determine total arrow weight, add the weight of the shaft, point or broadhead, RPS insert, nock and fletching. Where two models are shown for one size, the weight shown is for XX75. Letter codes A–C listed to the right of shaft weight indicate the relative stiffness of each aluminum shaft within that "Shaft Size" box ("A" being the stiffest, "B" less stiff, etc.)

"Shaft Model" column—designates arrow model
XX75 = Gamegetter, Gamegetter II, Camo Hunter, Autumn Hunter and PermaGraphic shafts
E = Eagle Hunter shafts
A/C/H = Aluminum/Carbon/Hunter shafts
A/C/C = Aluminum/Carbon/Comp shafts

Determining Actual Bow Weight or Actual Peak Bow Weight

Actual Bow Weight of a recurve bow and Actual Peak Bow Weight of a compound bow can be determined at your archery pro shop.

Although Easton has attempted to consider most variations of equipment, there are other style and equipment variables that could require shaft sizes other than the ones suggested. In these cases, you'll need to experiment and use stiffer or weaker spine shafts to fit your situation.

SHAFT SELECTION CHART

25½"- 26" -26½"			26½"- 27" -27½"			27½"- 28" -28½"			28½"- 29" -29½"			29½"- 30" -30½"			30½"- 31" -31½"			31½"- 32" -32½"			32½"- 33" -33½"		
Shaft Size	Shaft Model	Shaft Weight	Shaft Size	Shaft Model	Shaft Weight	Shaft Size	Shaft Model	Shaft Weight	Shaft Size	Shaft Model	Shaft Weight	Shaft Size	Shaft Model	Shaft Weight	Shaft Size	Shaft Model	Shaft Weight	Shaft Size	Shaft Model	Shaft Weight	Shaft Size	Shaft Model	Shaft Weight
1913 1816 3L-04	XX75 XX75,E A/C/C	217 A 241 A 180	1913 1816 1818 3-04	XX75 XX75,E XX75 A/C/C	225 B 251 B 289 A 194	2013 1916 1818 3L-18	XX75 XX75,E XX75 A/C/C	252 A 281 A 300 B 209	2013 1916 1918 3L-18 3-18	XX75 XX75,E XX75 A/C/C A/C/C	261 B 292 B 336 A 216 226	2113 2016 1918 3-18	XX75 XX75 XX75 A/C/C	279 A 317 A 347 B 234	2113 2114 2016 2115 2018 3-30	XX75 XX75 XX75 XX75 XX75,E A/C/H	266 C 306 B 327 C 334 A 381 A 251	2213 2114 2115 2018 2020 3-30	XX75 XX75 XX75 XX75,E XX75 A/C/H	315 A 316 C 345 B 393 B 432 A 259	2312 2213 2215 2117 3-39 4-18	XX75 XX75 XX75 XX75,E A/C/C A/C/H	310 A 324 B 352 A 397 A 277 298
1913 1816 1818 3-04	XX75 XX75,E XX75 A/C/C	217 B 241 B 278 A 187	2013 1916 1818 3L-18	XX75 XX75,E XX75 A/C/C	243 A 271 A 289 B 201	2013 1916 1918 3L-18 3-18	XX75 XX75,E XX75 A/C/C A/C/C	252 B 281 B 324 A 209 219	2113 2016 1918 3-18	XX75 XX75 XX75 A/C/C	270 A 306 A 336 B 226	2113 2114 2016 2115 2018 3-30	XX75 XX75 XX75 XX75 XX75,E A/C/H	279 C 298 B 317 C 323 A 366 A 243	2213 2114 2115 2018 2020 3-30	XX75 XX75 XX75 XX75,E XX75 A/C/H	305 A 306 C 334 B 381 B 418 A 251	2312 2213 2215 2117 2020 3-39 4-18	XX75 XX75 XX75 XX75,E XX75 A/C/C A/C/H	301 A 315 B 341 A 385 A 432 B 269 289	2312 2314 2215 2117 2216 3-49 4-28	XX75 XX75 XX75 XX75,E XX75 A/C/C A/C/H	310 B 301 A 352 B 397 B 397 A 286 306
2013 1916 1818 3L-18	XX75 XX75,E XX75 A/C/C	234 A 261 A 278 B 194	2013 1916 1918 3L-18 3-18	XX75 XX75,E XX75 A/C/C A/C/C	243 B 271 B 313 A 201 211	2113 2016 1918 3-18	XX75 XX75 XX75 A/C/C	260 A 296 A 324 B 219	2113 2114 2016 2115 2018 3-30	XX75 XX75 XX75 XX75 XX75,E A/C/H	270 C 286 B 306 C 312 A 356 A 235	2213 2114 2115 2018 2020 3-30	XX75 XX75 XX75 XX75,E XX75 A/C/H	295 A 296 C 323 B 368 B 405 A 243	2312 2213 2215 2117 2020 3-39 4-18	XX75 XX75 XX75 XX75,E XX75 A/C/C A/C/H	291 A 305 B 331 A 373 A 418 B 261 280	2312 2314 2215 2117 2216 3-49 4-28	XX75 XX75 XX75 XX75,E XX75 A/C/C A/C/H	301 B 341 A 341 B 385 B 385 A 277 297	2413 2314 2315 2216 2219 3-49 4-28	XX75 XX75 XX75 XX75 XX75,E A/C/C A/C/H	343 A 351 B 385 A 397 B 454 A 286 306
2013 1916 1918 3L-18 3-18	XX75 XX75,E XX75 A/C/C A/C/C	234 B 261 B 301 A 194 203	2113 2016 1918 3-18	XX75 XX75 XX75 A/C/C	251 A 285 A 313 B 211	2113 2114 2016 2115 2018 3-30	XX75 XX75 XX75 XX75 XX75,E A/C/H	260 C 276 B 296 C 302 A 344 A 227	2213 2114 2115 2018 2020 3-30	XX75 XX75 XX75 XX75,E XX75 A/C/H	298 A 286 C 312 B 356 B 391 A 235	2312 2213 2215 2117 2020 3-39 4-18	XX75 XX75 XX75 XX75,E XX75 A/C/C A/C/H	282 A 295 B 320 A 361 A 405 B 252 271	2312 2314 2215 2117 2216 3-49 4-28	XX75 XX75 XX75 XX75,E XX75 A/C/C A/C/H	291 B 330 A 331 B 373 B 373 A 268 288	2413 2314 2315 2216 2219 3-49 4-28	XX75 XX75 XX75 XX75 XX75,E A/C/C A/C/H	333 A 341 B 373 A 385 B 441 A 277 297	2512 2413 2315 2219 3-60 4-39	XX75 XX75 XX75 XX75,E A/C/C A/C/H	336 A 343 B 385 B 454 B 305 322
2113 2016 1918 3-18	XX75 XX75 XX75 A/C/C	242 A 275 A 301 B 203	2113 2114 2016 2115 2018 3-30	XX75 XX75 XX75 XX75 XX75,E A/C/H	251 C 266 B 285 C 291 A 332 A 219	2213 2114 2115 2018 2020 3-30	XX75 XX75 XX75 XX75,E XX75 A/C/H	275 A 276 C 302 B 344 B 378 A 227	2312 2213 2215 2117 2020 3-39 4-18	XX75 XX75 XX75 XX75,E XX75 A/C/C A/C/H	272 A 285 B 309 A 349 A 391 B 244 262	2312 2314 2215 2117 2216 3-49 4-28	XX75 XX75 XX75 XX75,E XX75 A/C/C A/C/H	282 B 318 A 320 B 361 B 361 A 260 278	2413 2314 2315 2216 2219 3-49 4-28	XX75 XX75 XX75 XX75 XX75,E A/C/C A/C/H	322 A 330 B 362 A 373 B 427 A 268 288	2512 2413 2315 2219 3-60 4-39	XX75 XX75 XX75 XX75,E A/C/C A/C/H	326 A 333 B 373 B 441 B 296 312	2512 2315 2317 2219 3-60 4-39	XX75 XX75 XX75 XX75,E A/C/C A/C/H	336 A 385 B 438 A 454 B 305 322
2113 2114 2016 2115 2018 3-30	XX75 XX75 XX75 XX75 XX75,E A/C/H	242 C 258 B 275 C 280 A 319 A 210	2213 2114 2115 2018 2020 3-30	XX75 XX75 XX75 XX75,E XX75 A/C/H	255 A 266 C 291 B 332 B 364 A 219	2312 2213 2215 2117 2020 3-39 4-18	XX75 XX75 XX75 XX75,E XX75 A/C/C A/C/H	263 A 275 B 299 A 337 A 378 B 235 253	2312 2314 2215 2117 2216 3-49 4-28	XX75 XX75 XX75 XX75,E XX75 A/C/C A/C/H	272 B 309 A 309 B 349 B 349 A 251 269	2413 2314 2315 2216 2219 3-49 4-28	XX75 XX75 XX75 XX75 XX75,E A/C/C A/C/H	312 A 319 B 350 A 361 B 413 A 260 278	2512 2413 2315 2219 3-60 4-39	XX75 XX75 XX75 XX75,E A/C/C A/C/H	315 A 327 B 362 B 427 B 287 303	2512 2315 2317 2219 3-60 4-39	XX75 XX75 XX75 XX75,E A/C/C A/C/H	326 A 373 B 424 A 441 B 296 312	2512 2514 2317 3-71 4-49	XX75 XX75 XX75 A/C/C A/C/H	336 B 374 A 438 B 322 339
2213 2114 2115 2018 2020 3-30	XX75 XX75 XX75 XX75,E XX75 A/C/H	256 A 256 C 280 B 319 B 351 A 210	2312 2213 2215 2117 2020 3-39 4-18	XX75 XX75 XX75 XX75,E XX75 A/C/C A/C/H	254 A 265 B 288 A 325 A 364 B 227 244	2312 2314 2215 2117 2216 3-49 4-28	XX75 XX75 XX75 XX75,E XX75 A/C/C A/C/H	263 B 298 A 299 B 337 B 337 A 242 260	2413 2314 2315 2216 2219 3-49 4-28	XX75 XX75 XX75 XX75 XX75,E A/C/C A/C/H	302 A 309 B 338 A 349 B 399 A 251 269	2512 2413 2315 2219 3-60 4-39	XX75 XX75 XX75 XX75,E A/C/C A/C/H	305 A 312 B 350 B 413 B 277 293	2512 2315 2317 2219 3-60 4-39	XX75 XX75 XX75 XX75,E A/C/C A/C/H	316 A 362 B 411 A 427 B 287 303	2512 2514 2317 3-71 4-49	XX75 XX75 XX75 A/C/C A/C/H	326 B 353 A 424 B 312 329	2514 2317 2419 3-71 4-49	XX75 XX75 XX75 A/C/C A/C/H	374 B 438 C 480 A 322 339
2312 2213 2215 2117 2020 3-39 4-18	XX75 XX75 XX75 XX75,E XX75 A/C/C A/C/H	244 A 256 B 277 A 313 A 351 B 219 235	2312 2314 2215 2117 2216 3-49 4-28	XX75 XX75 XX75 XX75,E XX75 A/C/C A/C/H	254 B 287 A 288 B 325 B 325 A 234 250	2413 2314 2315 2216 2219 3-49 4-28	XX75 XX75 XX75 XX75 XX75,E A/C/C A/C/H	291 A 298 B 327 A 337 B 386 A 242 260	2512 2413 2315 2219 3-60 4-39	XX75 XX75 XX75 XX75,E A/C/C A/C/H	295 A 302 B 338 B 399 B 268 283	2512 2315 2317 2219 3-60 4-39	XX75 XX75 XX75 XX75,E A/C/C A/C/H	305 A 350 B 398 A 413 B 277 293	2512 2514 2317 3-71 4-49	XX75 XX75 XX75 A/C/C A/C/H	316 B 351 A 411 B 302 318	2514 2317 2419 3-71 4-49	XX75 XX75 XX75 A/C/C A/C/H	363 B 424 C 466 A 312 329	2514 2419 3-71 4-49	XX75 XX75 A/C/C A/C/H	374 B 480 A 322 339
2312 2314 2215 2117 2216 3-49 4-28	XX75 XX75 XX75 XX75,E XX75 A/C/C A/C/H	244 B 277 A 277 B 313 B 313 A 225 241	2413 2314 2315 2216 2219 3-49 4-28	XX75 XX75 XX75 XX75 XX75,E A/C/C A/C/H	281 A 287 B 315 A 325 B 372 A 234 250	2512 2413 2315 2219 3-60 4-39	XX75 XX75 XX75 XX75,E A/C/C A/C/H	285 A 291 B 327 B 386 B 259 273	2512 2315 2317 2219 3-60 4-39	XX75 XX75 XX75 XX75,E A/C/C A/C/H	295 A 338 B 385 A 399 B 268 283	2512 2514 2317 3-71 4-49	XX75 XX75 XX75 A/C/C A/C/H	305 B 340 A 398 B 293 308	2514 2317 2419 3-71 4-49	XX75 XX75 XX75 A/C/C A/C/H	351 B 411 C 451 A 302 318	2514 2419 3-71 4-49	XX75 XX75 A/C/C A/C/H	363 B 466 A 312 329	2419	XX75	480 A
2413 2314 2315 2216 2219 3-49 4-28	XX75 XX75 XX75 XX75 XX75,E A/C/C A/C/H	270 A 277 B 303 A 313 B 358 A 225 241	2512 2413 2315 2219 3-60 4-39	XX75 XX75 XX75 XX75,E A/C/C A/C/H	275 A 281 B 315 B 372 B 250 264	2512 2315 2317 2219 3-60 4-39	XX75 XX75 XX75 XX75,E A/C/C A/C/H	285 A 327 B 371 A 386 B 259 273	2512 2514 2317 3-71 4-49	XX75 XX75 XX75 A/C/C A/C/H	295 B 329 A 385 B 283 298	2514 2317 2419 3-71 4-49	XX75 XX75 XX75 A/C/C A/C/H	340 B 398 C 437 A 293 308	2514 2419 3-71 4-49	XX75 XX75 A/C/C A/C/H	351 B 451 A 302 318	2419	XX75	466 A			
2512 2413 2315 2219 3-60 4-39	XX75 XX75 XX75 XX75,E A/C/C A/C/H	265 A 270 B 303 B 358 B 240 254	2512 2315 2317 2219 3-60 4-39	XX75 XX75 XX75 XX75,E A/C/C A/C/H	275 A 315 B 358 A 372 B 250 264	2512 2514 2317 3-71 4-49	XX75 XX75 XX75 A/C/C A/C/H	285 B 317 A 371 B 273 288	2514 2317 2419 3-71 4-49	XX75 XX75 XX75 A/C/C A/C/H	329 B 385 C 422 A 283 298	2514 2419 3-71 4-49	XX75 XX75 A/C/C A/C/H	340 B 437 A 293 308	2419	XX75	451 A						

If you use one of the following sizes: 2312, 2314, 2315, 2317, 2413, 2419, 2512, 2514 with an aluminum RPS insert, add the weight of that insert to your point weight, then subtract 25 grains and re-enter the point weight column within which this adjusted point weight falls.

How to use the
EASTON SHAFT SELECTION CHARTS

1. Determine your **Correct Arrow Length** and your **Actual, Actual Peak, Calculated** or **Calculated Peak Bow Weight**.
2. Under the column for recurve or compound bows, locate the box that includes your **Actual, Actual Peak, Calculated** or **Calculated Peak Bow Weight**.
3. Move across the row in a horizontal direction to the right until you locate the column including your **Correct Arrow Length**.
4. One or more recommended sizes are listed in the "Shaft Size" box located where your "**Actual, Actual Peak, Calculated** or **Calculated Peak Bow Weight**" row and "**Correct Arrow Length**" column intersect.

The "Variables" listed below will affect the **Actual Bow Weight** and **Actual Peak Bow Weight** as noted. Combine all the adjustments that apply to your equipment to figure your **Calculated Bow Weight** or **Calculated Peak Bow Weight**.

Variables to the "standard" set-up:

- High Energy Cam – add 10 lbs.
- Dacron String – subtract 3-5 lbs.
- Release Aids – subtract 3-5 lbs.
- Bow efficiency – subtract 3-5 lbs. for older less efficient bows
- Compound bow lengths 44" or less, and draw lengths over 28" – add 4-6 lbs.
- Point Weight – add 1.5 lbs. for every 10 grains your point weighs more than:
  -7% F.O.C. point, aluminum shaft
  -8% F.O.C. point, A/C/C or A/C/H shaft
  -recommended point weight, A/C/E shaft

Reading the **EASTON SHAFT SELECTION CHARTS**

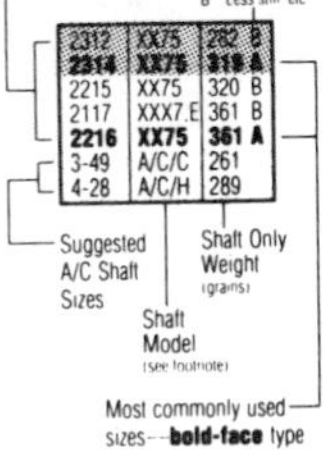

Suggested Aluminum Shaft Sizes
Relative Stiffness
A Stiffest
B Less stiff etc
2312 XX75 282 B
2314 XX75 318 A
2215 XX75 320 B
2117 XXX7.E 361 B
2216 XX75 361 A
3-49 A/C/C 261
4-28 A/C/H 289
Suggested A/C Shaft Sizes
Shaft Only Weight (grains)
Shaft Model (see footnote)
Most commonly used sizes--bold-face type

Fletch Preparation

Feathers do not usually require cleaning or other preparation, but plastic vanes do. Most have some residue on their surfaces from the manufacturing process; this must be removed to ensure that the glue will bond well. Certain residues cause glues to break down over a period of weeks and the fletching will fall off the arrow. That's always a pleasant event at a big tournament!

You can use denatured alcohol or acetone to clean plastic vanes. Do not soak your vanes in acetone, however, as prolonged contact can deteriorate some plastics. Place the vane in a glue clamp and use a paper towel dipped in the cleaning agent. Wipe the base of the vane with the towel. Clean all of the vanes you intend to use and lay them aside to dry. Be careful not to touch the bases of the vanes so that they remain free from skin oil and dirt.

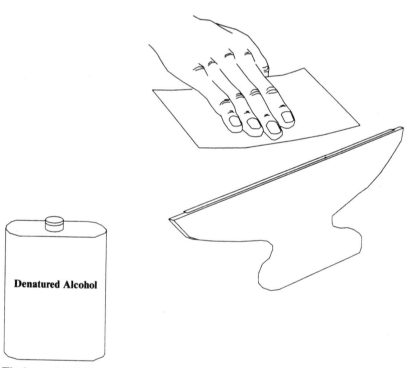

Denatured Alcohol

The base of each plastic vane should be cleaned with denatured alcohol before glue is applied.

The Fletching Procedure

Begin with one arrow and one fletch. Put the arrow in the fletching jig and the plastic or feather fletching in the glue clamp. Place the clamp on the magnet of the jig and slide it close to the arrow. Adjust the angle of the clamp according to the directions supplied with the jig so that both ends of the fletch are making contact with the shaft.

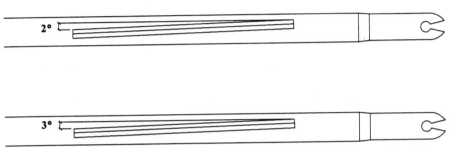

Vanes or feathers should never be put on arrows in line with the shaft. Instead, 2 or 3 degrees of offset should be used so the fletching spins the arrow in flight.

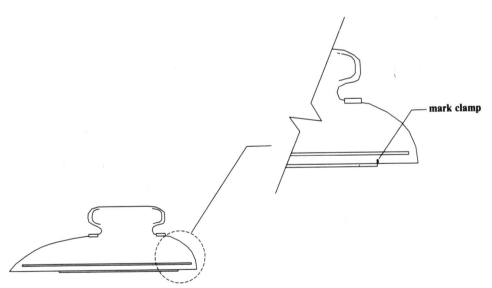

mark clamp

A pencil mark should be placed on the glue clamp so that each fletch can be installed at the same position relative to the nock of the arrow.

Do not align the fletch with the shaft. Use some offset — 2 to 3 degrees should be sufficient — so that the fletch will make the arrow rotate on its axis while in flight. The more angle you use, the more quickly the arrow will stabilize during flight.

Before you begin gluing, make a pencil mark on the clamp at the rear of the fletch. Then you can place each fletch at this same location in the clamp so that all of the fletching will wind up the same distance from the nock end of the arrow shaft.

Once you have angled the clamp correctly, remove it from the jig and apply a thin line of glue along the entire base of the fletch. Replace the clamp on the jig and slide it so that the entire length of the fletch is in contact with the shaft; there should be no gaps. If you are using a quick-drying cement, don't try to move the clamp after the initial contact between the fletch and the shaft. A slower-drying glue is better for beginners, as it gives you time to spread the glue and position the fletch so that there are no gaps.

Allow this to stand for at least fifteen minutes, then remove the clamp by opening it and sliding it away from the shaft. This little trick will keep you from pulling the newly glued fletch off the shaft.

Rotate the arrow in the jig 120 degrees if you are installing three fletches or 90 degrees if you are installing four fletches (105 and 75 degrees on some jigs). Repeat the gluing process for each fletch. When the last fletch has had time to dry, remove the arrow from the jig and place a drop of glue on the ends of each fletch. This will prevent the ends of the

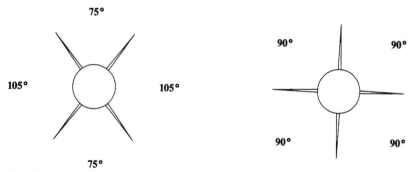

Four-fletch arrows can be placed on the shaft in two different arrangements. The 75–105-degree version is most common.

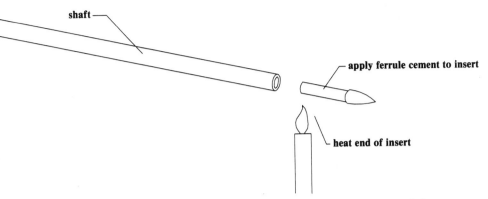

shaft

apply ferrule cement to insert

heat end of insert

Use pliers to hold the point shank to a flame for twenty to thirty seconds, rub it on a hot-melt glue stick, and insert it into the aluminum shaft.

fletching from coming loose when the arrow passes through a target butt. Allow all of your newly fletched arrows to dry for at least a day before shooting them.

Point Installation

Once you have selected the point weight for your aluminum arrows, glue the points into the shaft with hot-melt glue. First, heat the shank of the target point or the screw-in point insert adapter by holding it with pliers in or near the flame of a gas torch. Rub the warmed point or insert over a stick of hot-melt glue and then push it into the shaft. Be sure to push the point against a hard surface so that it goes all the way into the shaft. Some glue always remains on the outside of the shaft; let this harden and then peel it off.

To remove a point or insert, simply reheat the point, not the shaft, and use pliers to pull the point from the shaft with a twisting motion.

Nock Installation

After the point is secure, it is time to glue the nock onto the swaged end of the arrow shaft. Remove the nock that you twisted onto the arrow and place a drop of glue near the very tip of the swage, or beveled end. Replace the nock and twist it several times to spread the glue evenly. Align the nock so that the fletching will clear the arrow rest. (This is detailed in chapter 3.)

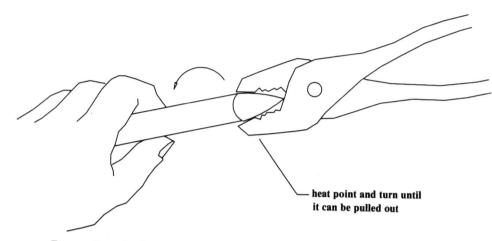

heat point and turn until
it can be pulled out

Remove the point from an aluminum arrow by heating the point — not the shaft — for twenty to thirty seconds and pulling on the point with pliers using a twisting motion.

Spin the shaft in your hand so that you can watch the nock rotate. If it wobbles as the arrow shaft spins, then it is not straight with the shaft. Realign the nock and spin again. Do this until the nock does not wobble. If you're a beginner, do not use quick-drying cement for this job as you won't be able to adjust the nock. For best results, allow the glue to dry for about a day, but an hour will do if you're in a hurry.

Maintenance Tips

Aluminum arrows are very tough and can withstand hundreds of shots without becoming bent. Bends often do occur, however, if arrows strike a tree, a rock, or the wooden frame around a target butt. If the shaft is not kinked anywhere, you can straighten it with a mechanical straightening device. Some people with keen eyes can even straighten them without tools. Kinks usually can't be straightened.

The mechanical method is the easiest way to get an arrow as straight as new, but you can also do it by hand. You locate the bend by looking down the shaft, then use the heel of your hand to do the straightening. With proper lighting you'll be able to see bends, and you can bend the shaft in the opposite direction until it is near straight.

Use soap and water to clean grimy aluminum arrows. Stronger cleaning agents can be used without harming the shaft. For dirty plastic vanes, use soap and water or denatured alcohol.

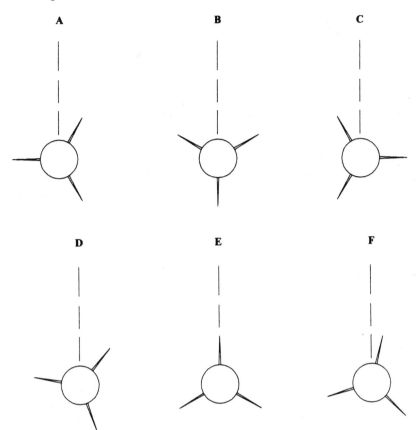

Nocks should be placed on your arrows so that fletching passes the arrow rest without making contact. Position A is standard for right-handers; B is for double-prong or double-launcher rests; C is standard for left-handers; D is for right-handed shoot-around rests; E is for single-launcher rests; F is for right-handed shoot-through rests.

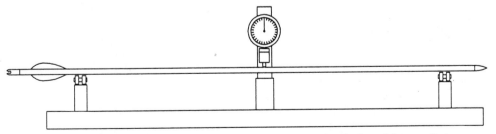

Bent aluminum arrows can be straightened with a mechanical straightener that has a gauge that detects bends to the nearest thousandth of an inch.

If feathers become worn and matted down, place them in the steam of a tea kettle to bring them back to their original shape. If small pieces of feather are missing, this should not affect the arrow's flight and the feather need not be replaced. If most of a feather is missing, however, it should be replaced.

Plastic vanes will withstand a great amount of punishment. Tears and holes will develop in them after a great amount of use, but they will still perform properly. You can trim torn pieces with scissors and not affect the flight of the arrow. When most of a vane is missing, you should consider replacing it.

When an arrow becomes lodged in a tree or board, you can remove it by untwisting the shaft from the field point. If you have installed target points, heat the end of the shaft with a lighter and pull the shaft from the lodged point. You can remove a screw-in field point with a point puller, but a target point may be permanently lodged and serve as a reminder of one of your "finer" shots.

Another method you can use to remove arrows lodged in wood is to hammer a screwdriver several inches into the wood beside the shaft. This should relieve the pressure around the arrow point so that the arrow can be pulled from the wood. Don't use this method on your neighbor's good walnut tree, however.

If a nock becomes damaged in any way, replace it immediately. If a nock should break upon release of the string, damage to you or the bow could result. This event is called a *dry fire* and is basically the same as shooting your bow without an arrow on the string. All of the stored energy of the bow is released through vibrations, which can cause a lot of damage.

With proper care and good backstops of straw, hay, foam, or grass mats, aluminum arrows can last for years. I still have several of my first aluminum arrows from 1960. I also have a large box full of arrow pieces that I plan to take to the recycling center some day.

ALUMINUM-CARBON ARROWS

Carbon fibers are strong, stiff, and lightweight. When these fibers are wrapped around an aluminum arrow shaft, they help create a very stiff, lightweight projectile. The increased stiffness allows the arrow manufacturer to significantly reduce the diameter of the shafts and still provide arrows strong enough for today's compound and recurve bows. Decreasing the diameter of the shaft also decreases the weight, which translates into faster arrow speeds and, for a target archer, higher scores at long range.

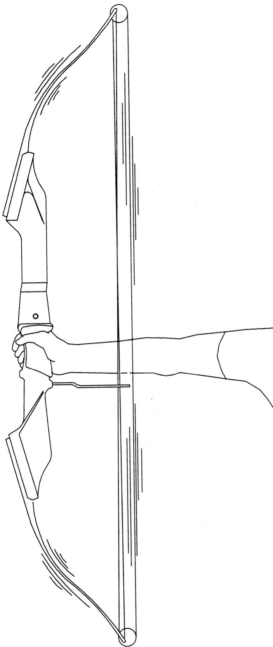

Never release any bow without an arrow on the string and arrow rest, as all of the available stored energy of the bow will be dissipated in vibrations that could break the bow.

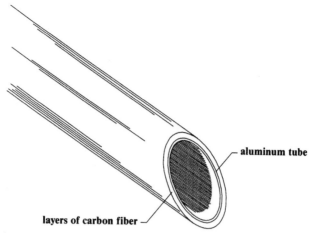

aluminum tube

layers of carbon fiber

The aluminum-carbon arrow is constructed by wrapping carbon fibers around a thin aluminum shaft to form a much stronger shaft than a much larger all-aluminum arrow.

The construction of the aluminum-carbon arrow begins with a very small aluminum tube. The tube can be about 25 percent smaller in diameter than a regular aluminum shaft, with a reduction in weight of about 10 to 20 percent.

The advantage of the aluminum-carbon arrow is increased arrow velocity; the disadvantage is the increased price of production. The arrow velocity that is gained is nearly 15 percent. Translated into shooting terms, an archer can shoot 80 yards with the faster arrows using a sight setting that was good for 70 yards with the aluminum shafts. The cost for these high-tech arrows is about twice that of the best all-aluminum shafts, but to the top tournament archers that is a small price for the possible gain in points.

Easton Aluminum is currently the only manufacturer of the aluminum-carbon arrow. There are nine different sizes to choose from. Their arrow size selection chart shows the best size for a given bow weight and a given arrow length. As with other types of arrows, it is best to test-shoot before buying.

Fletching Aluminum-Carbon Arrows

The procedure for fletching the aluminum-carbon arrow is basically the same as that for the all-aluminum arrow, with a few slight variations and precautions. The differences are detailed in the following paragraphs.

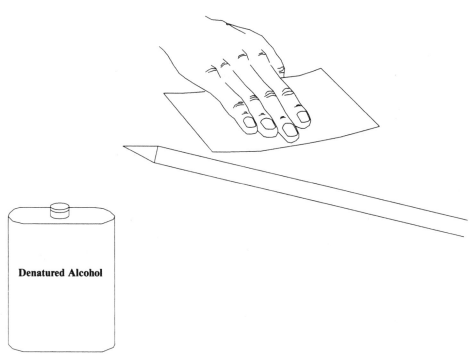

You can clean an aluminum-carbon shaft using a clean cloth and denatured alcohol.

Consult the section on fletching aluminum arrows for the remaining instructions.

Shaft Preparation

Have your local archery dealer cut the arrow shafts to the desired length with a high-speed cutoff tool. Sand off any burrs on either end with very fine sandpaper, using a motion across the end of the shaft at a 45-degree angle.

Clean the surface of the arrow with acetone or denatured alcohol. Do not use sandpaper or other abrasives for this purpose. You can clean the entire shaft or just the last six inches at the nock end, then allow the shafts to dry. Be careful not to handle the area of the shaft to be fletched.

Choose your fletching cement carefully. Some cements and glues do not bond well with carbon, and the fletching will separate from the shaft after a short period of time. It's best to get the recommendation of your local archery dealer.

Nock Preparation

The aluminum-carbon shaft is not tapered on the nock end like the all-aluminum shaft, so the nock must be inserted into the end. Don't use glue at this time; instead place a piece of a plastic sandwich bag over the end of the shaft, then insert the nock. The nock will fit tightly in the shaft while you're fletching the arrow, and you can later simply pull it out, remove the plastic, and glue the nock into its proper position.

Fletch Preparation

Follow the instructions given for aluminum arrows.

The Fletching Procedure

Smaller-diameter shafts like the aluminum-carbon ones need less offset angle for their fletching. When you set the clamp on the fletching jig, adjust it so that each fletch is offset about 1 or 2 degrees relative to the arrow shaft.

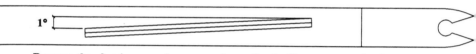

Because the aluminum-carbon arrow is smaller in diameter, you should use only 1 degree of offset when installing fletching.

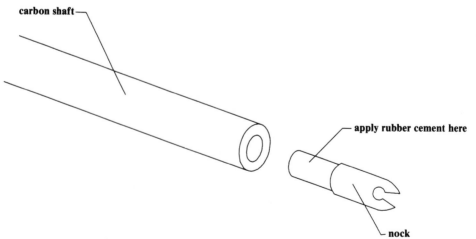

You should use rubber cement to install the insertable nocks in aluminum-carbon arrows so that they can be easily removed.

Point Installation

Follow the instructions for aluminum arrows.

Nock Installation

After the point has cooled, you can glue the nock into the shaft. Use a simple rubber cement for this purpose. A small drop on the end of the nock that inserts into the shaft is all that is necessary to keep the nock in place for hundreds of shots. If a nock ever breaks off flush with the end, rubber cement will enable you to remove the stub that's left in the shaft.

Maintenance Tips

The main purpose of the aluminum-carbon arrow is to supply speed and higher scores at long range. Because it is made with a much smaller aluminum tube, it is not as sturdy as the all-aluminum arrow and will not withstand as much battering.

With this in mind, you should always be careful what kind of target butt you use. Also, if you shoot too many arrows into one target, some of them will take hits on the sides of the shafts and the carbon fibers will become damaged and broken. You can feel these broken fibers by rubbing your hand over the shaft. Not much can be done to repair this kind of damage, but the arrows will still perform well. You can cover the broken fibers with epoxy to possibly prevent further fraying.

Not much can be done about bends in aluminum-carbon arrows either. You may be able to straighten some minor bends by hand, but often the shaft will break if you try to use a mechanical straightener.

To clean these shafts, use soap and water, denatured alcohol, or acetone. Do not use anything abrasive as it may damage the carbon fibers.

If a nock becomes damaged, you need to remove and replace it. Twist the nock to loosen the rubber cement. If the nock's end is broken completely off but its shank is still in the arrow shaft, thread a small screw into the remaining portion. After several turns, just pull on the screw and turn clockwise with a pair of pliers to remove the piece.

As you may have guessed by now, these arrows are not for beginners. They are very high-tech projectiles that have but one purpose: flying fast. When used and cared for properly, they can provide hundreds of shots with no problems.

CARBON ARROWS

The newest shaft on the market, developed in the late 1980s, is made of resin-soaked carbon fibers that have been pulled through a forming device

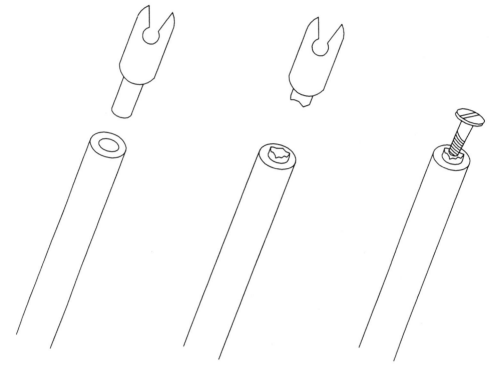

When a nock breaks off in the aluminum-carbon shaft, turn a small screw into the shank that is in the shaft and pull it out using a twisting motion.

into the shape of a tube. The tube is then cut into arrow-size lengths. The result is a very small-diameter shaft that is much stiffer than aluminum tubing and lighter in weight.

Several companies manufacture carbon arrows. They come in about ten different sizes that vary in outside and inside diameters to match the most common draw weights and draw lengths of today's bows. These diameters are significantly smaller than those of all-aluminum shafts, which gives the carbon shaft advantages in weight and speed, and the resins that hold the carbon fibers together make these shafts very durable.

Fletching Carbon Arrows
Shaft Preparation
Carbon shafts should be cut with the same high-speed cutoff tool that is used for aluminum arrows. Cut the carbon shafts about one inch longer

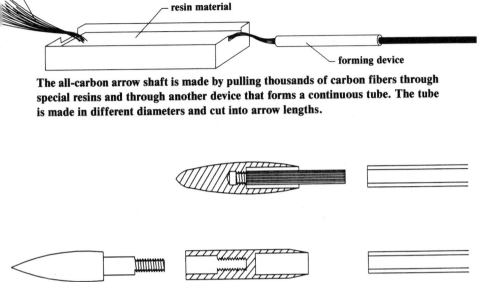

carbon fibers

resin material

forming device

The all-carbon arrow shaft is made by pulling thousands of carbon fibers through special resins and through another device that forms a continuous tube. The tube is made in different diameters and cut into arrow lengths.

The ends of the carbon arrow must be protected by using slip-over points and nocks. At the top is a slip-over target point with a weight pin that inserts in the shaft; second is a field point adaptor; at the bottom is a nock adaptor.

than you would an aluminum arrow because the point and nock adapter each slip over a half inch of shaft.

Like other arrow shafts, the carbon tube needs cleaning before you apply glue. For carbon shafts use lacquer thinner or denatured alcohol. Acetone leaves some residue that may destroy the bond between the glue and shaft. If you do use acetone, finish with denatured alcohol.

Another effective method of cleaning carbon shafts is to use very fine sandpaper. Sand only the last five inches where the fletch is going to be attached, then wipe clean with a dry cloth. The carbon shaft is a little temperamental when you are applying glue, so take great care in this cleaning step.

MAX II V–MAX EXACTA	ALUMINUM		DIVA
	X 7	XX 75	
—1800	—1616	—1618 / —1714 / 1713—	
—1880	—1714 / —1716	—1718 / 1716— / 1813—	—17S
—1960	—1814	—1814 / 1815—	
	—1816	—1816 / —1913 / 1818— / 1914—	
	—1914	—1915 / 1916—	—18S
—2100	—1916	—1917 / —2014 / 2013—	—19S
—2200	—2014	—2016 / —2018 / —2020 / —2114	20S 40/60
	—2115	2115—	21S 50/70
—2300		—2213 / 2117—	22S 60/80
	EXAMPLE: A 2300 WILL SHOOT SIMILAR TO A 2117 AND 2213	—2216 / —2217	
—2400		—2219 / —2317 / —2413	
—2540			

Use the arrow comparison chart by finding your current aluminum size and matching it with the AFC Carbon Arrow number. This chart assumes equivalent balance points.

Nock Preparation

The carbon arrow requires more preparation for nock installation than any other type of shaft because of the construction of the tube. Thousands of fibers held together by resins run from end to end, so the ends of the shaft must be protected from wear and tear. For this reason, an adapter onto which the nock can be glued slips over one end of the shaft, and the point slips over the other.

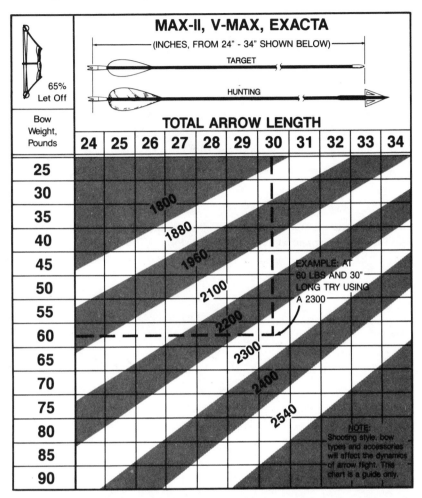

Use the bow weight chart by finding your average draw weight and moving across the chart to your arrow length. The Carbon Arrow size numbers within the bands are suggested.

To ensure that the nock adapter will stay bonded to the shaft, you must take care in preparing the end. Lightly sand the last half inch of the shaft and bevel the end slightly, then wipe clean with a dry cloth. Clean the inside of the nock adapter with denatured alcohol and allow it to dry.

Install the nock adapter on the shaft with a small amount of epoxy. You can also use a hot-melt glue that has a high melting temperature. Place a drop of glue on the end of the shaft and push the adapter on. Twist

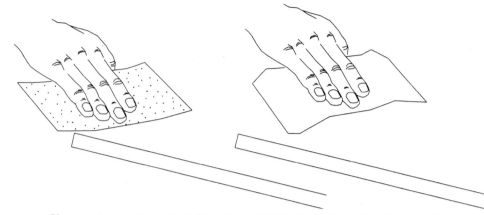

You can prepare the ends of the carbon shaft for the point and nock by sanding with fine sandpaper and wiping with a clean cloth.

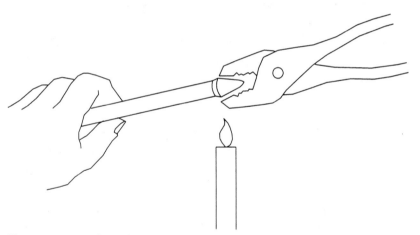

You can remove the point and nock adaptors by heating their ends for short periods of time and pulling straight off the shaft with pliers.

it several times to spread the glue. Allow this to stand for thirty minutes before you peel any excess glue from around the adapter. When you are ready to fletch a shaft, just twist a nock onto the adapter.

Should you ever need to remove the nock adapter from the shaft, a little heat will do the job. Heat the adapter for thirty seconds and try to pull it from the shaft with pliers. If it is not loose, try another thirty seconds of heat. Do not overheat the end of the shaft or the resins bonding the fibers will break down and the shaft will be destroyed.

Fletch Preparation
This step is the same as for other arrow types. Consult the section under aluminum arrows for details.

The Fletching Procedure
Fletching on carbon arrows should not have as much offset as that on the bigger aluminum arrows. Fletch the carbon shaft with an offset of 1 to 2 degrees. Use a helical curved clamp to install fletching that is longer than three inches so that the entire base of the fletch will make contact with the shaft.

The fletching operation from this point on is the same as for the aluminum arrow except that you must use a quick-setting cement or Saunders' fletching glue.

Point Installation
Lightly sand the point end of the carbon shaft and then bevel it. Wipe clean with a dry cloth.

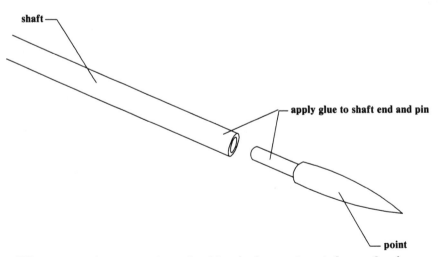

shaft

apply glue to shaft end and pin

point

When you use the target point and weight pin, be sure to put glue on the pin as well as the end of the shaft.

Carbon arrow points are composed of two parts. The actual point fits over the outside of the shaft, and a screw-in weight pin fits inside the shaft. Clean both parts with denatured alcohol before installation. Glue the pin into the point with a drop of epoxy, then cover the pin with epoxy and also place a small amount of it on the end of the shaft. Push the point and pin into the shaft with a slow, clockwise twisting motion to spread the glue evenly. After thirty minutes you can peel away any excess glue.

Nock Installation

Now that the arrow is fletched, you also need to glue on the nock. Remove it from the adapter and place a drop of fletching cement on the adapter. Push the nock back on and rotate it several times to spread the glue evenly. Align the nock so that the fletching passes the arrow rest with no contact. There are several common positions. (For more information, see chapter 3.) Allow the nock to set for an hour before using.

Maintenance Tips

Through a great deal of use over the last four years it has been found that carbon arrows are very durable. They can withstand impact with trees, boards, and even rocks. Over time, however, this kind of treatment will do damage to any kind of arrow shaft and repair work will have to be done. With the carbon shaft, some things can never be repaired while others never have to be repaired.

Something that can't be repaired is a split in the shaft. After a great amount of use or some abuse a crack may develop between the fibers. You can detect these by flexing the arrow in your hands and examining the length of the shaft. If you find one or several, discard the arrow since it is unsafe to shoot.

Carbon arrows won't become bent from use or from hitting solid objects. Their straightness is determined when they are manufactured and can't be altered by hand or by machine. In fact, machine straightening will break a carbon shaft, so don't try it.

Several things that *can* be repaired are points, nocks, nock adapters, and fletching. To remove a point, first heat it for thirty seconds and then pull it straight out with pliers. Keep heating and pulling in thirty-second intervals until the point comes out. Do not twist, as this might separate and crack the carbon shaft. Clean the end of the shaft with fine sandpaper and install another point following the directions given earlier.

You can cut cracked or broken nocks from the adapter with a knife. Clean the adapter with fine sandpaper, then wipe with a dry cloth. Install a new nock according to the instructions given previously.

If you need to remove a damaged nock adapter, apply heat in thirty-second intervals as was recommended for the points. Pull the adapter from the shaft with pliers and do not twist. Use fine sandpaper to clean the end of the shaft and denatured alcohol for the inside of the nock adapter. Install a new nock adapter according to the instructions given earlier.

If you wish to replace fletching, remove it with a knife. Cut the fletch material as close to the shaft as possible, being careful not to cut into the carbon. Any fletch material remaining on the shaft can be removed with acetone and a cloth. Be sure to clean the shaft with denatured alcohol to remove the acetone. Refletch as per the instructions given earlier.

A carbon arrow can provide thousands of shots over a period of years. Proper care and the use of a good backstop are the key ingredients for arrow longevity.

3

Selecting and Adjusting Arrow Rests

AN ARCHER'S OBJECTIVE is to project an arrow in a given direction at a specific target. Sometimes the arrow strikes the target and sometimes it doesn't. Success or failure depends on two aspects: the shooting form of the archer and the dynamic events that take place as the arrow is passing the handle of the bow. The latter is the subject of this chapter.

To achieve good arrow flight and tight groups, you need to use shafts that bend in the correct sequence as well as the proper device on which to position your arrows before launch. The right arrow rest made of the appropriate material can greatly enhance the flight characteristics of the arrow even if the shaft is not matched to the bow. The arrow rest is just as important to good shooting as the bow and arrows are, and it usually must be installed before an arrow can be shot.

RESTS FOR BOWS WITH NO CENTER-SHOT ADJUSTMENT

Up until fifty years ago, bow handles had no arrow rests. Instead, archers used the knuckle of the index finger on the bow hand or a siper, a device held in the bow hand, on which to rest the arrow. In either case the arrow

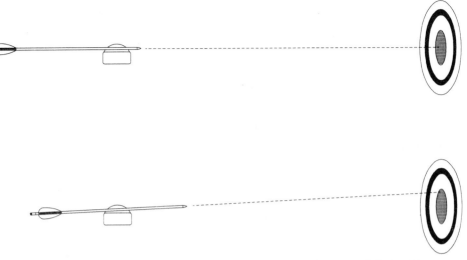

In a drawn wood-handled bow, the arrow can be pointed at the target (left sketch), but when the string is let up to the brace position, the nock stays in the center line forcing the point to the left. "How does the arrow hit the target when it is shot?" is the archer's paradox.

was shot around the bow handle, and choosing the arrow that had the proper bending characteristics was necessary to achieve accuracy. About the only material used on the bow handle was a leather or cloth wrapping to prevent the arrow from making noise when it passed the handle and to provide a better grip for the hand.

More recent wood-handled longbows and recurves have been built with an arrow shelf incorporated into the handle design. A small amount of the handle was cut away so that the arrow could rest on the shelf without falling off during the draw stroke and the power stroke.

The shelf saved the hand from wear and tear but did not do much for arrow flight because it was very rigid compared with one's knuckle. Soft materials were then placed on the shelf to cushion the flight of the arrow across it. Eventually feathers, bristles, and other materials were fastened to the shelf area to support the arrow underneath as well as on the side. This was the beginning of the science of arrow-rest tuning.

With newer, laminated handles that were strong enough that a hole could be drilled through them, a new technology for arrow rests came about. If a hole was drilled through the middle of the handle perpendicular to the arrow and above the arrow shelf, a side support for the arrow

could be mounted securely. This eliminated the stick-on style of side support and introduced the cushion style. A support that used small springs and would yield in the horizontal direction could be placed at the side of the arrow shaft. Cushioning on the side helped to dampen the bending of the arrow during the power stroke and added a large degree of control to the rest-tuning process.

RESTS FOR CENTER-SHOT HANDLES

The cushion plunger aided the tuning process, but the arrow still had to pass around most of the bow handle instead of through the middle of it. The development of the metal handle was the next step in the improvement of the bow and arrow. Metal added enough strength to the handle that it could be cut away around the arrow shelf. In fact, it could be cut through its vertical center so that the arrow could actually be launched directly through the center line of the bow. Now the arrow could be pointing at the target both before and after the bowstring was drawn.

The center-shot handle has opened the door to a wide variety of arrow rests. There are probably two hundred different kinds of rests on the market today, each offering the shooter a slightly different approach to the adjustments for center shot, plunger tension, and launcher tension. Some use metal parts, some plastic, and others wire springs. Their objective is the same: to support the arrow and guide it during its first thirty inches of flight.

Today's arrow rests take into account the complete center-shot alignment of the arrow and the need for a different kind of support. This support must yield as much in the vertical direction as it does in the horizontal, if not more. The amount of bend tension in both directions is critical for achieving good flight for arrows equipped with broadheads or target points.

There are two major types of arrow rests designed for bows with center shot. The shoot-around rest requires that the arrow bend around or move to the left side of the rest (for right-handed shooters) as it passes the handle riser. This is an acceptable procedure since most arrows do some kind of bending or vibrating as they pass by the arrow rest. The shoot-through rest provides support on the side and the bottom of the arrow with two separate rest parts. This allows the bottom hen fletch of the arrow to pass between the supports.

Both arrow-rest types have advantages and disadvantages. The shoot-through rest offers the capability of independent tension adjustment on

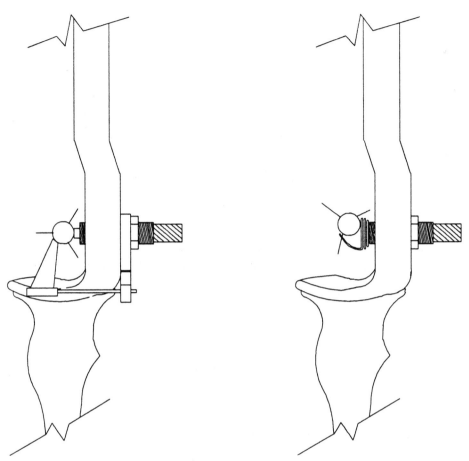

Arrow rests come in two basic varieties: the shoot-through type pictured on the left and the shoot-around on the right.

each support, but if the rest is not adjusted properly, the arrow will fall between the two parts. The shoot-around rest is simple and durable, but it does not have much tension-adjustment capability.

Try different arrow rests until you find the combination that works best with your arrows and bow system. I wish I could name one specific rest that would work for all bows and all shooters, but that is not the case so be open-minded and try several.

Arrow-rest selection is an ongoing process. Each bow you use may shoot better with another rest. Your shooting form may change during the

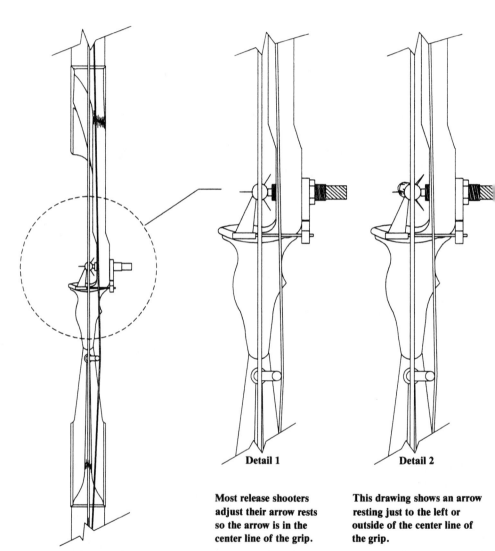

Detail 1

Detail 2

Most release shooters
adjust their arrow rests
so the arrow is in the
center line of the grip.

This drawing shows an arrow
resting just to the left or
outside of the center line of
the grip.

With the shoot-through handle design, the arrow rest can be adjusted so the arrow
sets in the center line of the handle. True center shot (middle sketch) is used by
most release shooters, while most finger shooters prefer to set their arrow just
outside of center as shown on the right.

weeks you spend practicing, and then you may need a different rest in order to improve the grouping ability of your bow. A switch in arrow sizes may also require that you change rests or adjust the tension on the one you are using. Don't do this every time a problem arises, but do be aware that a change in rests or in the relative stiffness of its springs and launchers can bring about tighter arrow groups if the conditions are right.

CENTER-SHOT ALIGNMENT OF THE ARROW

The center of pressure between the archer's hand and the bow handle determines the center line of the bow system. The arrow will try to shoot through this center line of pressure, and the arrow rest must be aligned accordingly. When the arrow is not in this line, it may not react well with the rest and flight problems may result. Arrow groups may not be as tight as they would be with better alignment.

Many finger shooters position their arrow rests so that the center of the arrow will be slightly to the outside of the center of pressure: Thus for right-handed shooters, the arrow lies to the left of center, and for left-handed shooters, to the right. Two-time Olympic gold medalist Darrell Pace uses this center-shot alignment for his recurve bows. He recommends that you begin bow tuning with the rest in this position. This is a suggestion, however, and not a rule; you may want to experiment with your arrow rest closer to or on the center line of pressure at the start of the tuning process.

Most release shooters move their rests left or right until the arrow is in the center line of pressure. When shot with a release aid, the arrow tends to leave the compound with very little bending and almost always flies best when shot through the center of pressure. From this location I seldom move the center-shot adjustment. Some pros, however, do make center-shot adjustments with their spring-coil or launcher rests to improve arrow flight. If it helps make your groups of arrows become smaller, tighter together, then by all means make the adjustment.

FLETCH CLEARANCE

The purpose of an arrow rest is to support the arrow and guide it during the initial stages of its launch. Contact between the fletching and the arrow rest or the side of the bow will cause each arrow to be launched differently. Therefore you must establish fletch clearance when you shoot the first dozen arrows from your bow. Achieving fletch clearance is part of the bow-tuning process, which is detailed in chapter 7.

4

Installing and Using Accessories

THE HUMAN MIND is never satisfied. Look what it has done to the simple game of bowling. Imagine what the inventor of the game, who tried to knock down a couple of sticks with a smooth stone he or she found in a river, would think of the modern bowling alley with its big sign outside and smoothly polished lanes inside, the electric pinsetters and the ball-return track, and the little air blower that dries your hands before each shot. That person may not even recognize the game!

Archery has undergone similar kinds of changes because of the human mind's ever-present desire to "make it better." A simple bent stick and a vine have given way to high-tech laminated limbs, composite handles, and a bowstring made of the strongest man-made fiber ever. Today's bow can send an arrow 100 yards to strike a five-inch spot, while the bent stick was used from a distance of 5 yards to hit a one-hundred-pound target.

Man is never satisfied with just utilizing an invention, but must constantly add to it so that it becomes more effective or easier to use—hence the multitude of devices known as accessories. These are the things that modern archers feel they need in order to become better marksmen.

In many cases accessories do help, but other times they don't because they are not used correctly or haven't been installed properly. I often see beginners using several accessories that perform the same function. More is not necessarily better. Understanding some of the essential accessories should help you around this situation and enable you to enjoy the sport a little more.

The following accessories are listed in order of importance from greatest to least; some are necessary and others are optional. It's up to you which ones to use, so read about all of them. The arrow rest is so vital—not only to accuracy but also to understanding the arrow's action during the shot—that it has already been described in depth in its own chapter.

THE BOWSTRING

The bowstring, of course, is a necessary part of the bow-and-arrow machine. Without it all you have is a pair of sticks. The bowstring is attached to both ends of the bow and enables the transfer of energy from the point where your hand pulls the string to the limbs of the bow. Then, when the string is released, it transfers the energy from the two limbs back to the one point on the string where the nock of the arrow is attached.

Since the limbs of a bow can store a great deal of energy, the bowstring must be strong. The first bowstrings were probably vines and were not strong enough to do the job for any length of time. Sinew from animals was the next choice and, with proper treatment, could last for many shots. Today the materials used are B-50 Dacron and high-performance polyethylene Fast Flight, which will last for thousands of shots over many years.

The modern bowstring is made to withstand the stress and strain placed on it by the limbs of the bow and the nock of the arrow. The string's ends and middle are reinforced and protected with serving thread to prevent wear and breakage; in fact, the whole string-building process is designed to ensure great strength and longevity.

The process begins with the laying of six to ten loops of string material around four pins in a rectangular formation. The number of strands depends on the peak weight of the bow on which it will be placed—the heavier the bow, the more strands required to support the weight. Each strand of B-50 Dacron has a rating of 50 pounds test weight, and the stronger Fast Flight strands have ratings of 80 to 100 pounds.

The loose ends are held tight while thread called serving is wound around the strands for several inches. This is done on each end to bind the

strands

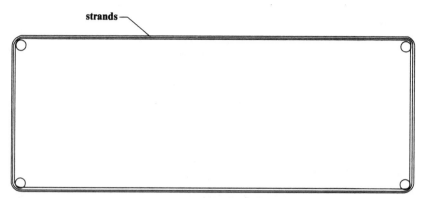

You begin making the bowstring by wrapping loops of string around the four pins of the string jig. Ten loops will make a twenty-strand string.

2″

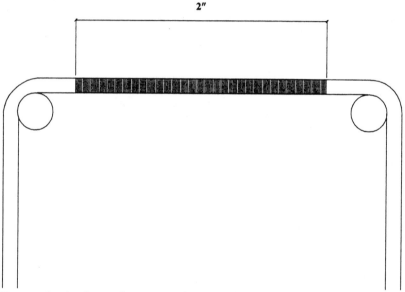

You can begin the serving process by wrapping two inches of serving thread around the ten strands between the pins at either end of the string jig.

strands so that they won't pull free. Sometimes the loose ends are tied in a knot before the serving thread is applied.

The end serving is completed by stretching the loops around only two pins. More serving thread is then wrapped around the doubled bowstring.

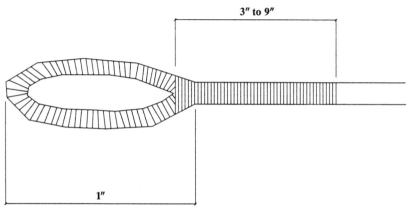

When the ten loops are folded and hooked on two pins, one at either end, the end serving will help to form the end loop. Finish the loop by serving three to nine inches toward the middle of the string.

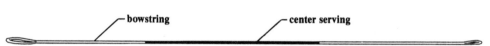

The center serving of monofilament should be about eight to ten inches long and is best applied when the string is on the bow under high tension. Be sure to serve two or three inches above the nocking point location.

This finish serving is applied for about four to eight inches up the string from each end. When completed, these ends are strong and durable and have loops that fit over the tips of bow limbs or onto the anchors of the cables of a compound bow.

The final step is the application of the center serving, which will strengthen and preserve that part of the string where the nock of the arrow and the fingers or release aid are placed. Nylon, Dacron, monofilament, or woven Fast Flight is wrapped for three to four inches in either direction from the middle of the string. Again, the loose ends are secured underneath the wraps of the serving material.

Normal use of your bow should not cause much wear to the string, and it should last for several years. If the strands begin to fray or a strand gets cut, however, you need to replace the string. Covering the exposed strands of the string with beeswax will help to protect them from the weather and normal wear.

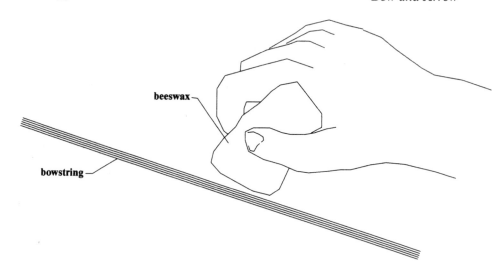

Rub beeswax on the strands of your bowstring to protect it from wear. Use a hair dryer to melt the wax into the strands.

To attach the string to a longbow or a recurve, you simply place the end loops around the tips of the bow limbs. The string is shorter than the bow, so it will take some effort to attach the second loop. Place the lower tip of the bow (with the string attached) over one foot and the center of the bow behind the opposite leg; now you'll be able to bend the bow with one hand and place the string on the upper limb tip with the other.

The compound bow is somewhat more difficult to deal with if it is not strung. Generally, the string is on the bow when it's sent from the factory, but if for some reason yours does not have a string on it, you must compress the limbs with a bow press. This is a mechanical device that pulls down on the handle while holding the limbs in a fixed position. Because of the stiffness of the compound bow's limbs, you will not be able to do this with your hands.

On the compound bow, the loops of the string fit around the anchors on the ends of the cables. These metal anchors come in several different shapes, but all have a hook around which the string wraps. The anchor is molded onto the end of the steel wire cable and is strong enough to withstand a lot of abuse.

Some newer compound systems totally omit the metal anchor and the cable end that usually wraps around the wheel; instead, the string itself wraps around the wheel and hooks onto a post in the wheel's center. By eliminating the potentially weak link, this compound system has fewer parts and is stronger.

NOCKSET LOCATORS

Another necessary accessory is a nockset locator. Whatever material is used to make the device, its purpose is the same: to locate a fixed position on the bowstring at which the nock of each arrow can be placed prior to

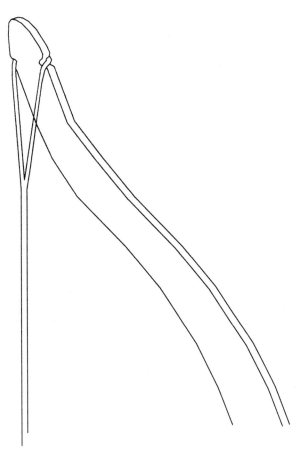

The end loop for a longbow string should be two to three inches long to facilitate the bow-stringing process.

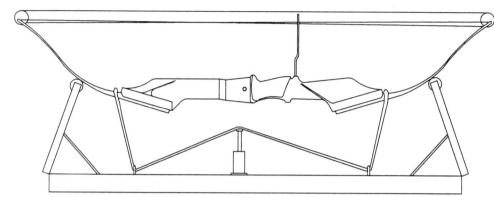

You should place your compound bow in a bow-press device to replace the bow-string.

every shot. Consistent arrow placement is of primary importance for achieving accuracy.

The nockset is most often a small metal ring that can be placed around the bowstring and then pinched with special nockset pliers so that it fits snugly. The ring usually has a plastic inner layer so that it won't cut the strands of the string. Other materials that can be used are heat-shrink tube and nylon serving thread.

The location of the nockset ring is of primary importance to shooting accuracy. If it is too low or too high, the arrows will fly with either a fishtailing or a porpoising motion instead of straight toward the target. The nockset must be movable to enable its adjustment during the bow-tuning process. A change of one-eighth of an inch can make a big difference in how close together your arrows will be in the target. (For bow-tuning details, see chapter 7.)

To install the nockset ring, you'll need two simple tools: a bow square and a pair of nockset pliers. Place the bow square on the bowstring so that the lower edge of the extended measuring arm is level with the spot on the arrow rest that supports the bottom of the arrow. Put the nockset ring on the string about one-fourth of an inch above that. The scale of inches on the vertical edge of the square next to the bowstring will help you find this setting.

Once you've positioned the nockset ring at the one-fourth-inch mark, squeeze it with the specially shaped nock pliers so that it's tight on the bowstring, but remember that you will need to move this ring during the test-shooting stage of bow preparation. If the ring is *too* tight, some damage may be done to the serving around the string or even to the strands of the string under the serving. Once this happens you must replace the string or risk sudden string failure.

Another popular method is to tie on nylon serving thread as a nocking point. Begin at the same location on the string as described above, looping the thread around the bowstring at the one-fourth-inch level and tying a snug overhand knot. Then pull the ends to the opposite side of the

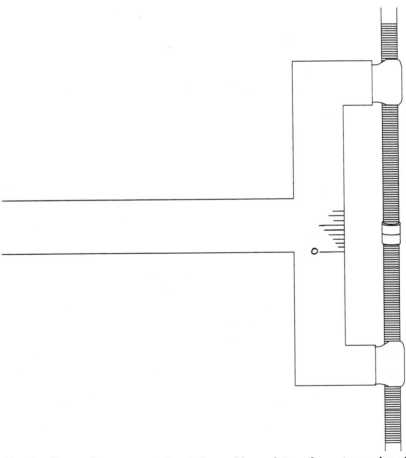

You should use a bow square to locate the nocking point on the center serving of your bowstring.

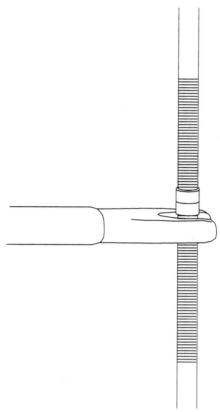

Place at least two nockset rings on the serving at a location several sixteenths of an inch above the level of the arrow rest. This will allow the bottom side of your arrows to be level with the arrow rest.

bowstring from the first knot and snugly tie another knot just below the ring of thread already in place. Tie seven more knots above the first two, alternating sides up the bowstring. After the ninth knot is made but not pulled tight, insert a loop of another thread under the ninth knot; then tie a tenth knot on the opposite side of the bowstring and pass the ends of the nylon thread through the loop of the other thread. Now pull this loop down through the ninth knot, bringing with it the ends of the nylon serving thread.

Pull these ends tight, then cover the knots with fletching cement. After the glue hardens, you can trim the ends of the nylon thread. The

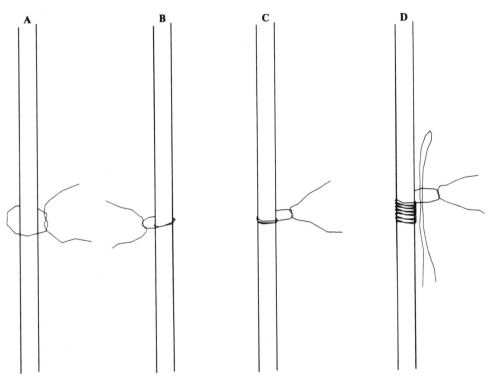

The tie-on nocking point begins with one loop and an overhand knot in **A**. The second knot shown in **B** is tied below and on the opposite side of the string. Knot three is tied directly above knot one as in **C**. To finish the process, slip an extra loop of thread up under knot nine as in **D**. Tie knot ten, then slip the loose ends of serving through the extra loop. Pull the ends of the extra loop down through knot nine along with the ends of serving.

result is a hardened nocking point. You'll be able to twist it up and down the serving of the bowstring like a nut on a bolt, but it will not move up the string with normal shooting. For security you can place a metal nockset ring directly above the hardened thread.

Once you've installed a nocking point locator, you can begin shooting the bow.

BOW SIGHTS

Not everyone who tries archery (or any other shooting sport, for that matter) has the high degree of eye-hand coordination required to become

80 to 90 percent accurate without using some sort of sighting aid. Accuracy through pure instinctive shooting is a real gift that few people have, especially with a bow and arrow. I learned to shoot without any sighting aids and became good enough that I stopped losing all of my arrows. But I wanted more, of course, and when I had the chance to put a sight on my bow, I took it. My accuracy improved greatly within a short period of time.

The bow sight used for hunting is a simple device, but much more sophisticated ones have been developed for target archery. My first bow sight was a straight pin taped onto the back of the bow. After a few shots I moved it up, down, left, or right, depending on where the arrow hit the target. Once I'd made the right adjustments, all I had to do was hold the pin on the middle of the target and release smoothly, and the arrow would hit the bull's-eye.

The key words here are *release smoothly*. The bow sight demands that you anchor, aim, and release the same way each time you shoot. If you don't, the arrow will miss the intended target and your human error once again will be in your face. But that is the challenge of shooting with a bow sight: improving your performance.

My next step up in bow sights was a machined metal bar with a sliding block through which a threaded sight pin was inserted. When the metal bar was screwed onto the back of the bow, I could adjust the pin's position by sliding the block up or down the bar. The windage — left/right adjustment of the sight pin — was accomplished by turning the threaded sight pin through the block.

With such a pin, once the windage is set correctly any yardage can be shot. For shorter distances you slide the pin up the sight bar, and for longer distances you slide it down. You can mark the points for different distances on the bar and shoot them with consistent accuracy simply by moving the sight pin to the appropriate mark and aiming at the target.

Much more sophisticated sights are being made today to perform the same task with greater precision. Some sights used by top professional and amateur archers cost as much as three hundred dollars. Microadjustment features for elevation and windage make very small changes in sight settings possible so that a high degree of accuracy can be achieved.

The first sight a beginner should have is a pin sight. This simple but very effective sight consists of a flat metal plate with slots in which a series of sight pins can be attached. You can adjust the pins up and down in the slots so that each is set for a different distance. Start with this basic sight until your skill level requires a more accurate adjustment system.

Most pin sights have a standard mounting-hole arrangement that will fit any bow following Archery Manufacturers Organization standards. Two or three screws hold the sight bracket or plate to the side of the bow. Do not overtighten the screws and strip the threads in the holes of the bow handle.

To start the sighting process, place one pin near the top of a slot. Remember, the higher pins will be used for the closer targets. Begin shooting at either 10 or 15 yards. If your anchor position and release are relatively consistent, you'll be able to shoot several arrows into a six-inch spot from this distance.

If you've shot a group of arrows and they are not near the middle of the target, move the sight pin to a new location on the mounting bracket. If the arrows are above and to the right of center, move the sight pin higher

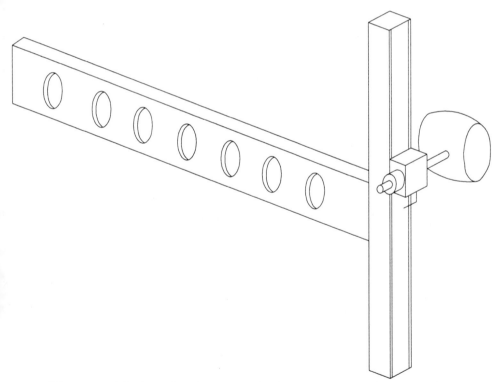

Most target sights have a bar that extends the sight away from the aiming eye and a vertical bar to which a movable block with a scope or sight pin is attached.

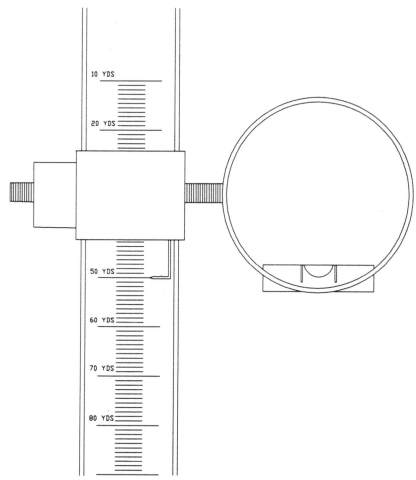

You can place sight marks on the sight bar for different distances. Sliding the sight down the bar causes you to hold the bow higher for a more distant target.

and to the right, or if they are hitting below and left of center, move the sight pin down and to the left, until your arrows hit the middle of the target.

You can make the vertical adjustment by loosening the locking nut holding the pin to the mounting bracket, sliding the pin up or down in its slot, and retightening the nut. Adjust the windage by turning the threaded sight pin to the right or left within its mounting block or housing.

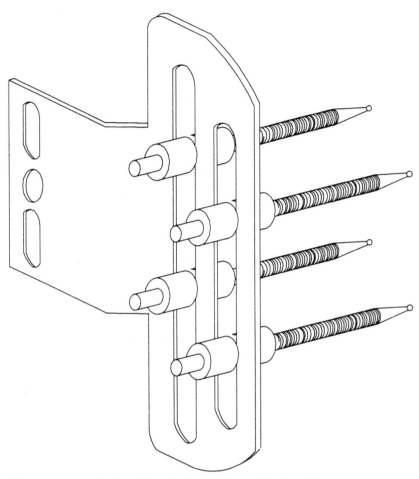

You may want to begin with a simple pin sight, which is nothing more than a flat plate of metal or plastic through which several straight sight pins are mounted.

After you've made the adjustments to the sight pin, shoot several more arrows. The next group should be closer to the middle of the target. If it isn't, make another adjustment and try again. If the second group of arrows hits on the opposite side of center from the previous group, you have overadjusted. Correct the overadjustment and shoot several more arrows.

The rule to remember when sighting in is to *match the sight pin to the impact point of the arrows*. Then when you shoot another group of arrows

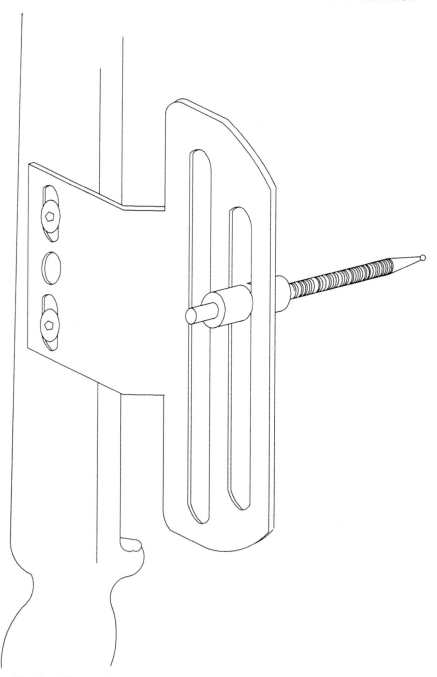

You should begin with one sight pin from a distance of 10 or 15 yards.

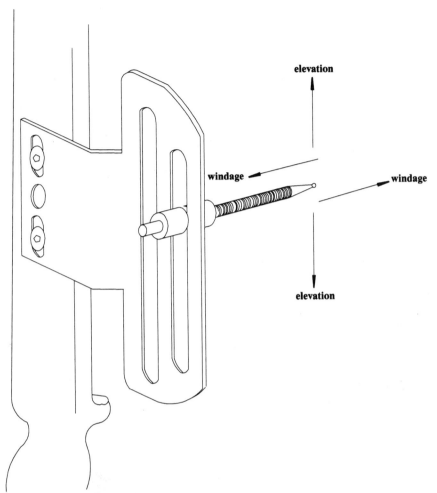

You must adjust the sight pin so that it matches the impact point of your arrows. Do that by moving the pin up if your arrows hit high on the target, down if they hit low, right if they hit to the right, and left if they hit left on the target.

while aiming at the middle, they will hit the middle. This rule holds true for adjusting the front sight of any device that launches a projectile. The rear sight, however, must be adjusted in the opposite direction.

To hit targets at longer distances, the arrow must be pointed higher, so install other pins at lower positions on the sight bracket. Again, shoot some arrows and adjust each pin until it matches the arrows' impact point.

Four or five pins should be sufficient to get you started at any archery club where outdoor shooting is enjoyed. Pins set for 15, 25, 35, and 45 yards are enough for me to hit any target from 2 to 50 yards. Archery clubs usually keep their casual outdoor shooting events within this range. Most indoor archery is shot at 20 yards, and for this you'll only need one pin.

There are more sophisticated sights with sliding blocks, magnifying lenses, levels, and microadjustment knobs for finer sight settings, but with all of these you still follow the same rule: Move the sight to match the impact point of the arrows. These sights give you the ability to hit a five-inch spot at 80 yards with great consistency. A major advantage is the ease with which you can attain different sight settings. You use only one sight pin or scope for all the distances you wish to shoot, and with only one pin to look at you won't pick the wrong one!

REAR SIGHTS

As I've mentioned, using a bow sight requires that you anchor and release consistently. Unless you're using a rear sighting device, the anchor position acts as the rear sight. If your anchor is not consistent, your eye will not be positioned the same on each shot and you will not achieve high accuracy.

To help you achieve a consisent anchor point, you can place a rear sighting device in the bowstring. This peep sight is a small disk with a hole through which you can look while at full draw so that your eye will be

Target Scope

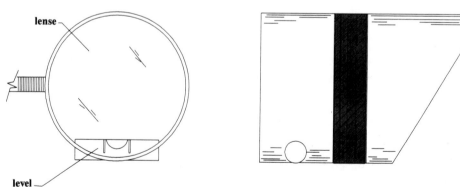

More sophisticated sights have magnifying lenses to enlarge the target and levels to help you hold the bow in the vertical plane.

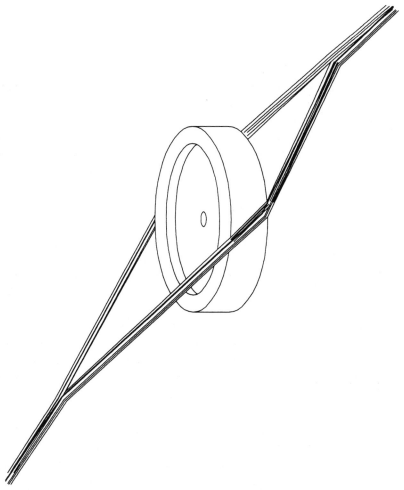

You may want to mount a peep sight in your bowstring to serve as a rear sight and improve your accuracy.

positioned the same on each shot. Stabilizing your aiming eye behind a fixed rear sight greatly increases your shooting accuracy. Since two fixed points—in this case the front and rear sights—determine a straight line, you need only release each shot the same way in order to hit your target with consistency.

Most peep sights are disks of metal or plastic about three-eighths of an inch in diameter and three-sixteenths of an inch thick. A groove around the disk's perimeter allows it to be placed between the strands of the string. Serving thread can be wrapped around or above and below the sight to hold it in place. Be sure that an equal number of strands of the bowstring are on either side of the sight so that it is centered in the string and not off to one side.

As long as the peep sight does not move up or down the string, your head and eye will be in the same relative position for each shot. The peep sight hole needs to be facing your eye at full draw, but since the bowstring twists while the bow is being drawn, the sight does not always wind up in the right position. The simplest way of dealing with this problem is to install the sight in the string so that it is rotated away from your eye until after the bow is drawn. When the peep starts out turned the appropriate amount away from the eye, it will end up facing the eye as the bow reaches full draw. With time and patience you can adjust the peep to the proper position.

The optimum level for setting your peep sight depends on the head position you want to use. To set your peep sight, draw the bowstring to full draw with your eyes closed until you are anchored comfortably, then open your eyes and adjust the peep so that you can look through it. If you align your sight correctly, when you open your eyes the next time you should not have to move your head at all to view through it; if you do, you need to readjust the peep.

An alternative to the peep sight is the kisser button, another string-mounted device. As its name suggests, this accessory positions your lips at the same point on the string for each shot. The result is similar to that achieved by the peep sight.

The kisser button is a plastic disk with a center hole that enables it to be placed around the bowstring. It is fastened in place with serving thread or several nockset rings.

You determine the location of the button in a similar manner as with the peep sight. Draw the bow, anchor, and get comfortable. Have someone mark the spot where your lips touch the string. Secure the button at this location. After that, for each shot, just draw the string and button to the corner of your mouth and aim with the sight pins; you should get consistent results.

The advantage of the kisser button over the peep sight is that nothing is in front of your eye while you are aiming. This is especially good for

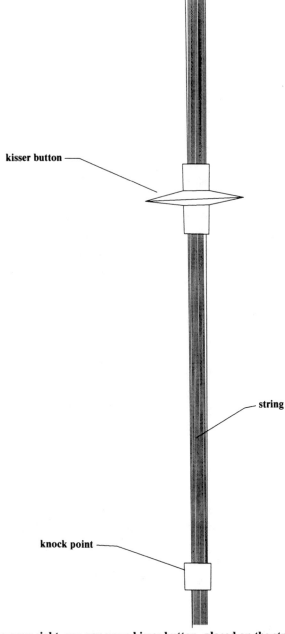

kisser button

string

knock point

Instead of a peep sight, you can use a kisser button, placed on the string above the nocking point, to serve as your rear sighting aid since it will help your head keep the same position on each shot.

bowhunters, who need to see more than the bow sight when aiming. The kisser is not as accurate as the peep sight, however, because you must aim alongside of the bowstring instead of through its center, and you might vary your aim slightly to the left or right without realizing it.

SHOOTING GLOVES, FINGER TABS, AND RELEASE AIDS

One of the biggest decisions you will make in archery, next to choosing your bow type, is whether to draw the bowstring with your fingers or with a release aid. The choice you make will determine several other very important features of your archery game: whether you will use a sight pin or a scope with a magnifying lens, how you will practice, the arrow size you will need, and so on. Make this decision with great care.

If you elect to use your fingers, you'll probably want to cover them with a shooting glove or a finger tab so that they don't get sore and blistered, although some of the hardier archers I know don't use any finger protection. The function of the glove or tab is to protect your fingers as the bowstring moves across them during the release.

Both the tab and the glove require the same basic shooting form. As you draw the bow and aim at the target, you must maintain, and even increase, tension in your back muscles until you release the shot. Failure to maintain a high level of back tension will cause arrows to fly inconsistently. At the moment of release you simply relax the fingers; the tension in the back muscles then causes the arm to fly backward in the opposite direction from the arrow.

The Shooting Glove

The shooting glove is the simplest method of covering your fingers. It should be made from leather and fit your hand snugly. Many hunters use a regular leather glove in cold weather and get good results.

A full glove does the job, but a specialized shooting glove will work better for both protecting the fingers and providing a smooth release. The shooting glove has protective leather coverings for the two end joints of three fingers. You don't need to cover more than that since it's just these two end sections of the fingers that should hold the bowstring; gripping with more will cause poor arrow release.

Straps to hold the glove on the hand are attached to each of the finger covers, run the length of the fingers, and join together on the back of the hand, where a wrist strap is fastened. A quality shooting glove will have an adjustable wrist strap and good stitch work at all of its seams.

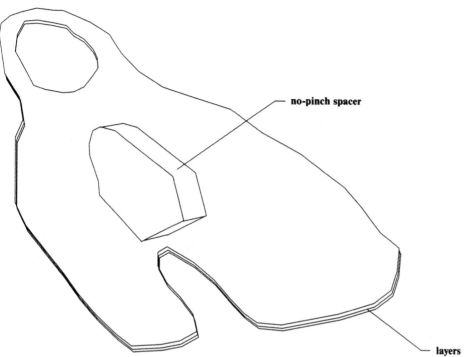

no-pinch spacer

layers

Most archers begin shooting with a finger tab that protects the fingers from the string and also allows a smoother release.

The Finger Tab

The majority of finger shooters seem to prefer the finger tab, a single flat piece of leather that fits over the three fingers that hold the bowstring. Because the tab is just one piece, all three fingers must work together when the string is drawn and released; therein lies the advantage of the tab.

As with the glove, the tab need only cover the first two joints of the fingers. To secure the tab so that it does not fly from the hand when the arrow is shot, the middle finger is put through a hole cut into an extension of the leather.

Some tabs have several attachments to assist the archer in making smooth releases. The most notable is the quarter-inch spacer, which keeps the index and the middle fingers apart so that they don't pinch the nock of the arrow. If they do so while the arrow is still on the string, arrow flight will be affected and accuracy will be compromised.

Thumb Ring

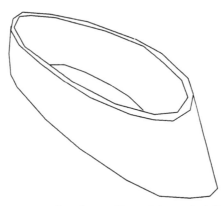

The thumb ring was an early release aid used to protect the thumb as it was wrapped around the bowstring. The bow was then drawn with the index finger wrapped around the end of it. As the finger slipped off the thumb, the bowstring was released.

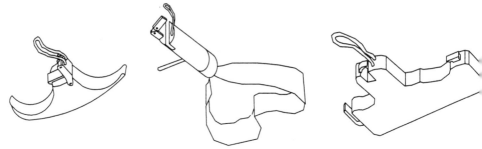

You may want to try one of these three types of release aids. The left one is a tension release held with the index and middle fingers and rotated to disengage from the bowstring. The middle release is strapped around the wrist and released by the index finger on a trigger. The release on the right is held with four fingers and released with the thumb on a trigger.

Many finger shooters prefer tabs with multiple layers, either two layers of leather or one of leather with another of felt or rubber. The feel of the tab between your fingers and the string is very important in order for you to release smoothly and consistently, so it's an individual decision as to what material and how many layers to use. To achieve a clean release, it's vitally important that you disturb the string as little as possible.

The Mechanical Release Aid

The release aid has been around since the first archer in history to get sore fingers. A thumb ring, made of wood or bone, was one of the first inventions used for hooking the bowstring in the hand, drawing the string, and releasing the arrow smoothly.

Many devices have since been used for drawing and releasing the bowstring. The thumb strap, the ledge hook, and the rope-spike are just a few. Today the mechanical release aid is extremely popular and is used by about half of all archers.

The mechanical release aid has put to use today's high technology in the form of machined internal parts and molded exterior cases. Metal sears and spring-loaded pins fit precisely inside and provide instant release of the bowstring when the archer operates a trigger mechanism.

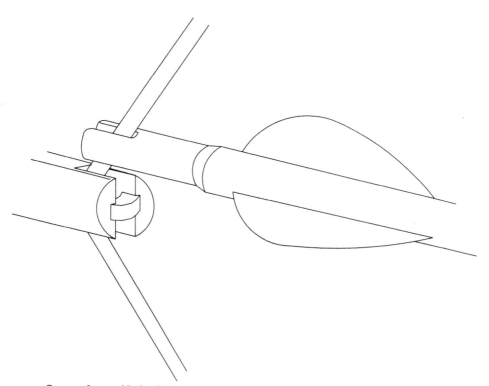

Some release aids hook directly onto the string, as shown, while others have a built-in rope that wraps around the bowstring and into the jaws of the release aid.

One type of release aid has a slot that fits around the bowstring and a metal gate that then closes around the string. When the trigger is operated, the gate releases the string. Another kind has a small rope that fits around the bowstring and hooks into a slot and gate. The latter type is preferred by most target shooters, and the former by most hunters.

Using a release aid is much like using the trigger of a gun: You must squeeze it slowly while aiming at the intended target. If you set off the release quickly, you will get inconsistent results. Proper form for shooting with a release aid requires good back-muscle tension throughout the aiming process, which causes the release hand to fall away in the opposite direction from the arrow after the device has been triggered.

STABILIZERS

A stabilizer is nothing more than a small weight suspended at some distance from the front of the bow handle by a metal rod. Adding the same weight directly to the handle would not have as much effect as when it is located some distance away. The purpose of the suspended weight is threefold: It dampens any torque applied to the bow handle by the bow hand when the arrow is released; it adds weight to the handle, giving it a different balance and feel; and it can make the bow steadier in the hand while you aim by absorbing the vibrations of the bow caused by movement in the hands and arms.

One important factor when adding weight to your bow is how it makes the bow feel in your hand. Some archers like the weight close to the handle, while others like it as much as three feet away. Some prefer weight added to the top of the handle, others the middle, and still others the bottom. Some add weight to all three locations.

For hunting, a short stabilizer is generally used. Long attachments to the bow catch a lot of brush and get in the way while you walk in the woods. A short stabilizer usually is six to twelve inches long — six inches is long enough for the hunting bow — and has a 12- to 20-ounce weight. The rod that holds this weight is about half an inch in diameter and is made of solid steel or aluminum tubing. Like most stabilizers, it screws into the bushing in the front of the bow handle just below the grip.

Longer stabilizers are better suited to target shooting. The longer extension rod is better than a short rod at balancing the bow and at damping bow handle torque after the arrow is released. And since most target archery doesn't involve walking through brush, the long extension rod does not get in the way.

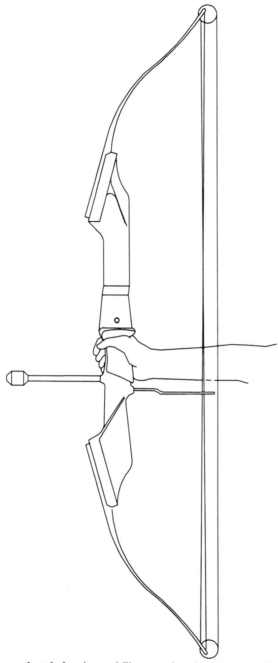

Bowhunters use short balancing stabilizers so they do not get tangled in the brush.

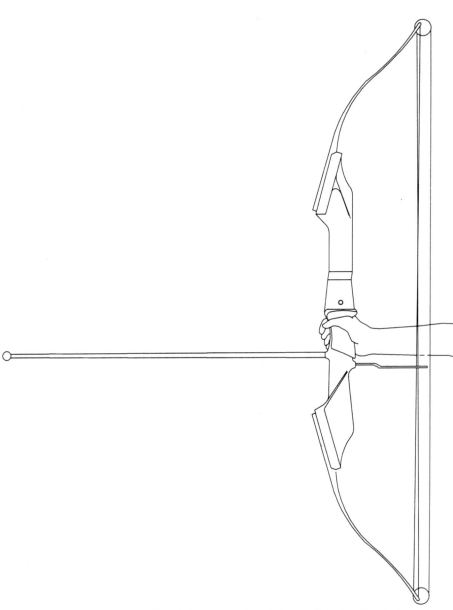

The longer target stabilizer balances the bow before and during the shot and also absorbs some of the vibrations after the shot.

Most of the longer stabilizer rods are made from some kind of tubing. Aluminum and carbon are the preferred materials because they both have some flex but a quick recovery rate. Each end is fitted with threads so that a small weight can be mounted on the one, and the other can be screwed into the bow handle.

Many archers experiment with the amount of weight on their stabilizers. Others try placing several different stabilizers on their bows in different locations. When they find the right balance and amount of weight, their shooting accuracy improves and reaches a peak. To this end some Olympic archers use as many as seven stabilizers on a bow.

QUIVERS

Any archer who plans to carry more than one arrow will need some kind of quiver to hold them. The term probably brings to mind the deerskin quiver on Robin Hood's back. Although the back quiver served its purpose throughout history, it has little popularity today and has been replaced by the belt-held quiver and the bow-attached quiver.

The bow quiver has been around for about forty or fifty years. It was designed to hold the arrows next to the bow so that stalking game through the woods would be easier and quieter. A bow quiver commonly holds four to six arrows and has a foam-lined plastic cup on the end to hold the points of the arrows, thus protecting them from damage and shielding the archer from the sharp tips.

The hunting bow complete with bow quiver and arrows is quite easy to carry for long periods of time; although the bow quiver adds weight to the bow, it is not so much that it makes this bow uncomfortable to hold. The tournament bow, however, becomes quite cumbersome when equipped with a bow quiver, and the extra weight added to the side of the bow while you make sixty or seventy shots over several hours would detract from your accuracy and endurance. For this style of archery, a belt quiver holding ten or twenty arrows is much more suitable.

Most bow quivers are made from plastic and metal and are as lightweight as possible; belt quivers, on the other hand, have no weight restrictions and are made from leather, leather imitation, or cloth. The belt quiver may have one or more large compartments to hold two or three dozen arrows for tournament shooting and several small pockets on the side to hold small tools and spare parts.

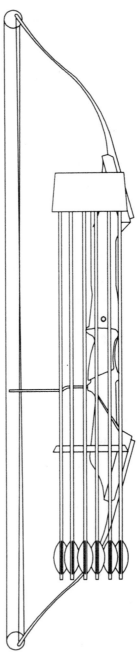

The bow-mounted quiver is ideal for hunting.

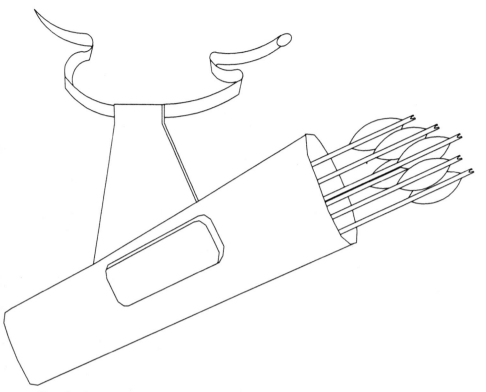

You should use a belt quiver for target archery so you can carry more arrows and not overweigh the bow.

WRIST SLING

Many tournament archers avoid gripping the bow handle so that they will not apply torque. A tight grip cannot be duplicated shot after shot, and the accuracy of the bow would be affected. A loose grip, in contrast, can be duplicated time after time and is preferred by the large majority of tournament archers. To prevent the bow from flying from your hand with this loose grip, you can tie a sling of rope or cord around your wrist and the bow handle. With the sling to hold the bow, you can concentrate on relaxing the fingers and pressing only the palm of the hand into the grip of the handle.

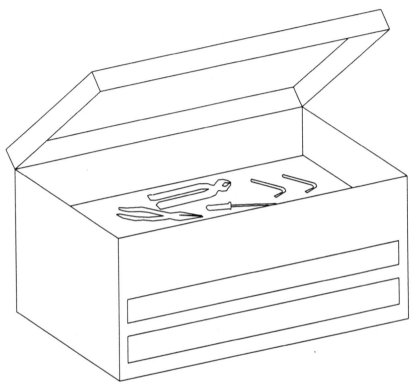

You will need tools and a tool box so you can make repairs and adjustments quickly.

TOOLBOX ITEMS

Almost everyone who has been in archery for some time has a collection of small tools and spare parts. Of course, you need a toolbox to hold all of these little goodies. Following is a list of items that are important if you plan to do any small repairs on your own equipment. Do not buy these all at one time, however, but as the need arises.

Tools:

Nockset pliers
Knife
Small level
Straight-end screwdriver
Phillips screwdriver
Needle-nose pliers
Open-end wrench set
Allen wrench set
Scissors
File
Bow square

Repair materials:

Hot-melt glue
Fletching cement
Instant glue
Monofilament serving
Nylon serving thread
Dental floss
Extra nocks
Extra fletching

5

Safety Rules for Archery

ARCHERY IS A very safe sport as long as safety rules are observed, but the bow and arrow can be a dangerous weapon if not used properly. Because arrows can penetrate objects at least as deeply as bullets from some handguns, the bow and arrow must be treated with utmost respect and care or serious injury may be inflicted on the user or a bystander.

The safety rules apply every time you have a bow and arrow in your hand, not just when you are shooting with other people. Safety must be in your mind anytime you are near a shooting range, whether you are looking for lost arrows or are actually shooting. Safety must become habit just as drawing an arrow, aiming, and releasing become habit. So read this chapter now and reread it just before you go out to shoot for the first time.

SHOOTING LOCATIONS

Safety begins with your selection of an area for shooting. If you're building your own practice target, you must set it up either in front of a steep dirt bank or with a clear area that extends behind it for at least 40 yards: Arrows that pass by or through a target can travel another 30 or more yards before coming to rest. A dirt bank will stop the arrows without doing damage to them.

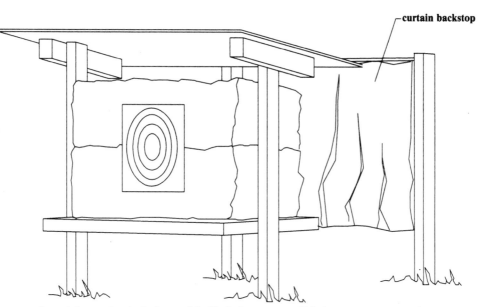

curtain backstop

A curtain or sheet of plywood behind the target will help prevent arrows from traveling a long distance beyond the butt.

If you do not have that much space, you can build a backstop from plywood. Hang a cloth, canvas, or mesh curtain in front of it to knock the arrows down before they get to the plywood: Although the plywood would stop the arrows, you might have a hard time getting them out of it.

On the shooting side of the target, have as much distance as possible but take care that no person will be able to walk between you and the target while you are shooting. Don't shoot across a street or a sidewalk or set up in any location where someone could approach without being seen and wind up either in front of or behind the target, such as alongside a building.

If you have an indoor practice area, before you shoot be sure to lock any doors between the shooting line and the target and cover any windows behind the target with plywood so that arrows that miss or pass through the target don't go through a window.

SELECTING TARGET MATERIALS

You also need to give a great amount of consideration to the target. Take the time to find the right material—it must stop the arrows and not allow any to pass through, yet not damage them. An outside target has to be able to stand up to the weather or you'll need to build a protective roof over it. It's important that an indoor target not be a fire hazard, and it should probably be movable so that if arrows pass through it they can be pulled from behind the target.

Several materials meet all of the above requirements. Tightly baled straw makes an excellent backstop as long as it is covered by a roof. The best bales are those made in a stationary baler and wrapped with two or three wires instead of twine. Wood fiber or excelsior bales make even longer lasting targets. They are heavier and more expensive but they do a great job when roof protected.

Common hay bales from a farm or ordinary cardboard boxes don't make very effective backstops; most of your shots will pass through them, making them both unsafe and hard on your arrows.

Indoor archery clubs and shooting lanes often use layers of heavy cardboard that are stacked and compressed so that you can shoot into the corrugated edges. Many such target butts have wooden or metal frames and are compressed by the use of bolts on threaded rods. When the target becomes well used in certain areas, the cardboard layers can be taken apart, shuffled, and restacked, resulting in an almost new target butt.

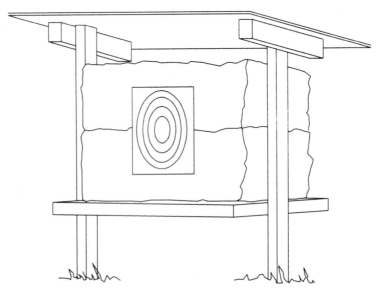

A roof and stand should be built to protect your outside target butt from the weather.

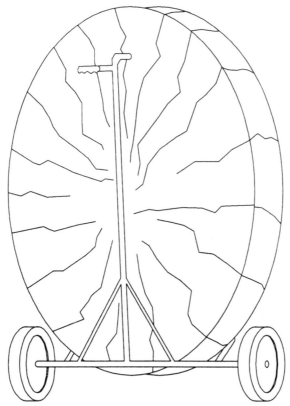

A simple grass mat on a portable stand can serve as an indoor target or an outdoor target. Be sure that you use a wall or plywood for a backstop.

Ethafoam also does a great job of stopping arrows. It is more expensive than most other materials but does not need to be covered and is very lightweight and easy to move. These targets can be used indoors and out. Buy the type with replaceable round cores so that when the center becomes well used you can pull it out and insert a new one.

Broadhead points that are used for hunting should never be used on the practice targets mentioned here, with the exception of the ethafoam target with replaceable cores. Broadheads will either cut the targets to pieces or become impossible to remove. If you plan to shoot broadheads, make sure that a dirt, sand, or sawdust mound is behind the target to stop the arrow.

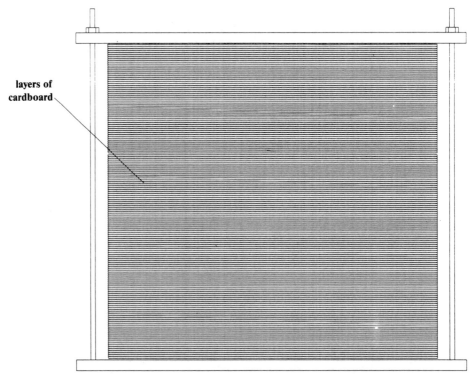

layers of
cardboard

Many archery clubs compress layers of cardboard to form an indoor target 20 to 24 inches deep. When the center begins to show some wear, reshuffle the layers to form an almost new target.

EQUIPMENT INSPECTION

Before every practice session, inspect all of your equipment for possible safety hazards. Arrows, bow limbs, cables, and strings need to be checked for cracks, frays, and any other damage that might possibly cause a break or other failure during shooting.

Check all arrows for bends and cracks. A cracked arrow can break at the instant the string is released and cause serious injury to you, another archer, or a spectator. Broken or cracked nocks must be replaced before you can shoot the arrow again. Bent arrows need to be straightened so they will not damage the arrow rest when shot and so they don't miss the target or backstop. Destroy all cracked arrows and do not use any arrows with points missing or loose until you've repaired them.

One of the most dangerous situations in archery is the arrow that is too short for the user. The short arrow can be drawn so that its point

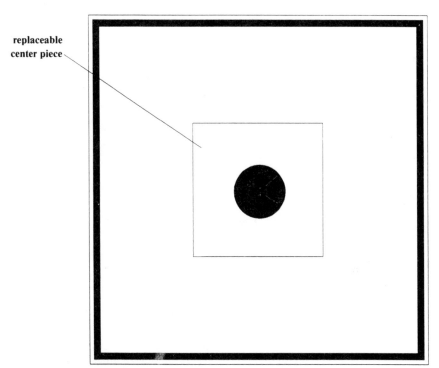

replaceable center piece

Ethafoam targets with replaceable centers can be used inside or outside with great success. Always place them in front of a safe and suitable backstop.

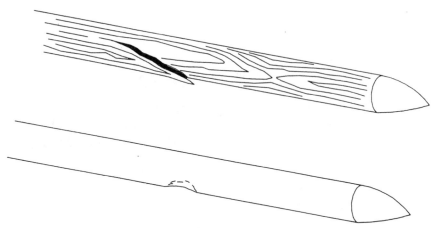

Cracked wooden arrow shafts should not be shot again. Kinked aluminum arrows that remain straight can be shot but may not hit the intended target. Most kinks cannot be straightened.

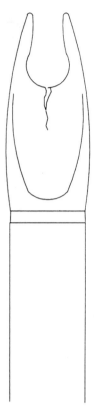

Shooting a cracked nock will risk injury to the shooter and damage the bow. Replace damaged and cracked nocks immediately.

passes the arrow rest and falls onto the bow hand of the archer. It could then lodge in the hand or stick between the string and the bow handle and cause damage to the bow.

Closely inspect your bow for cracks in the limbs. This doesn't often happen, but if it does, it's potentially dangerous: A cracked limb could break when the string is released, causing the arrow to fly unpredictably, and the limb tips might hit you or another person.

Frayed strings and cables can also break and cause injury: The arrow may fly unpredictably, and you could be hit by the cable ends.

SHOOTING-LINE RULES

When two or more archers plan to shoot together, several simple rules must be followed. All members of the group must step to the same shoot-

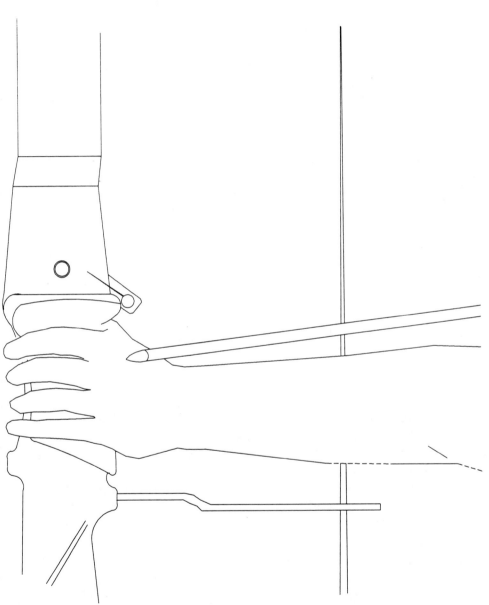

Arrows that are too short for you can fall off of the arrow rest and cause injury to your hand or to a bystander.

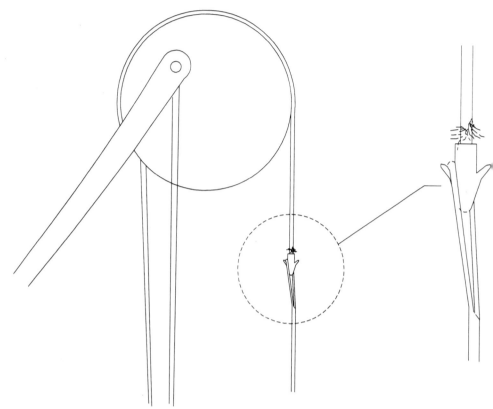

A frayed steel cable should be replaced immediately to prevent injury to you and damage to the bow.

ing line so that no one is in front of or behind the rest of the group. A designated group leader should give signals to start and stop the shooting. No one should start toward the target until the shooting has ceased and the leader has given a signal.

In tournament situations a single whistle blast signals the start of shooting and two blasts the end of shooting. When an emergency arises in the shooting area, three or more blasts are sounded to stop all shooting immediately.

If an arrow or other piece of equipment falls in front of the shooting line while shooting is in progress, don't step out to get it: Use your bow or an arrow to drag it back to the line. If you can't reach it, leave it there until the shooting has stopped.

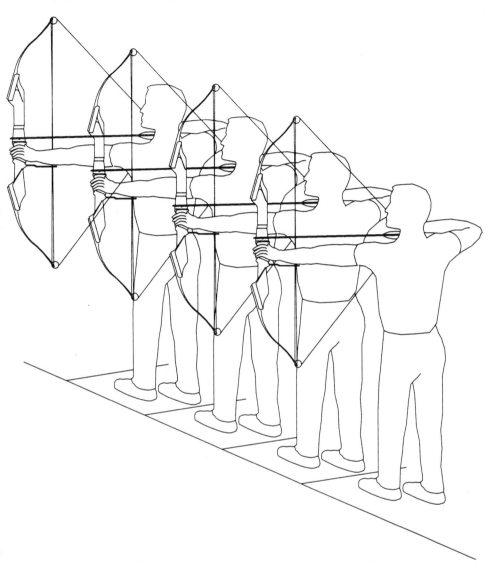

When you are shooting in a group, always stand on the same shooting line with no one ahead of or behind another shooter.

Never place an arrow on the string of the bow unless you are facing the target and the target area is clear. And never shoot an arrow in any direction other than at the target, especially not straight up in the air.

During a timed shooting period, those finishing before the allotted time has elapsed can step back from the shooting line. It is customary, however, to remain at the shooting line if the person next to you is at full draw. After he or she has released the arrow, then step back.

APPROPRIATE CLOTHING

Your shooting can be unsafe just because of the clothes you are wearing. If your sleeves are too loose and interfere with the bowstring, your arrows may not fly well or in the proper direction. It's best to wear shirts or sweaters that fit tightly around your bow arm and chest. Not only will you be less of a safety hazard, but you also will shoot more accurately.

Always wear shoes when practicing. Stepping on an unseen arrow lodged in the grass in front of the target can cause injury to bare feet.

RETRIEVING ARROWS

After you have shot your arrows and after the whistle blasts signal the end of the shooting period, walk to the target to locate your arrows. Don't

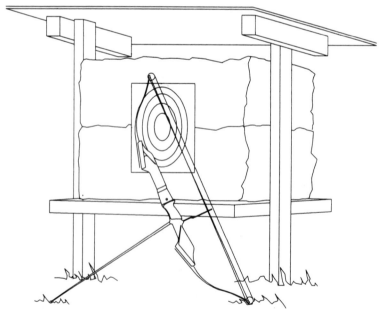

A bow propped in front of the target is a clear signal that someone is in the area and you should not shoot.

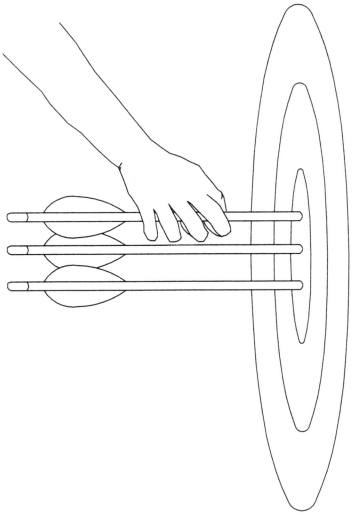

Always walk when you approach your target, and pull the upper arrows first so you don't injure yourself on the nocks.

run; you might trip and fall into the arrows stuck in the target. If you didn't store your bow behind the shooting line, prop it against or beside the target in plain sight.

To pull the arrows from the target, place one hand on the target face near the arrows. With the other hand, grasp an arrow where it enters the target and pull straight out. This method will not tear the target face or

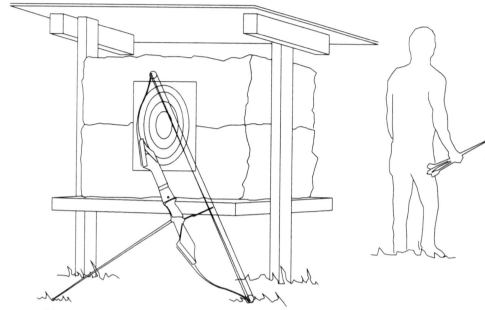

If you go behind the target for any reason, leave your bow in front of the target in plain view.

bend the arrow. It is best to pull the arrows in the upper part of the target first. If you bend over to pull the lower arrows first, the arrows in the upper portion of the target may injure your eyes or face. This also determines who should pull his or her arrows first while the others stand clear.

Should you need to go behind the target butt to locate an arrow, have someone stand in front of the target to ensure that everyone knows it's not safe to shoot another round. If you are by yourself, leave your bow in front of the target so others will see it and know not to shoot. If others are waiting for you to return to the shooting line, spend only a few minutes looking for your arrow. You can look more after the shooting has finished for the day.

If you lose an arrow in the grass, you may need a small rake to find it. A long stick with a bent nail in the end also makes a great arrow finder. Just drag the nail or rake in a line perpendicular to the shooting direction at intervals of about two feet. You can cover a large area in a short time and find your arrow—if it is there. Sometimes an arrow will skip a great distance and is not where you think it is, and other times it will deflect in an unknown direction and be lost forever.

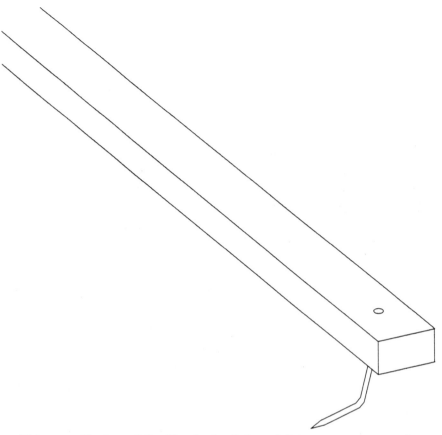

**Make yourself a long stick with a bent nail through it to use as an arrow rake.
Pulling the rake through the grass at intervals of two feet and perpendicular to the
path of the arrow will uncover buried arrows.**

You can use a metal detector to find arrows, but it's not as effective as
the rake or nail. The metal detector will only register when the point is
found. Aluminum, carbon, and wooden arrow shafts will not cause a
reaction in the sensors.

6

Shooting Form Basics

BUILDING GOOD ARCHERY form is like building a house: You begin with the foundation. This means that the feet must be positioned properly so the rest of the body can do whatever it must do to achieve a clean and consistent release of the bowstring. Only if the feet provide you with the most stable foundation possible can you perform consistently at peak efficiency.

As a beginner in archery you should experiment with foot position during the initial stages of form development. When you find the best position for you, stick with it and build the rest of your form over it.

There are basically three different foot positions. The most commonly used is the open position and the least used is the closed, while the perpendicular, or even, position falls somewhere in between.

To understand the positions of the feet, place an arrow on the ground parallel to the target face. Imagine that it's the shooting line. Place another arrow across and perpendicular to the first arrow, so that it's pointing toward the target. Straddle the arrow representing the shooting line and, with your feet shoulder width apart, touch your toes against the arrow that's pointed toward the target. If you are right-handed, your left side will be toward the target, and vice versa. This is the perpendicular, or even, stance.

The open stance is attained from this point by turning your face, chest, hips, and feet slightly toward the target. Your left foot is now pulled back away from the arrow that's pointed toward the target. You have opened your stance toward the target. The degree to which you do this depends on how you feel and perform while shooting in that position. If you open too much to the target, however, you lessen your ability to use your back muscles in a push-pull relationship during the aiming process.

For a closed stance, simply turn your body slightly away from the target face, at the same time pulling your right foot several inches away from the arrow that points toward the target and letting the toes of your left foot touch that arrow. The degree to which you close your stance again depends on how you feel and perform. If it doesn't feel good to you, change your stance until it does.

Be patient: Finding the best stance may take weeks or even months. Some archers I know have changed their stances after several years just to perk up their concentration or to help a sore arm or shoulder. Like everything else in this sport, there are no guarantees and never say never.

BACK AND HEAD POSTURE

When your stance is stable, your back and head can be trained to perform consistently on that strong base. This takes weeks and weeks of muscle conditioning. It will not happen overnight because too many muscles are involved. Eighty shots a day for six weeks may get you close to being in condition, but you can't start by shooting eighty shots your first day in

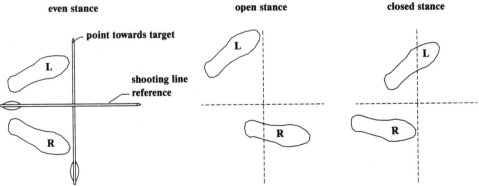

Two arrows can be used to get your stance correctly set for shooting. The stance you find most comfortable and consistent is the stance you should use.

archery. You have to build up to that, which alone could take several weeks. Be patient but determined. Consistent effort in archery will be rewarded. Besides, you'll learn a lot about yourself by meeting the challenge that this sport offers.

You might think that the arm and shoulder muscles do all the hard work in archery, but it's actually the small groups of muscles in the back between the shoulders that make or break an archer. These muscle groups work together and in opposition to create good, clean releases and cause good follow-through. If they are not involved in the action of the shot, there will be no follow-through and eventually your releases will get ragged and the groups of arrows in the target will become large and scattered.

To get the best performance from these muscles, your back should be straight and upright. If you bend at the waist, all of your back muscles will not be involved in holding and controlling the aiming of the bow. And without good control, the follow-through breaks down along with the rest of the shot.

Head position plays an important role here because of the muscles and tendons that run from the skull to and through the back. If your head is bent over or tilted to one side or the other, the muscle groups in the back will not work as efficiently as they should. The best possible way to shoot is with your head upright and turned toward the target.

BOW ARM, BOW HAND, AND GRIP

The next piece of anatomy that comes into play as you prepare to make a shot is the shoulder of your bow arm. This shoulder must support the weight of the bow as you lift and push it toward the target. It must also work against the draw force of the bow as your other hand and shoulder pull the bowstring.

Most archers keep the bow shoulder locked in the down position. If it is allowed to ride up during the draw and aim sequence, performance will be inconsistent, stability will be lost, and the release and follow-through will break down.

Conditioning the shoulder to stay in the down position takes regular training and can be done by pushing against a door frame. Just push and lock the shoulder for thirty-second intervals. Twenty repetitions about three times a day will condition the shoulder in a few weeks.

You can extend your bow arm in one of two ways. One school of thought believes the bow arm should be slightly bent at the elbow during the aiming process; the other thinks it should be locked straight. As with the other facets of your form, you must decide which works best for you. I

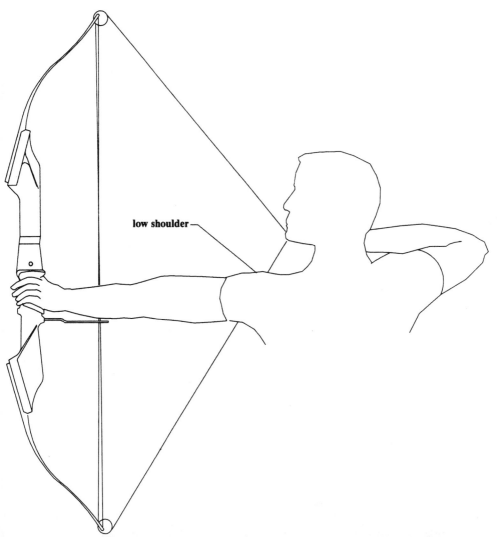

low shoulder

When you draw to full draw, keep your head and back erect so that both sides of your back muscles can work directly against each other for more consistent releases. Try to keep your bow shoulder as low as possible to prevent collapse on the release.

prefer to lock my elbow while aiming because I'm most consistent when shooting that way, but everybody is different.

Though there may be some difference of opinion over the position of the elbow, there is little over how the hand should grip the bow handle:

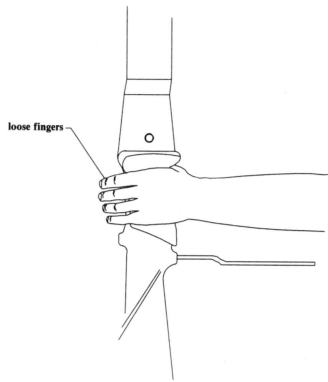

loose fingers

The best grip for the bow hand is no grip at all. The fingers should be relaxed and away from the grip of the bow handle so that no torque is applied to the bow during the release of the shot.

Most of the professionals I know don't grip the handle at all. Instead, they simply push against the handle with part of the palm, relax the fingers, and use a wrist sling to keep the bow from flying out of the hand. Closing the fingers on the bow handle creates tension in the bow hand and forearm, which will not allow the bow to freely react to the release of the string. Instead, it will react differently to each release and cause each arrow to hit a different spot.

The palm of the hand can be placed either high or low on the grip. The high grip requires a stiff, straight wrist, while the low grip has a bent wrist and more of the base of the thumb rides against the bow grip. Try both methods to find which one helps you to be the most consistent.

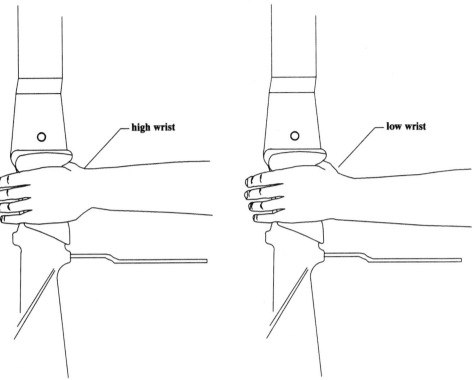

During your first several months of shooting you will need to decide on the best grip for you. The high wrist places the pressure point nearest the arrow, but the low wrist is stronger.

DRAWING THE BOWSTRING

As I mentioned earlier, you can draw the bowstring either with your fingers or with a release aid. When drawing and shooting with the fingers, you place the crease of the first knuckle around the bowstring. With a release aid you hook the jaws or the rope of the release around the bowstring.

Once the string has been engaged by the release aid or the fingers, the draw stroke begins. Regardless of the method of engaging the string the draw is the same. The shoulder and back muscles should do most of the work. Keep your arms as relaxed as possible during the draw so that built-up tension does not cause any torque in the bow handle or on the bowstring as the string is released.

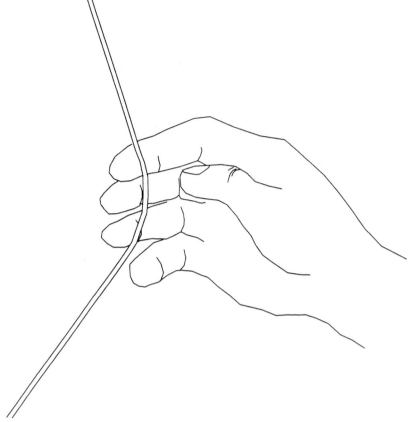

Most finger shooters place the fingers on the string so that only half of the first section of finger is around the string.

First, raise the bow to address the target. Extend the bow arm toward the target and either lock or slightly bend the elbow. Now draw the bowstring to your face without bending your face to the string. Remember to keep your head erect so that the back muscles can do the job they're supposed to do.

When the drawing hand reaches your face, you must then place it at the anchor position, or anchor point. You will determine the appropriate spot only through many practice sessions, basing your decision on how smooth and consistent the release is from a given anchor position. Most target archers prefer the low anchor, which places the fingertips of the drawing hand on or just under the lower jawbone. The bowstring is then directly in front of the aiming eye.

Some bowhunters and a few target archers use the high anchor, which places the fingertips at the corner of the mouth or just under the cheekbone. They feel there is an advantage in being able to look directly down the arrow shaft as they are aiming. This is good for short-range shooting, but it has its limitations for longer distances.

When using a release aid, anchoring is usually done in the low position. The string runs next to the face, and you can aim with the head erect.

An anchor point may feel uncomfortable until you've conditioned your muscles through practice. After you have achieved a good level of conditioning, you can begin experimenting with different anchors. Again, be patient.

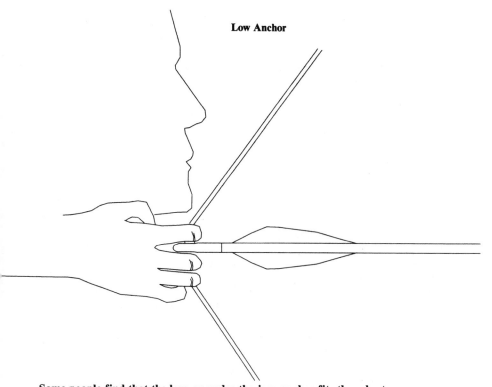

Some people find that the low, or under-the-jaw, anchor fits them best.

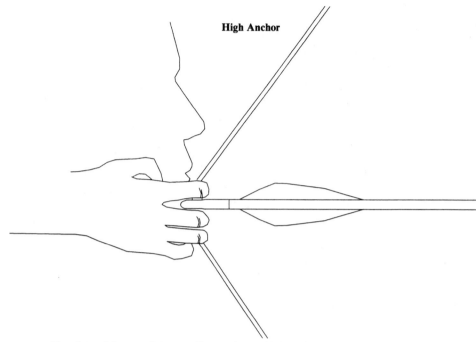

Shooting without a sight usually requires a higher anchor so that the point of the arrow can be seen and used as an aiming reference. Some sight shooters find the high anchor more comfortable.

Keep the bow arm firm and at shoulder height during the entire drawing process and while you aim and shoot. Once you release the string, the bow arm will fall downward as a natural reaction to the relieving of the pressure that had been on it. Too much arm tension will cause the bow arm to do something other than that.

AIMING

The aiming phase of the shot process begins when you reach your anchor point. Steady your bow arm and lock the shoulder and back muscles. Now place the sight pin on the middle of the target. Use your back muscles to push the bow arm toward the target while pulling the other arm in the opposite direction. These two motions must be in direct line with the arrow so that upon release the arrow will be propelled straight to the target without any torque applied to it. Remember that this push-pull

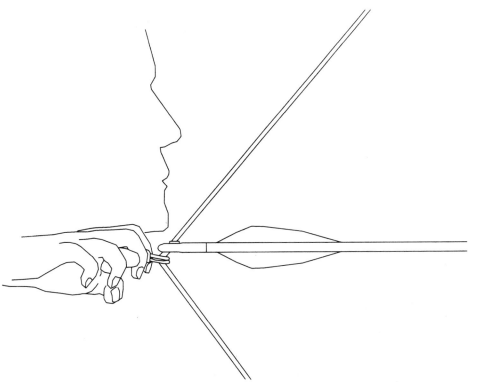

If you plan to use a release aid, anchorings on the side of your face or under your jaw need to be tried to see which will be most comfortable for you. This anchor is the low, or under-the-jaw, anchor.

effort must be exerted by the back muscles, while the arms are kept as free from tension as possible.

During this push-pull motion you are pushing the sight pin toward the center of the target. Most archers focus on the sight pin and allow the target to appear in the background, although some focus on the target and allow the pin to appear in front of it. Try both to see which you prefer.

THE RELEASE

During the push-pull sequence of the aim the brain will signal the finger shooter to release. This must occur while the release hand is being pulled directly away from the target so the string will be released cleanly and that hand will fall directly away from the target and back behind the shooter. If the release hand is not being pulled away from the target, the fingers tend to hang on to the string for a small amount of time and distort the release, which will cause the arrow to impact the target at some undesired location.

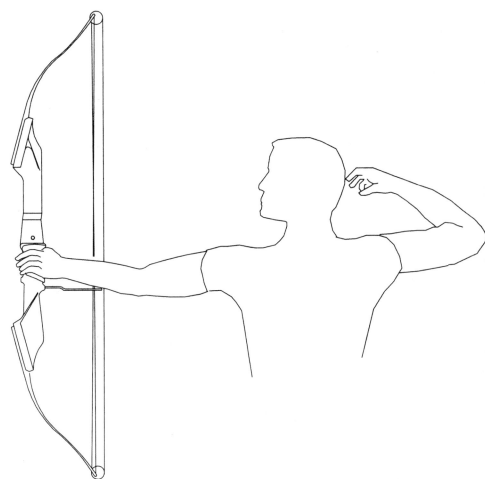

When you use good back tension while aiming and releasing a shot, the release hand will often fall back after the release of the string while the bow arm will fall slightly downward. These motions should be a direct result of push-pull tension and not manufactured or exaggerated by the archer.

The release shooter uses a slightly different sequence, but only in that he or she must squeeze a trigger or rotate the handle of the release aid while the push-pull motion is in progress. When the sight pin is moved to the middle of the target, the archer must begin the push-pull motion and simultaneously begin squeezing the trigger. If the push-pull does not exist or if it relaxes during the aiming process, then the release hand will not be pulled directly away from the target and the string will be adversely affected. For this reason, many shooters prefer a tension release that requires rotating a handle rather than squeezing a trigger. This type of release helps you maintain good back tension throughout the entire aiming process and is the one I prefer for all my target shooting.

THE FOLLOW-THROUGH

The follow-through is the natural reaction of the muscles as built-up tension is suddenly released. It is not a contrived or controlled motion; it just happens. The desired follow-through occurs when the push-pull motion is executed correctly during the aiming phase of the shot. When the string is released, the bow arm will fall downward because the tension of the back and shoulder muscles has been keeping it level with the shoulder during the drawing and aiming sequence, and the release arm will fall backward and down because it was being pulled straight back by the shoulder and back muscles during the aiming sequence.

If something else is happening during your follow-through, have someone watch you as you shoot to see what might be causing the flaw. Or you can use videotape to watch yourself shoot. You will be surprised what a few minutes of video will tell you about yourself.

While the arms and shoulders are relaxing after the release of the tension, the eye and head should still be focused on the target center, and the arrow should enter your sight as it falls into that center. Do not look for the arrow as it leaves the bow or is halfway to the target. Your concentration must remain focused on the target and not on the arrow so that you will follow through properly. If you begin looking for the arrow, your head and shoulders will begin moving, your arms will follow them, and the arrow will be pulled off course before it clears the arrow rest. Keep focused on the target.

7

Bow Tuning

WHEN YOU DRAW a bow and arrow, you have but one objective: to hit the intended target. Sometimes you'll meet that goal and sometimes you won't. When you do not hit the target, you have three choices: quit shooting and use your bow for a walking stick, practice your shooting skills, or improve the bow and arrow you're using.

The most difficult question is when to use which alternative. If you're just learning to shoot and you don't have a coach, the decision is tougher because you don't yet know the limits of your own ability and won't be able to judge when it's your shooting or when it's the bow that is the problem.

After you have practiced for several weeks and have developed some muscle conditioning, you must entertain the thought of making adjustments to your bow. Improved shooting skill demands that the bow be more consistent than you are. So you adjust the bow and practice some more to improve your performance. Once you improve, you adjust the bow some more, and so on. Does the cycle end? Only if you are ever satisfied with your skill level. I'm very seldom satisfied, so for me the cycle goes on and on.

Bow tuning begins with adjustments to draw length, then to fletch clearance and nocking point. Next, the arrow must be matched to the bow and to the arrow rest to achieve good arrow flight. Since superior arrow flight leads to tight groups in the target, test-shooting first at short range and later at long range is the final phase of bow tuning.

ADJUSTING DRAW LENGTH

You will enjoy archery more if your bow feels good. When you can relax and feel confident about your shooting, you can concentrate more and perform with greater consistency. If the bow feels too stiff and you are constantly fighting it while drawing or aiming, good concentration and accuracy will be hard to achieve.

The primary question when adjusting a bow is how to make it feel comfortable. To answer this you must understand the bow's draw length and make the necessary adjustments to it so that the feel of the bow will allow you to perform at your best.

Recurve and Longbows

The draw lengths of recurves and longbows are determined by the bowyer. The stiffness of the material in the limbs, as well as their length and width, determine how they bend and where in the draw stroke the "sweet spot" will be located.

As shown in chapter 1, the force-draw curves of the longbow and the recurve are both very near to a straight line. The recurve bow is more likely to deviate from the straight-line graph and is also more likely to have a certain position in its draw stroke that feels better for the purpose of aiming. The force-draw curves of these bows and where the archer might feel most comfortable when aiming each are shown in the illustrations on the next two pages.

Also mentioned in that chapter is that understanding the draw-stroke traits of the bow you plan to shoot is vitally important to your future shooting success. Both the recurve bow and the longbow should be shot before the weight begins to increase at its fastest rate. If you shoot at another position in the draw stroke, you won't be able to take full advantage of the shooting characteristics that have been designed into the bows.

Very little can be done to adjust the location of the sweet spot of either the longbow or the recurve, but small changes can be achieved by altering string length. A shorter string can make the bow produce slightly

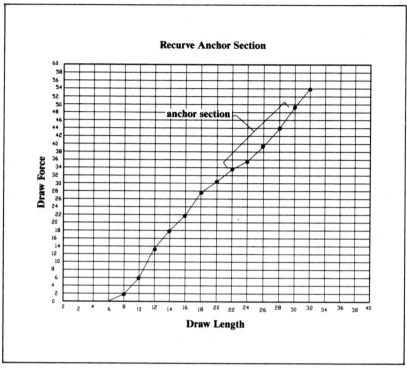

The recurve bow should be shot at a draw length that falls within the sweet spot or
section that is not increasing as fast as the beginning of the curve.

more draw weight and, perhaps, feel better or worse than before. Twisting
the bowstring is one way to make it shorter, and untwisting it will make it
longer. The exact effects may be different from bow to bow, so you'll have
to experiment.

The three-piece takedown recurve bow offers a different approach.
Since the limbs can be removed, you can test different limbs until you find
a pair that feels and shoots exceptionally well. This can be an expensive
proposition, considering the price of limbs, but many top Olympic archers
use this procedure to build their best bows.

Compound Bows

The design of the compound bow offers several avenues of adjustment for
draw length: You can change the string length, cable length, cable posi-

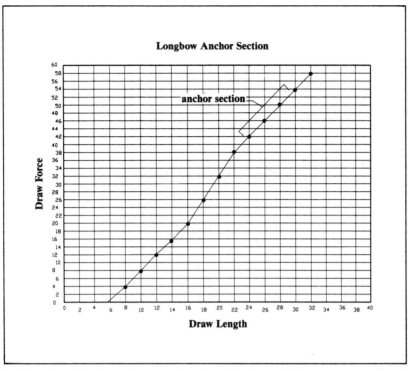

The longbow should be shot at a draw length in front of the steepest increase of weight at the back end of the draw stroke.

tions within the wheel, and wheel sizes. Most compounds can be made to fit any archer and allow him or her to feel comfortable when drawing and aiming.

The force-draw curve of a typical round-wheel compound bow is illustrated on the next page. You should anchor, aim, and release in the valley. This has a span of about one inch on compounds with a 2.5-inch wheel, while compounds with smaller wheels have shorter valleys. If you anchor within this region, the bow will perform consistently, shot after shot. Outside the valley, the weight on the string constantly changes and any variation in anchor position will give you a different draw weight. Thus it's difficult to shoot tight groups of arrows when overdrawing or underdrawing.

It is possible to adjust your bow so that the valley matches the location where you anchor and release. You can make major adjustments to the

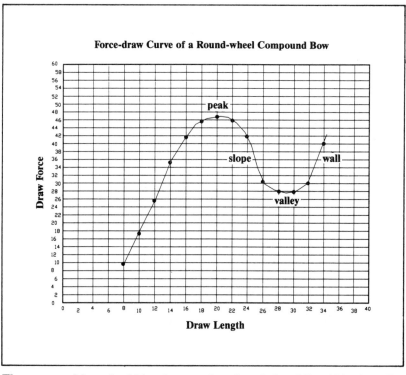

The compound bow should be shot at a draw length that falls within the valley region of the draw stroke.

draw length of a compound by changing its wheel size; finer adjustments are made by changes to cables and strings.

Major Adjustments

The compound bow you buy should have the correct wheel size for your draw length. Most archery shop dealers are skilled at fitting bows to buyers' draw lengths. This task has been made easier with the development of the multiple-draw-length wheel. Most wheels today can accommodate a three-inch span of draw lengths, and it's fairly easy to find the right size for you. Nevertheless, errors do occur and wheels do need to be changed.

Here are some simple rules of thumb for choosing the correct wheel size. The largest wheels on compounds are about 2.5 to 2.75 inches in diameter. This size wheel on a 44-inch-long bow will produce a traditional draw length of 28 to 30 inches. That same wheel size on a 48-inch bow will yield draw lengths of 30 to 32 inches. A wheel diameter of 2 inches on a 44-inch bow will place the valley between 26 and 28 inches, depending on how it's adjusted. A 48-inch bow with a 2-inch wheel will fit draw lengths from 28 to 30 inches. If you need a bow with a short draw length, buy one that's 44 inches long with a 1.75-inch wheel.

If you feel that the wheel size on your bow is not correct, you can change it yourself or have it done where you purchased the bow. The change is rather simple. You place the bow in a bow press, which compresses the limbs to relax the cables and string so that the wheel system can be removed and replaced.

Don't change wheel sizes without changing cable lengths. A bigger wheel has a larger circumference, so more cable will wrap around it during the draw stroke and you will need longer power cables.

When you install a larger set of wheels, both the draw length and draw weight of the bow increase. The draw length increases because the circumference of the wheel is greater and the string must be drawn a longer distance to roll the wheels to full draw. The draw weight increases because the limbs are now bending over a longer distance. Each inch of increase in draw length will increase draw weight by three to five pounds, depending on the design of the wheel and the limbs.

Minor Adjustments

Most eccentric wheels have cable slots for adjustment purposes. These are designed so that the string cable attached to the wheel can be placed in one of several different positions to vary draw length. Moving one of the cables one slot position will give you a half-inch change in draw length. If you adjust the other cable in the same manner, you'll get another half-inch change. If you move both cables one slot in the same direction, you will have a one-inch change in draw length.

Some eccentric wheels have been designed to provide a great number of adjustments so that you can very easily and quickly make modifications to fit your exact draw length. A wheel that has two anchor pins for the bowstring and three slots in which it can be placed after it is hooked on a pin can provide more than thirty different draw lengths over a three-inch span. The chart on the next page shows the various draw-length settings for the eccentric wheels made by Indian Industries.

How do you know when the draw length is correct for you? The following description of how the eccentric system works will help you answer that question. You should understand by now that larger eccentric

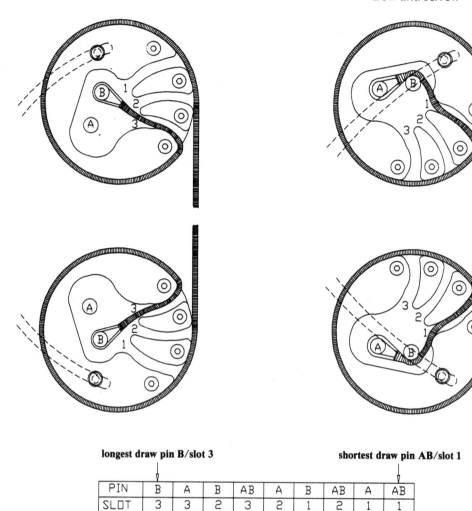

longest draw pin B/slot 3   **shortest draw pin AB/slot 1**

PIN	B	A	B	AB	A	B	AB	A	AB
SLOT	3	3	2	3	2	1	2	1	1

**Some eccentric wheels have no slots or pins for draw length adjustment, others
have two or three slots, while still others have both pins and slots. Two pins and
three slots can allow you to adjust the draw length of the bow to thirty or more
different settings within a 3-inch range.**

wheels roll over a longer distance, and that bigger people should have
bigger wheels and smaller people need smaller ones so that the valley of
the draw stroke will be near their anchors. The wheel, therefore, is the key
in knowing when you are shooting in the middle of the valley.

To help you determine when the wheel has rolled to the middle of the valley, mark on it a visible timing point that one of your friends can watch as you draw and shoot. Imagine a line that begins at the axle hole of the wheel, runs through the center, and continues to the other edge. At this edge opposite the axle hole, make a mark on the wheel. The location of the mark relative to the string cable of the drawn bow will let you know if the draw length of your bow is too short or too long. When the bow is at full draw, the mark will indicate that the middle of the valley has been reached when it is positioned at the point where the string cable is leaving the edge of the wheel.

If the wheels are rolling too far, the timing marks will go past the point where the string cable leaves the edge of the wheel, indicating that the draw length of the bow is too short for your anchor position. If the timing marks don't roll far enough to reach the position where the string

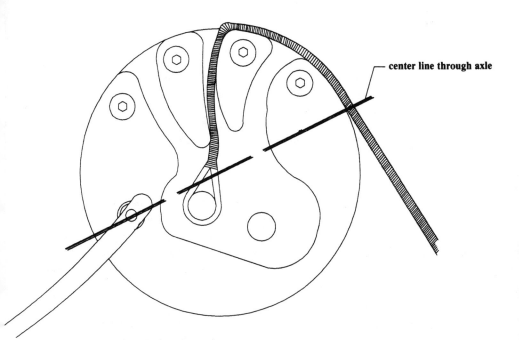

center line through axle

The line of maximum leverage for a round wheel can be found by drawing a line from the axle through the center of the wheel to the opposite side. This timing line can show you if you are in the middle of the valley.

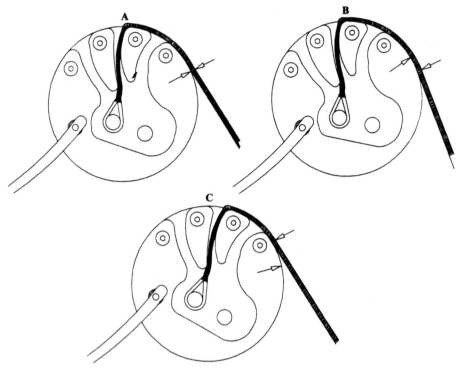

When you reach the middle of the valley with a round wheel, the center line from the axle matches the point on the wheel where the string is leaving the circumference, as in A. If the draw length of the bow is too long, the center line does not roll far enough, as in B. If the wheel rolls too far, as in C, the draw length of the bow is too short for you and should be adjusted.

cable leaves the edge of the wheel, the draw length of the bow is too long for you. In either case, you need to modify the bow to fit your draw length.

If both wheels are not rolling the same amount, this means the power cables of the wheels are not the same length, and one of the cables should be adjusted. Again, a bow press is needed to make the adjustment, and your local dealer can assist with this operation. When the bow is in the press, you can loosen the set screw that locks the cable in position and change the cable length slightly. Don't move it more than a sixteenth of an inch. Remove the bow from the press and draw it several times as someone checks the timing marks. If the wheels are not synchronized, make another adjustment. You'll know when it's adjusted correctly by the position of the timing marks.

If your bow has a Fast Flight cable system made from bowstring material, you can easily synchronize the wheels by twisting one of the cables. These usually have thirty or more twists in them when they are installed. Adding twists to one cable while the bow is in a bow press will make it shorter than the other, and the corresponding wheel will then roll farther than the other wheel. When the timing marks on both wheels roll the same amount, stop adjusting.

Once both wheels are synchronized, you can set the draw length with some accuracy. If the draw length of the bow is too long for you, you must place the string cable in a new position that shortens the length of string between the two wheels. If the draw length of the bow is too short for you, reposition the string cables in the wheel slots so that the string between the two wheels is longer.

You can also twist the bowstring to make very small adjustments to draw length. Several twists added to the bowstring will shorten it by a small amount. Make only three or four twists at a time, then shoot the bow to see if it feels better. If it needs more adjusting, add a few more twists and test-shoot again. Changing the string length by half an inch will change draw length by about three-fourths of an inch.

When making any of these adjustments, remember that *a longer string or cable extension means longer draw length and a shorter string or cable extension means shorter draw length.*

If you are using a Fast Flight cable system and don't want to twist the bowstring for fear of altering your peep sight, you can also adjust draw length by twisting the power cables. In this case there is an inverse relationship: *A longer power cable means shorter draw length and a shorter power cable means longer draw length.* Adding several twists to both power cables will shorten them and slightly increase the draw length. Test-shoot the bow after three or four twists to each cable. If it is not right, add or subtract twists and shoot again.

Adjusting the draw length of the compound bow is the single most important step in making the bow shoot well. Take some time to make it correct. Keep checking the draw length, especially during the first several months while you are learning to shoot. You will find yourself changing during these months, and the draw length of the bow must change with you. Your primary objective at the end of the beginner phase of archery is to feel comfortable when shooting your bow. Only then can you begin to perform consistently and improve your shooting ability.

ESTABLISHING FLETCH CLEARANCE

Stable arrow flight depends on two basic ingredients: the right size arrow for your bow and clear flight around or through the arrow rest. Before you can analyze the arrow's flight on its downrange voyage and determine if it is the proper size for your bow, you have to be certain it's passing through or around the parts of the arrow rest without making contact. First, make sure the arrow rest is aligned with the center line of the bow. You should have set this center-shot adjustment when you installed the arrow rest on your bow according to the instructions in chapter 3.

There are seven possible factors that may be contributing to fletch contact: the nock rotation on the arrow, the nocking point location on the string, the tension of the cushion plunger or other side plate material of the rest, the tension of the underneath support, the closeness of the parts of the arrow rest, your arrow shaft sizes, and the styles of fletching.

To check fletch contact, you can spray white powder on the fletching and the nock end of the shaft and on the side of the sight window around the arrow rest. White-powder foot spray, found in any drugstore, can be used for this purpose. Once you've sprayed on the powder, shoot the arrow from close range. If the fletching is making contact with either the rest or the sight window, markings will appear on the white powder.

Contact with the arrow shaft is acceptable, but any contact between the fletching and the rest is not, as this will distort the flight of the arrow. Each arrow will be affected differently.

Slight contact between the fletching and the rest can be corrected by several adjustments. If the lower hen fletch, the fletch next to the bow handle, is striking the rest, then raising the nocking point on the string can sometimes eliminate the contact. Usually, however, this problem has to be corrected by rotating the nock on the end of the arrow to change the position of the fletch so that it can pass the arrow rest without making contact. Simply cut the nock off the arrow and replace it with a new one turned to a slightly different position. Spray, test-shoot, and adjust until you have succeeded in eliminating the contact. Glue nocks on all of your arrows in this same position.

Sometimes all that is needed to eliminate contact is an adjustment on the arrow rest. The shoot-through and the single-launcher rests are often

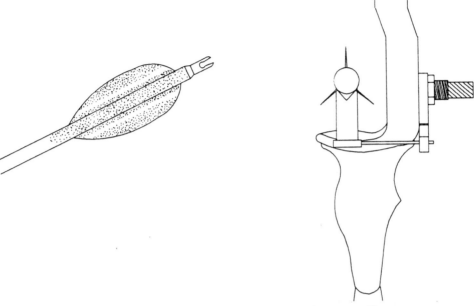

Spraying the fletching with white powder and shooting the arrow will uncover any contact between fletching and arrow rest. Here the points of the single launcher have left drag marks across the vanes of the arrow. The points need to be trimmed shorter and closer together.

installed with the launcher too close to the cushion plunger or side plate. This does not give the fletching space to pass between the rest parts or between the launcher and the bow handle. Move the launcher away from the sight window and plunger to create a larger gap for the lower fletching to pass through.

The single launcher is a popular and easily tuned rest. Arrow flight is usually very good with this rest, but fletching contact can cause the arrow to leave the bow with the nock end higher than the point end. To avoid contact between the two points of the launcher and the fletch, you can trim the launcher with tin snips along the dotted lines.

Fletch contact with a springy rest, or any rest with an extended support arm for the arrow, can be eliminated by one or two adjustments. The support arm is often too long and in the way of the lower fletching. Cutting this arm so that it's shorter will often take care of a contact

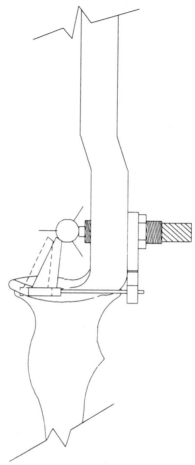

If the launcher is too close to other parts of the rest, the fletching will not pass cleanly. Move the launcher outward as indicated by the dotted outline.

problem. You can also rebend the arm of a springy rest if there is contact with the upper fletch.

Severe contact between the fletching and the arrow rest may require changes in nock size or arrow spine. Nocks that don't fit the string properly can cause the fletching to strike the arrow rest or sight window and should be replaced. The nock should snap onto the string but then slide up and down easily. A nock that fits the string loosely may come off at full draw and cause a dry fire, which can damage the bow.

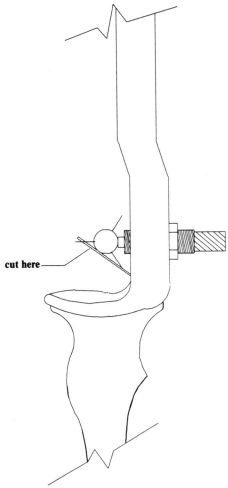

cut here

The support arm of a springy rest or a flipper rest, as shown here, may be too long to allow good clearance. Trim away any excess beyond the center of the arrow shaft.

If the shafts are too stiff, the fletched ends will hit the sight windows; if they are too weak, the fletched ends will move away from the sight window to an extreme degree. Either of these conditions can be corrected by using the proper spine.

Another cause of contact can be the improper gripping and twisting of the bowstring with your fingers. Take care to establish finger and wrist

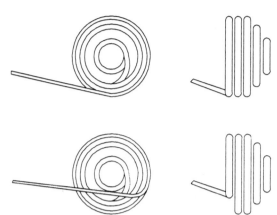

The arm of the springy rest sometimes hangs too low to allow the top fletch to clear the top of the spring coils. Bend the arm upward as shown.

positions that allow the string to keep its vertical alignment during the drawing and releasing of the arrow. Here's where a friend can spot the problem for you and help you correct it. When you can hold and release the bowstring consistently without twisting, then resume the fine-tuning process.

Arrows with four fletches or extra-large fletches may make contact with the rest that can never be eliminated. A fourth fletch on the arrow shaft means there will be less area between fletches and a greater chance of contact. Large fletching will wrap around the shaft for a longer distance and will not pass the rest as easily as smaller fletching. Fletching that is installed with a helical curve will have difficulty passing around or through the rest without making contact. Regardless, you should use helical fletching for broadhead shooting, which means that you may have to tolerate a small amount of contact between rest and fletching as long as good flight and good groups are still possible.

In general, though, persistence in eliminating contact is a must for reliable performance. You need to check for contact on a continuing basis throughout the tuning process and beyond. A good bow tuner always does so even when the arrows are grouping well.

NOCKING-POINT ADJUSTMENT
The job of the arrow rest is to guide the arrow through its first thirty inches of flight and establish its direction toward the target. Directly related to

this is the position of the nock end relative to the point as the arrow leaves the bow. The nocking point on the string determines this location in the vertical plane and, therefore, has a direct effect on the initial flight of the arrow: If the nocking point is too high on the string, the arrow begins its flight with the fletching higher than the point; if it is too low, the arrow leaves the bow with the fletching lower than the point. In either case, the arrow may not fly to its intended target.

A simple paper test can tell you how your arrow is leaving your bow. Fasten a piece of newspaper over a picture frame and hang it about 5 feet in front of your target butt. Stand 10 feet from the frame and shoot an arrow through the paper and into the target butt. The hole the arrow makes in the paper is a record of its flight 10 feet from the bow.

There are several possible hole shapes you might encounter. If the fletching is slicing through the paper above the entry hole of the point, move your nocking point down and shoot another arrow. Usually you will see a difference: The fletching should now be slicing a little lower through the paper. If the fletching is slicing the paper below the entry hole of the point, your nocking point is too low, so move it up the bowstring and shoot another arrow through the paper. Readjust your nocking point until the slices made by the fletching are close to the entry hole of the point.

Perfect holes through the paper are not always possible. Some bows and some arrow rests will always have a tendency to shoot arrows with the fletched end high or to one side. Your objective is to dampen these tendencies and improve arrow flight as much as possible.

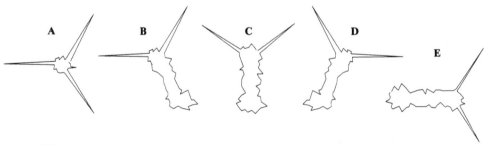

The hole made by an arrow as it passes through a piece of paper will indicate its flight characteristics. Hole A is perfect flight, while B indicates a slightly weak arrow. Hole C shows a high nocking point and D shows a stiff arrow and high nocking point. Hole E indicates an arrow that is much too stiff for the given draw weight. Holes A, B, and C are all acceptable for right-handed shooters.

COORDINATING ARROW SPINE
WITH BOW AND REST

The paper test also works well for testing how the spine of the arrow matches the draw weight of the bow. If the holes through the paper for right-handed shooters show the fletching slicing to the left of the point, this means the arrow is too weak in spine for the draw weight; if the fletching is slicing to the right of the point, the arrow is too stiff. The opposite is true for left-handers.

Both the stiff arrow and the weak arrow can be made to shoot well if they are close to being correct in spine. The stiff arrow needs to be shot at a higher draw weight. If you're using a compound bow, add a few pounds; with a recurve bow, twist the string several more times to increase the draw weight slightly. You can adjust a cushion plunger so that it is weaker, or even try using a heavier point on the arrow to make it act weaker.

Weak arrows need to be shot at a lighter draw weight. You can decrease the draw weight of a compound bow, make a cushion plunger's tension stiffer, or both. You can also try subtracting weight from the point to make the arrow act stiffer.

Longbows don't offer much adjustability in this department. Twisting the string can add some draw weight, but it may not be enough to make a difference. Adding or removing a layer of leather on the side of the sight window where the arrow rests can change the way the arrow leaves the bow and may improve arrow flight.

Arrows that are much too stiff or too weak for your draw weight will not improve in flight with these adjustments; no amount of adjusting plunger tension or draw weight will have much effect. If you are not getting the desired results, you'll need to change arrow sizes.

CHANGING ARROW SIZES

Chapter 2 illustrated the use of an arrow size selection chart to find two or three sizes of arrows that should work well for your bow. These charts usually are very accurate and give good results, but if you're not getting good arrow flight, as indicated by the paper test, consult the chart again and make another selection. If the arrows you have tried are too stiff, select another that is one or two sizes weaker and test again. Remember, this is not an exact science; charts are merely indicators of what should work and are not infallible.

Continue using the paper test to check for a correct match of arrow spine and draw weight. Make adjustments until you get holes in the paper that are less than one inch long. Holes that are less than a quarter inch long are most desirable but not always possible.

At this point, it's best to borrow arrows of several different sizes rather than buying them just to test. When you find a size that gives good results through the paper, try test-shooting it from short and then long range.

TEST-SHOOTING FROM SHORT RANGE

Short-range bow testing is done between 5 and 35 yards. These distances serve well to indicate major tuning problems and to establish groups of arrows that match your ability. Several systems of bow tuning can be applied at these shorter distances and are outlined here.

The Fletched-Arrow Method of Bow Tuning

Begin the fletched-arrow method of bow tuning at 15 yards using at least four but not more than six arrows. You want to use enough arrows to make a pattern in the target but not so many that you get tired and shoot poorly.

A three-inch spot to shoot at should be sufficient from 15 yards, but if you need a larger spot, by all means use one. Have several more spots available for use after tuning adjustments have been made.

Begin by shooting several four-arrow ends at the target spot. Set your sight pin so that you are near the spot with your practice arrows. Now shoot three ends of four arrows each into a new target spot. Shoot as well as you can, then examine the target. The arrow impact holes indicate the tendencies of the arrows and of the shooter. A new shooter tends to miss randomly around the target spot. The tendencies of the arrows may be some definite pattern either in the spot or off to one side of it.

If your arrows are missing mostly to the left and right, adjustments to the arrow rest and nocking point can improve your results. Horizontal groups may be the result of a too-low nocking point or a too-stiff cushion-plunger tension or launcher, so try raising the nocking point, making the launcher weaker, or resetting the plunger tension. Shoot three more ends of four arrows each. If you get no improvement after several adjustments, consider trying a weaker arrow size.

Vertical groups—high and low misses—need different adjustments. They often are the result of a high nocking point or a weak launcher. Lower the nocking point, make the launcher stiffer, and retest. If there is no change in the groupings of arrows, try making the cushion-plunger tension stiffer. Should this also prove unsuccessful, try a stiffer arrow size.

As discussed in chapter 2, point weight can affect arrow spine. At this time in the tuning process, changing point weight becomes an alternative to trying different sizes of arrows. Your arrows will act weaker if weight is added to the point and stiffer if weight is removed. Many experienced archers use 10-grain increments or decrements to fine-tune their arrows. This is a very effective technique to use when your arrows are grouping well but you would like to do better.

Compound bows have draw-weight adjustment features to assist in the tuning process. You can add draw weight to the bow if the arrows are grouping horizontally across the target. If that has no effect, try lessening the draw weight. For arrows that are grouping vertically in the target, try first decreasing and then adding to the draw weight. Use the twelve-arrow test after each adjustment to check for improvement. If you feel that you have not bettered the grouping ability of your bow, then try a different size arrow.

Success at 15 yards qualifies you to move back to 25 or 35 yards and repeat the twelve-arrow test. If you have done your homework at the shorter distance, you will have less work here. The same rules apply at 35 yards: Adjustments have to be made if your arrows are grouping vertically or horizontally. Follow the previously outlined strategies for tuning your arrow rest, draw weight, and nocking point.

Your skill level will be an important part of the tuning process when you move to 35 yards. Unconditioned muscles and form flaws need to be identified and improved before the bow-tuning process can be completed. If you're at a low skill level, you may not see any definite pattern in the target and won't be able to make the necessary tuning adjustments to the bow.

A paper-plate-sized target is good for the beginning archer at 35 yards. After two or three weeks of regular practice, your skill should improve to the point where nine of the twelve arrows will be in the plate. Your misses should be randomly distributed around the edge of the target. If they aren't, either more bow tuning is in order or your form needs some improvement.

The Bare-Shaft Method of Bow Tuning
The bare-shaft tuning method calls for one unfletched and three fletched arrows. As with other tuning methods, the objective is to examine how the arrow is leaving the bow and improve its initial flight.

Begin testing at about 10 yards. Start closer if you will feel more comfortable, however, or move to 15 or 20 yards if you feel confident. Shoot the three fletched arrows at a target spot and finish with the unfletched one.

Where the unfletched arrow hits the target relative to the fletched ones indicates how the arrows are leaving the bow. If the point of the bare shaft hits the target lower than the others did, the nock of the arrow is leaving the bow too high and you need to lower your nocking point; if the point of the bare shaft hits higher, raise the nocking point. Retest with four more shots.

The second phase of the bare-shaft test involves adjustments for impact positions to the left or right. A bare shaft that hits to the right of the fletched ones indicates a weak shaft, and you should make the corresponding adjustments: Use less draw weight if possible, stiffen the cushion-plunger tension, decrease point weight, shorten the arrow, or move the center-shot location of the rest to the right. If the unfletched arrow impacts to the left of the fletched ones, the shaft is too stiff: Add draw weight to the bow if possible, make the cushion-plunger tension weaker, increase point weight, use longer arrows, or move the center-shot location of the rest to the left.

Bare-shaft testing ends when the unfletched shaft hits the target with or very near to the fletched arrows. After you've accomplished this from a distance of 20 yards, move to 35 yards and test with fletched arrows, using the techniques outlined in the previous section.

TEST-SHOOTING FROM LONG RANGE

The archery event for the Olympic competitions is shot from 90, 70, 50, and 30 meters. Long-range accuracy is an absolute must if you ever plan to try out for such an event.

Short-range tuning adjustments work well to ensure that the arrows are as stable as possible when leaving the bow. Once the arrow has begun its downrange flight and stabilizes, it must guide itself in free flight to the target. If that target is a great distance away, the arrow may become unstable again because of the location of its balance point or the amount of fletching on the shaft.

For long-range stability, the projectile must be built so that it remains stable in free flight. If the balance point or center of gravity is too far forward or too far back, wind resistance on the shaft and fletching will cause the arrow to become unstable.

Changing the balance point is a primary tuning adjustment for long-range stability. After 60 meters, an arrow with a point that is too heavy will fall quickly, while one with a point that is too light may float erratically. In order to find the best balance point for the arrow, vary the point weight by 10 grains at a time and test each weight.

The amount of fletching on arrows has a similar effect on long-range arrow flight and grouping. After 60 meters, too much fletching may cause an arrow to fall quickly, while too little may cause it to float. Try larger or smaller fletching until you find the best grouping arrangement.

Long-range shooting is not for the absolute beginner; it's a long-term goal to shoot a scoring round at 90 meters. Novice archers need to be more concerned with learning consistent form from 20 or 30 meters. When the form is consistent, then move to a longer distance. Be patient.

8

Target Archery

TARGET ARCHERY IS a sport of shooting arrows accurately over long distances ranging from 30 to 90 meters (33 to 99 yards). Most often a set number of arrows are shot at several distances to complete a tournament round.

The target archer must compete on a flat surface in open terrain; thus all those who wish to participate in the target event will stand at the same shooting line at the same time in the same weather conditions and shoot at targets set at the same distance. The emphasis is then placed on the ability of the archer to shoot arrows into the middle of the target and not on any other skill.

The most common target rounds are the metric 900 round and the long FITA (Federation Internationale de Tir à l'Arc) round, which is used in the Olympic archery event. The 900 round is shot from 60, 50, and 40 meters. Thirty arrows are shot from each distance in five ends of six arrows for a perfect score of 900 points. Sometimes this round is altered to the metric 600 round, in which twenty arrows are shot from each distance for a perfect score of 600 points.

The target used in either metric round is the five-colored international face with ten scoring rings valued from ten points in the center to one point in the outer ring. Each scoring ring is designated by a thin, black circle; the two center rings are gold and are surrounded by two scoring rings of red, then two of blue, two of black, and an outer two of white. The scoring area has a diameter of 122 centimeters (48 inches), with the ten ring being 12.2 centimeters (4.8 inches) in diameter.

The longer FITA round used in Olympic and other tournaments is shot from four distances: 90, 70, 50, and 30 meters for men; and 70, 60, 50, and 30 meters for women. The two longer distances are shot in six ends of six arrows each and the two shorter distances in twelve ends of three arrows each, with a perfect score of 1440 points for the complete round of 144 arrows.

The 122-centimeter face is used at 90, 70, and 60 meters. As large as it is, this face is very difficult to hit from almost 100 yards, and this distance offers the most difficult challenge of archery. A smaller, 80-centimeter target face with narrower bands of ten scoring rings in five colors is used for 50 and 30 meters. Usually the two longer distances are shot on the first day of a tournament and the two shorter ones the following day.

The shooting of two distances takes about five hours, depending on the weather conditions and how fast scoring can be done after each end of shooting. When shooting that many ends from long distances, there is a great amount of walking to be done, about 3.7 miles per round, and that also takes time.

EQUIPMENT REQUIREMENTS

The Olympic competition in archery is open to those who have qualified with recurve bows using simple sight pins and drawing the bowstring with the fingers. No magnifying lenses, peep sights, or mechanical release aids are allowed. The rules are very restrictive so that the skill of the archer will play the major role in determining the winning score. They also prevent those countries that have greater technology from dominating the sport.

The equipment used in competition other than the Olympics is less restrictive. The local, regional, and national target-archery tournaments sponsored by the National Archery Association (NAA) have divisions for bows with no sights, crossbows, and compound bows in addition to those for recurve bows. The compound division, however, is designated as compound with mechanical release aid and has just recently been instituted within the NAA.

The NAA recognizes two basic styles of shooting in its tournaments: recurve bows shot with the fingers and compound bows shot with mechanical release aids. Within these two styles, the following divisions are established for both men and women: cadet, ages up to twelve; junior, ages twelve up to fifteen; intermediate, ages fifteen up to eighteen; and adult, ages eighteen and older.

For more information, see appendix I, in which the NAA constitution and bylaws have been reprinted with the organization's permission. You may reproduce the membership application if you wish to use it.

TARGET-ARCHERY ORGANIZATIONS

The NAA is recognized by the FITA and the United States Olympic Committee as the single organization in the United States responsible for selecting and training the men's and women's Olympic archery teams. The NAA is also responsible for presenting teams at the world championships and Pan-Am Games. The NAA also conducts annual national championships, which determine champions in all age groups and shooting styles.

The International Olympic Committee conducts the Olympic Games while, in the case of archery, the FITA sets the standards of entry and qualification as well as the rules for the events. Within each country a governing body must administer those rules and establish a team for the Olympics. The NAA, therefore, works closely with the United States Olympic Committee when team qualifications are being conducted.

The NAA has many state and local affiliates. These clubs and organizations provide year-long competition and training for target archery. This is where most target archers get started and where most continue their practice.

Two other NAA programs deserve mention. The Junior Olympic Archery Development (JOAD) program provides youths with training and practice in archery fundamentals. JOAD also provides tournaments for young people to show off their skills and adds great incentive for achievement. In the College Division program, college teams compete annually in the U.S. Intercollegiate Championships and other events throughout the country. Most Olympic team members come from the collegiate program.

The NAA and Indoor Archery

The NAA provides tournament opportunities throughout the year by being involved in indoor archery. NAA shooters participate in major tournaments in Las Vegas and Atlantic City, as well as NAA indoor regional and national tournaments. Most state championships have divisions for those shooting by FITA rules.

The indoor round shot by NAA members is the thirty-arrow or sixty-arrow round using the 40-centimeter, five-color international FITA target with ten scoring rings. The ten ring and nine ring are the center, gold-colored rings. The eight and seven rings are red and are surrounded by rings of blue, black, and then white. The ten ring is only 4 centimeters (1.57 inch) in diameter and offers a very demanding target with any kind of archery equipment. Not many archers can hit the ten ring thirty out of thirty times, and even fewer can hit it sixty out of sixty times.

The overall purpose of indoor archery is to improve your shooting form. Here, the obstacles of terrain and the elements are eliminated. With these out of the picture, you can think only of making every shot the same. The body and mind must be trained to repeat with great precision the motions and thoughts that produce near-perfect shots that hit the target in the ten ring. This shooting-form practice translates to better long-distance shooting when you move outdoors.

Indoor archery also offers a great chance to work on your bow. The bow will not always repeat itself on every shot, and you must adjust it to make it do just that at least to the same degree that you are repeating yourself. Before you can improve your shooting form and scoring, the bow must repeat itself more consistently than you do.

The NAA shooting program and styles of target championships offer something for everyone. If you're interested in shooting archery with a recurve bow, this is the organization to join. If you prefer to shoot the compound bow, the NAA has a growing division for the compound with a release aid, which may lead to a division in the Olympics in the not-too-distant future.

INTERNATIONAL TARGET ARCHERY
PRACTICE TIPS

DENISE PARKER: She is a recurve amateur sponsored by Easton Aluminum/Hoyt.

A bronze medalist at the 1988 Olympic Games in Seoul, Denise also took home a bronze medal at the 1989 World Championships and was a gold medalist at the Pan American Games in 1987 and 1991. She also won the Indoor National Championship four years straight from 1988–91 and was National Champion in 1990 and 1991.

Tips: Don't be too hung up on scoring all of the time. There is more to practicing than scoring. During practice, pay more attention to fixing details and making everything smooth.

Make it as fun as possible. Shoot at other things once in a while besides just a target.

Make sure you are practicing because you want to and that you enjoy shooting. It's your decision.

ED ELIASON: Ed is a recurve amateur sponsored by Easton Aluminum.

Ed captured the first place at the Olympic festivals of 1989 and 1991, won the NAA Outdoor title in 1991, and finished second at the 1991 Pan American Games in Cuba. He holds the U.S. record at 50 meters (347/360).

Tips: Always have fun.

Strive for consistency in your practice. Shoot every day even if it's for only fifteen minutes. Have a specific goal for each session.

Practice reaiming shots and keeping your bow hand steady.

Don't let your release hand leave your face after the shot.

Grip the bow string with equal tension on all three fingers while drawing the bow, then allow most of the pressure to be divided between the finger above the nock and the finger just below the nock. Too much top-finger pressure will cause high arrows while too much pressure on the lower finger will cause low arrows. Practice finger pressure at ten yards using a peep sight.

Don't let your fingers slip off of the bow string; slipping will cause arrows to impact left of the target center.

Always warm up for shooting by stretching and always stretch after shooting.

All good shooters start with these basics and stay with them throughout their careers.

Stay in the present when shooting. Don't try to relive the previous shot and don't try to shoot the next three shots now. Shoot *this* shot only.

9

Field Archery

FIELD ARCHERY IS just what its name indicates: archery shot in the field. The word *field*, however, has a broad meaning; field archery includes just about every kind of terrain imaginable, from open field to thick brush to open woods. It is shot up hills and down, over creeks and ponds, from bridges and from gullies. It can be enjoyed anywhere a target can be placed outdoors.

In the sport of field archery, you shoot at a sequence of twenty-eight targets positioned along a trail in natural terrain. After shooting at each target, you walk along the trail to the next. The targets vary in range from 20 feet to 80 yards and are set at marked distances. You shoot four arrows at each target, making a total of 112 shots for a complete field round. One additional target is shot as a practice target before official scoring is begun.

To me, the ultimate test of man and machine is the field-archery course. Shooting in the field combines your skills in physical conditioning, equipment preparation, shooting accuracy, and mental tenacity. You must be in good physical shape to spend three, four, or five hours hiking from target to target, shooting four arrows at each, both uphill and down.

The bow and arrows you use for field archery must be in top condition and remain reliable for the entire shooting round. The bow has to be well tuned to provide accuracy across the entire range of target distances. Take enough arrows so that you will be able to shoot all of the targets on the field course. Lost, bent, or damaged arrows will need to be repaired or replaced. Carry along some small tools for making simple adjustments or repairs to the bow or arrows.

Shooting accurately at one set distance requires practice and good form; shooting accurately at many distances demands far more practice and a shooting form that is reliable aiming both uphill and down, standing on flat and on slanted ground, and even after one hundred arrows have been drawn and released.

Shooting over a long period of time such as four hours is demanding on the mind as well as the body. Your mind must remain sharp for the entire round so that for each target you set your sight correctly and shoot at the proper face and from the correct distance marker. You must also demand that your body shoot each arrow as well at the last target as you did at the first. Mental fatigue can sneak in at any moment during a field round and destroy a good score in only a few minutes.

If you elect to shoot a formal field tournament, be well prepared to shoot the 112 arrows necessary to complete the round. No rest periods are given, and the only weather condition that stops a field round is lightning; rain, wind, snow, or hail will just make the round more difficult.

The field round has fourteen different target situations, each of which is shot twice in the twenty-eight-target course through two fourteen-target sequences. Each sequence forms a half, with a perfect score of 280 points per half and a perfect total score of 560 points.

The target situations from shortest to longest are as follows:
1) one shot each at 35, 30, 25, and 20 feet;
2) four shots at 15 yards;
3) four shots at 20 yards;
4) four shots at 25 yards;
5) four shots at 30 yards;
6) one shot from each of four markers at 35 yards;
7) four shots at 40 yards;
8) four shots at 45 yards;
9) one shot each at 45, 40, 35, and 30 yards;
10) four shots at 50 yards;
11) four shots at 55 yards;

12) four shots at 60 yards;

13) four shots at 65 yards;

14) one shot each at 80, 70, 60, and 50 yards.

The target situations are not laid out on the field-course trail in this sequence but randomly. The two halves are not set up in the same sequence either, so you must be prepared to shoot at any of the targets at any time. Each target is set in a unique position in different terrain—much like a golf course, except that you're mostly in the woods.

Archers shooting in any field tournament are assigned to targets by groups of three or four. When all participants have reached their assigned starting targets and are prepared to begin, a horn or a gun is sounded to start the shooting for the round. Most ranges have trails wide enough that two people can shoot side by side. After two shoot their arrows, the other one or two can step to the distance marker and shoot.

When all have completed shooting, they walk to the target to score the arrows. Generally two people keep score while the other two call the values of the arrows in the target. The value of any questionable arrow is decided by the group, but if a decision can't be reached or if there is any other problem on the course, a range captain—usually an appointed member of the host club—can be called upon to handle the situation.

Although the field course leads through the woods, you are never far from the clubhouse or pavilion where everyone started. Ten acres is sufficient for a safe field course. Many clubs have much more area to work with, however, and generally the more area available the safer the range can be made.

After shooting all twenty-eight targets, you can walk ahead on the trail to the clubhouse. Don't backtrack on the course since other archers may still be shooting. At the clubhouse the score cards can be totaled and posted for awards.

Many people prefer to shoot the field range by themselves. Being alone on the course is a great way to spend an afternoon of archery. Just the walk is good exercise. I built my own field course, and when I have thirty minutes I can shoot seven targets for practice or test a new piece of equipment.

EQUIPMENT REQUIREMENTS

Field archery is open to anyone with a bow and a few arrows who wants the challenge. Local archery clubs recognize shooters of every style, from those using a longbow and wooden arrows to those using sights and release aids. Every age group has a division in which to participate: Cubs are the youngest, under age twelve, while seniors are over age fifty-five. If you accept the challenge of field archery, you'll be able to find someone your age and skill level to shoot with. You can shoot in local tournaments or national championships, or you can shoot by yourself at your local club.

Field-archery competition is separated into different divisions, and within each division there are different styles of shooting. The divisions are as follows: cub, under age twelve; youth, ages twelve through fourteen; young adult, ages fifteen through seventeen; adult, age eighteen and older; professional; and senior, age fifty-five and older.

The styles of shooting, determined by the equipment the archer chooses to use, are freestyle, freestyle limited, barebow, bowhunter, bow-hunter freestyle, and bowhunter freestyle limited.

Limited indicates that the archer must draw and release the bowstring with the fingers. *Freestyle* allows the use of any kind of hand-held bow with the accessories of your choice. *Barebow* means that you may not use a sighting device of any kind on the bow. *Bowhunter* denotes the use of hunting-weight arrows and simple pin sights.

For more details of equipment regulations, check appendix II. There you will find the bylaws of the National Field Archery Association (NFAA), which will answer most of your questions.

FIELD-ARCHERY ORGANIZATIONS

The grass roots of field archery are the local archery clubs that participate in this kind of shooting. They can be found in all regions of the United States. Joining is easy and very inexpensive; just ask at any archery shop or sporting-goods store.

Most local clubs are affiliated with a state association that organizes championships and regional tournaments.

The NFAA is the governing body for field archery in the United States. Its membership numbers about twenty thousand throughout the fifty states. One director is elected from each state to attend an annual convention where the rules and policies are set for the coming year. Appendix II includes more details on the NFAA's structure.

Various national field-archery organizations have joined together to form the International Field Archery Association (IFAA). Its purpose is to promote field archery through the establishment of world-championship tournaments. These tournaments take place every two years. The host country is determined by a bid and selection process at least four years in advance of the tournament date. The IFAA recognizes the same divisions and styles of competition as the NFAA, with a few minor exceptions. The world tournaments are open to anyone who wishes to travel to them and offer a great way to meet people from other countries who have a common love of archery.

NFAA Indoor Archery

Like most other national and international archery organizations, the NFAA sponsors indoor archery events throughout the country. The country is divided into eight sections, which each have indoor sectional tournaments in early March. The NFAA then holds its National Indoor Championship in late March.

The round that's shot at these events is similar to other indoor rounds shot from 20 yards. The white center spot of the target face is about three inches in diameter and contains a 1.5-inch X-ring for use as a tiebreaker. The value of the center spot is five points, and there are four outer blue rings with point values of four, three, two, and then one.

An official round is made up of sixty shots divided into twelve ends of five arrows. Anyone hitting the center spot with all sixty arrows scores a perfect 300 points. The next step up the ladder is to shoot all sixty arrows into the smaller X-ring, a difficult feat from 20 yards.

Many local clubs use the NFAA indoor target for their indoor leagues, which usually take place during the winter months and finish sometime in March just before the NFAA Indoor Championship. The indoor archery league is quite popular in all parts of the country and keeps club members active during the winter months. Shooting at 20 yards all winter is great for developing good shooting form; I recommend doing as much of it as possible.

I would also recommend that anyone interested in learning more about indoor and field archery join the NFAA. You may reproduce the membership application if you would like to join the organization.

Many beginners spend great amounts of time practicing field archery. At least some of this time is wasted on practicing things that are not useful or are counterproductive. To help prevent this and to increase your enjoyment of field archery, I'm including some practice tips from several good friends who are members of the National Field Archery Professional Division.

FIELD ARCHERY PRACTICE TIPS

TERRY RAGSDALE: Terry and his wife, Michelle, and their two children live in Tucson, Arizona. Terry is employed by Precision Shooting Equipment (PSE) on a full-time basis and represents PSE on the pro tour.

Terry has won three IFAA World Field Championships, four NFAA National Field Championships, two NFAA Indoor Championships, and three Las Vegas Indoor Championships.

Tips: In my opinion, the most important thing for someone just getting started in our great sport is to: a) take the time to get properly fitted with good equipment; b) listen to other opinions to see if what they are passing on works for you; and c) start with good instruction and learn the basics!

I believe that too many folks try to do too much, too soon. Start out with a good basic set-up and learn proper shooting form (keep in mind that it takes time and quality practice to be able to repeat an accurate shot).

I mentioned listening to others, which is how we do learn many things. A word of caution: Don't make the mistake of constantly changing things without giving them a chance to work. When you do get a set-up you like, LEAVE IT ALONE AND TRY A BIT OF HARD WORK! Good luck!

MICHELLE RAGSDALE: She is an unlimited women's shooter sponsored by PSE/Easton Aluminum.

Michelle was the 1990/91 World IFAA Champion, 1981 NFAA National Champion, 1990 PAA Outdoor National Champion, 1979 Las Vegas Champion, and 1979 North American Indoor Champion.

Tips: Beginning archers should practice their form over and over until it becomes second nature. Once they develop muscle memory, then they can work on improving their scores. High scores will come later when they have put enough time into just the basics. Practice sessions should be short at first so as not to tire muscles and to build the right muscles without developing bad habits that will prove difficult to break later. Increase each practice session until you can shoot sixty to ninety arrows comfortably without form breakdown. Don't keep score; shoot for form and shoot for groups. Be patient when working on your form. Give a new technique a fighting chance before you decide another way is better.

JACK CRAMER: He competes in the unlimited division, is from Gettysburg, Pennsylvania, and is sponsored by PSE.

Jack is a former PAA National Champion, NFAA National Champion, IFAA World Champion, Las Vegas Champion, and Desert Shootout Champion.

Tips: I suggest all beginners start with a sight and a release aid. I would also suggest a nonmechanical release (Stanislawski release) so that beginners learn how to make good shots with proper back tension and follow through. Start at close range (about 10 yards) with a big bull's-eye and think only about form at first.

I also believe a beginning archer should have a professional archer or someone knowledgeable about release aids to teach the proper technique. Learning good habits at the beginning can make archery much more enjoyable.

MIKE LEITER: Mike is part of the field archer unlimited division, sponsored by PSE, and lives near Baltimore, Maryland.

Mike captured the 1980, 1982, 1985, and 1991 NFAA Outdoor National Championships in pro freestyle.

Tips: Learn the fundamentals, the proper stance, hand position, consistent anchor, and good back tension.

Learn the difference between a good shot and a bad shot. Many people blame their equipment for misses when, if they were a little more honest with themselves, they would know the misses were caused by their own errors.

Practice only quality shots. Two hours of quality shots is a zillion times better than twelve hours of poor-quality, bad-habit-forming shots.

Last, don't be afraid to seek the help and advice of a top-ranked archery professional. I don't know very many who wouldn't share the knowledge of their many years in the sport.

BUTCH JOHNSON: Butch competes in men's freestyle limited compound and is sponsored by Hoyt. He lives in Connecticut.

He's been the NFAA Outdoor National Champion seven times, the NFAA Indoor National Champion two times, the PAA Outdoor National Champion two times, and the PAA Indoor National Champion five times. He's also an eight-time winner of the Atlantic City Classic.

Tips: Practice making good shots. Don't worry about score; with good shots, the score will come. Don't overdo it. If you are tired, don't keep practicing. You will just develop bad habits and will end up getting frustrated. Don't try to rush practice. If you don't have much time, just shoot fewer arrows, but make all of your shots good ones.

If you use a clicker to control your release of the string, start your pull to come through the clicker. Don't stop even if the site moves. Keep pulling and remember, when the clicker clicks, the shot is not over—it has just begun.

TRICIA H. JOHNSON: Tricia competes in the Women's Pro Fingers sponsored by Hoyt and lives in Connecticut with her husband, Butch.

She was the IFAA World Champion in 1988, the Las Vegas Champion in 1987 and 1988, the NFAA Outdoor Champion in 1988, 1989, and 1990, and the NFAA Indoor Champion in 1989 and 1991. She also captured the PAA Indoor Championship in 1987 and 1988, as well as the PAA Outdoor Championship in 1991.

Tips: Practice good shots! It is much better to only shoot thirty arrows the very best you can than to just fling one hundred shots to say you practiced a lot. It will not help you. When you are practicing, don't worry where the arrows land on the target. It is more beneficial to just execute a technically perfect shot as many times as possible in short sessions. The scores will follow when you perfect your form.

In a tournament, do not concern yourself with what your score might be—it will kill you. Give each shot 110 percent and when you are through look at your score. Even if you don't win that day, you will know you did your best.

If you shoot with a clicker, never stop pulling! Once you begin your pull, try to make it constant and smooth. Remember, the shot is not over when the clicker clicks—it is just beginning. You must follow through with your bow arm and your pulling arm. Don't panic when your sight moves around the spot. Everyone moves. Let the sight float and just keep looking at the spot. Always, always aim consistently.

LINDA KLOSTERMAN: A participant in Women's Freestyle Release sponsored by Bear/Jennings and AFC. Linda lives in Ohio.

The Desert Shoot-Out Champion in 1990 and 1991, Linda was the NFAA Outdoor Champion in 1986, 1989, 1990, and 1991, the Las Vegas

Champion and PAA Indoor Champion in 1989, and the PAA and Big Sky Outdoor Champion in 1991. She also won the Atlantic City Classic in 1987, 1989, 1990, and 1991.

Tips: Concentration during practice is important. Think about what you are trying to improve. Don't just stand and shoot arrows with no purpose. Concentrate on improving each shot.

Stand close to the backstop and shoot some shots with your eyes closed. It will help develop your muscle memory so that each shot feels the same. With your eyes closed (not aiming), the rest of your body and brain can get a better feel of what a good shot is like.

10

Unmarked-Distance Archery

SHOOTING UNMARKED-DISTANCE tournaments is very similar to shooting field archery: The targets are set along a trail through the woods and fields in all kinds of terrain. The major differences lie in the kinds of targets, the number of arrows shot, the number of targets shot, and, of course, the fact that the distances to the targets are unmarked.

The unmarked-distance tournament is in many ways as much of a challenge to the archer as field archery. The forty targets of an official round are shaped and painted like various wild game animals. You shoot one arrow at each target in hopes of hitting a small circle representing the vital area on the side of the creature. This shot must be made carefully because it is the only one you will get at that target.

The distances to the targets range from 20 to 60 yards. Shooting markers denote the shooting position and the target number but not the distance to the target. You must make an estimate, set your sight, and take your one shot. After the other archers in your group have shot, you advance to the target and score the arrows.

Shooting forty targets in a tournament situation often takes four to six hours, so mental alertness and equipment preparation are essential, as is being in shape physically. Bow-tuning skills are equally important so that your equipment will perform flawlessly throughout the tournament.

An extra skill demanded by shooting unmarked targets is that of estimating distance, which is what makes this style of archery most like actual hunting. Like other skills, this must be practiced, and you'll need to devise a system of some kind to aid you in this estimating process. Shooting skill doesn't mean much if you can't judge distance; conversely, if you can't shoot, knowing the distance doesn't help either.

Most local archery clubs sponsor unmarked-distance tournaments before hunting season. These shoots start in the early summer and continue until midautumn when hunting season begins. A few tournaments occur after that, but most archers are spending their time on the live version of the targets they have been shooting at all summer.

EQUIPMENT REQUIREMENTS

As in field archery, anyone with a bow and a few arrows can shoot unmarked-distance archery. Various age groups are recognized, as well as different styles of shooting. The recognized classes are as follows: male compound aided, female aided, male compound unaided, female unaided, male bowhunter release, female bowhunter release, male bowhunter open, female bowhunter open, male recurve aided, male recurve unaided, youth aided, youth unaided, and cub.

Aided means that a fixed pin sight may be used, while *unaided* indicates that no sighting device of any kind may be used. The classes denoted as *open* allow any sight device that can be mounted on the bow and any method of releasing the bowstring. The youth classes apply to ages thirteen through seventeen; the cub class is for those ages twelve and under and has no equipment restrictions.

For shooting unmarked distances, an arrow that would remain perfectly horizontal after leaving the bow would be a great advantage. That is impossible, however, but making your arrow travel as fast as possible is still a worthy objective and a distinct advantage. For that reason an 80-pound draw-weight limit has been placed on the bows used in unmarked-distance tournaments sponsored by the International Bowhunting Organization (IBO).

The arrow used in IBO events is also subject to some restrictions. The arrow must have a total weight equivalent to no less than 4½ grains per pound of peak weight. There are no length restrictions, so many archers use short arrows and an overdraw arrow-rest mounting device. With short arrows the minimum weight can be attained and faster arrow speeds achieved.

The compound bow, because of its greater stored energy potential, is the predominant choice for IBO events. In fact, for a maximum of stored energy, most archers are choosing to shoot a compound with full-cam eccentric wheels. High stored energy and low arrow weight is the best combination for high arrow velocity.

The increase in stored energy usually means higher arrow velocities, but only if you are willing to spend some time tuning the bow. With lightweight arrows it's very often difficult to achieve good arrow flight. As mentioned earlier, weak-spined arrow shafts fly erratically unless some time is spent tuning the arrow rest, draw weight, draw length, and your shooting form.

Although arrow speed is a great advantage in shooting unmarked distances, the archer who wins will be the one who has the best grouping bow. In order to score points in any tournament, you have to be able to hit what you aim at.

UNMARKED-DISTANCE ARCHERY ORGANIZATIONS

As with other forms of archery, the local clubs are the foundation of the unmarked-distance tournament. These clubs sponsor events all year long but primarily in the months preceding hunting season. To find the club nearest you, inquire at your local archery store.

The major governing body for unmarked-distance archery is the IBO, which sponsors the annual Triple Crown of Bowhunting. This is a series of three events in three different states, all of which follow the same format and scoring rules and lead to overall national champions in all thirteen classes.

Consult appendix III for more information on the IBO. You may reproduce the membership application if you're interested in joining.

UNMARKED-DISTANCE ARCHERY PRACTICE TIPS

TODD HERRMAN: He is sponsored by Hoyt and lives in Harrisburg, Pennsylvania.

Todd has held many titles in the IBO. He won the Manufacturers Division of the 1989 Aurroraland Archers Championship (the first leg of the IBO triple crown), as well as the 1991 National IBO Triple Crown

Team Championship in the Manufacturers Team Division. He also captured the National Indoor IBO Championship three straight years, from 1988–90.

Tips: Always practice on a "bull's-eye" type target face. This will help the pinpoint concentration sometimes lost by shooting at animal targets with no aiming dots painted on them — the only type of target in the IBO.

Since speed and accuracy are the name of the game in the IBO, I suggest you use a dependable simple shoot-through or shoot-over rest like the "Star Hunter," "Pacesetter," or the "TM Hunter." I have found them to be very sturdy and simple. Also, at the higher speeds an arrow does some funny tricks if its fletches or vanes hit the rest. I have found that if a fletch or vane does hit one of these rests they will withstand this punishment without bending or breaking so you can go right on shooting.

Don't rely on the speed of your bow to make up for all of your mistakes in yardage guessing. Practice honing these skills as much as you do your shooting skills.

As a beginner, don't go "whole hog" into the speed game. Learn all of your fundamentals and achieve accuracy, then start trying to speed up your bow if you feel you need it.

A few of the ways to speed up bows like cranking the weight up or going to a weaker, lighter arrow are ways some beginners in the IBO mess up. Don't shoot any more weight than you can handle if you have to struggle to pull and hold a bow. Your fundamentals will suffer and therefore your accuracy also. Going to a weaker, lighter arrow can cause the arrow to become too weak-spined, and, even though you might have a faster setup, it will not be as accurate as a slightly slower one.

PETE TRESSLER: He's a member of IBO in Pennsylvania.

Tips: Begin by getting set up with proper equipment tuned to shoot at its maximum potential. Poorly tuned equipment causes a multitude of frustrations for young archers. Learn about your equipment.

Begin your new sport with a knowledgeable shooter who is able to help you with form as well as equipment functions, such as sight adjustment and wheel timing.

When first starting unmarked-distance shooting, get used to known distances and work up. Don't get yourself frustrated.

No matter how hard or easy the distance, always maintain the best form and posture you can. Knowing the distance doesn't always mean you will hit the highest scoring section on the animal.

MELANIE BUSE: An IBO competitor, she is sponsored by Indian Industries and lives in Indiana.

Melanie has won the Indoor Animal Championship in IBO, the IBO Triple Crown, the IBO Triple Crown Team Championship, and the Illinois and Indiana State championships.

Tips: In IBO shooting always start with good matched equipment and don't hesitate to ask questions of someone who knows how to shoot IBO events and how to adjust equipment.

Speed is important in unmarked-distance shooting. You cannot always judge the distance correctly, and speed can compensate for error since the arrow will not be falling as fast as a slower arrow and may still hit the big score area.

Guessing yardage will come with practice just as good form improves. Both are important. Once you have developed a system for guessing yardage, stick with your first guess and go for it. Second-guessing will ultimately cause doubt, and doubt will eventually cause your form to break down.

Don't give up. I am always outclassed in speed because of my short draw length but, if I work hard and shoot consistently during the entire tournament, particularly two-day events, I can still win. Often I win because I don't lose my shooting form under pressure when others do.

This should get you started in the great sport of archery or, if you're an experienced archer, help you improve your skills and find more ways of becoming involved. I'm sure you'll find it as rewarding as I do. Happy shooting!

Appendix I

CONSTITUTION OF THE NATIONAL ARCHERY ASSOCIATION OF THE UNITED STATES, INC.

Adopted March 1990

ARTICLE I

The name of this organization shall be "National Archery Association of the United States, Inc.", indicated in abbreviation as NAA.

ARTICLE II

The corporation is organized and shall be operated exclusively for educational and charitable purposes and to perpetuate, foster, and direct the practice of the sport of archery in connection with the educational and charitable purposes of this corporation and to raise funds for the carrying out of these purposes: it is authorized to accept, hold, administer, invest and disburse for said purposes any such funds as may from time to time be given to it by any person, persons or corporations, to receive gifts and make financial and other types of contributions and assistance to religious, charitable, scientific, literary or educational organizations which are exempt or are eligible for exemption under applicable Federal Internal Revenue Laws, and in general do all things that may appear necessary and useful in accomplishing the purposes herein set out. All of the assets and earnings shall be used exclusively for the purpose herein above set out, including the payment of expenses incidental thereto; no part of the net earnings shall inure to the benefit of any private individual and no substantial part of its activities shall be carrying on of propaganda or otherwise attempting to influence legislation.

In the event of dissolution, all of the remaining assets of the corporation shall be distributed only for educational, religious, charitable, scientific, or literary purposes.

ARTICLE III — MEMBERSHIP

1. There shall be seven classes of membership: Honorary, Life, Sustaining, Active, Youth, Family, and Associate.

2. Honorary membership, with exemption from regular dues, may be granted for exceptional merit or service, by the Board of Governors.

3. Life membership shall be granted to anyone, on payment of appropriate dues, and approval of the Executive Director.

4. Sustaining membership shall be granted upon application, payment of dues, and approval of the Executive Director.

5. Active membership shall be granted to persons who have attained their eighteenth birthday, upon application, payment of dues, and approval of the Executive Director.

6. Youth membership shall be granted to anyone under eighteen years of age, upon application, payment of dues, and approval of the Executive Director. Upon attaining their eighteenth birthday, a youth member shall automatically become an active member.

7. Family membership may be granted to a family, including husband, wife, and dependents under eighteen years of age, upon application, payment of dues, and approval of the Executive Director.

8. Associate membership is a non-voting and non-competitive category of membership and is open to everyone, upon application, payment of dues and approval of the Executive Director.

9. The Board of Governors may suspend or expel any member for any reason considered detrimental to the NAA; however, the member may be reinstated upon appeal, if approved by two-thirds of the membership voting.

ARTICLE IV— BOARD OF GOVERNORS

1. The Board of Governors shall consist of ten (10) elected members, two (2) from each of the four regions, the ninth member an active Archer Athlete, and the tenth member, the Athlete Advisory Council Representative of the USOC. The nominees for election, to the Board of Governors, shall be selected without regard to race, color, religion, national origin or sex.

2. The Chairman of the Board of Governors, who also serves as President of the NAA, and the Vice-Chairman of the Board of Governors, who also serves as Vice President of the NAA, shall be chosen by the Board from its ten elected members. The vote shall be taken as soon after the annual meeting of the NAA as practicable, but not to exceed thirty days. Any vacancy occurring in these offices shall be filled in the same manner.

3. Subject only to the provisions of this Constitution and to such action as may be taken thereunder from time to time by the NAA membership, the voting members of the Board of Governors shall control and manage the activities, policies and property of the NAA.

4. Any action required or permitted to be taken at a meeting of the Board of Governors or any committee thereof may be taken without a meeting if a consent in writing, setting forth the action to be taken, shall be signed by all of the Board

members or committee members entitled to vote with respect to the subject matter thereof. Such consent (which may be signed in counterparts) shall have the same force and effect as if the action were taken by a unanimous vote of the Board members or committee members at a duly called meeting at which all of the Board members or the committee members were present.

5. The Board of Governors shall meet at the call of the Chairman, and at such meetings six voting members present shall constitute a quorum. An agenda shall be furnished to the Board members fourteen days prior to any called meeting. A majority vote of those Board members present at a meeting of the Board of Governors shall decide matters on the agenda or new matters requiring immediate action, but all other matters shall require the approval of at least six voting members, and any such action of the Board of Governors taken in accordance with Paragraph 4 or taken at a later meeting in accordance with this Paragraph 5. Members of the Board of Governors or any committee thereof may participate in a meeting of the Board or committee by means of conference telephone or similar communications equipment by which all persons participating in the meeting can hear each other at the same time. Such participation shall constitute presence at the meeting for all purposes. No member of the Board of Governors or committee thereof may vote or otherwise act by proxy at any meeting of the Board or committee. A Board member who is present at a meeting of the Board of Governors at which action on any corporate matter is taken shall be presumed to have assented to the action taken unless such Board member's dissent shall be entered in the minutes of the meeting or unless the Board member shall file a written dissent to such action with the person acting as the secretary of the meeting before the adjournment thereof or shall forward such dissent by registered mail to the Executive Director of the NAA immediately after the adjournment of the meeting. Such right to dissent shall not apply to a Board member who voted in favor of such action.

6. Any vacancy occurring in an elective office of the NAA, including membership in the Board of Governors, except the Athlete Advisory Council Representative, shall be filled by the Board, and the officer thus chosen shall hold office until that officer's duly elected successor shall take office.

7. Committees with specific assignments may be appointed from the NAA membership by the Executive Director upon approval of the Board of Governors. Such Committees shall report to the Chairman who shall submit their findings to the Board for action.

8. The Board of Governors may elect Honorary Presidents and Honorary Vice Presidents who shall be distinguished persons whom the NAA desires to honor or persons who have distinguished themselves by their work for archery.

ARTICLE V— OFFICERS AND DUTIES
1. The officers of the NAA shall be: President, who shall serve as Chairman of the Board of Governors; Vice President, who shall serve as Vice Chairman of the Board of Governors; Executive Director and Treasurer.

2. The President/Chairman of the Board of Governors shall preside at all meetings of the Board and business meetings of the NAA; appoint standing and special committees upon approval of the Board of Governors; and initiate and develop activities of the Board which will accomplish the purposes of the Association, as set forth in Article II and the President shall serve as voting delegate to FITA Congress.

3. The Vice President/Vice-Chairman of the Board of Governors shall officiate when the President/Chairman of the Board of Governors is unable to serve.

4. The Executive Director shall keep all records of the NAA and of the Board of Governors; serve notices of meetings; conduct correspondence, and, to the extent permitted by the Constitution and the By-Laws of the NAA, take a vote of the membership by mail when so instructed by the Board of Governors; inform the membership of official actions of the Board of Governors when requested by them to do so; make a report at the Annual Meeting; and perform the other duties incident to the office of Executive Director.

5. The Treasurer shall oversee the receipt and the deposit of all monies of the NAA in the name of the Association in depositories approved by the Board of Governors; shall oversee the keeping of accurate accounts of all such transactions; present a report at the Annual Meeting, which shall have been audited as directed by the Board of Governors; prepare an annual budget for the approval of the Board of Governors, and shall, in general, perform the duties incident to the office.

ARTICLE VI – ELECTIONS: TERMS OF OFFICE

1. Four members of the Board of Governors shall be elected at the Annual Meeting of the NAA in every odd numbered year, one from each of the four (4) following geographical regions:

EAST REGION
Connecticut
Delaware
District of Columbia
Maine
Maryland
Massachusetts
New Hampshire
New Jersey
New York
Pennsylvania
Rhode Island
Vermont
Virginia
West Virginia

NORTH REGION
Illinois
Indiana
Iowa
Kansas
Michigan
Minnesota
Missouri
Nebraska
North Dakota
Ohio
South Dakota
Wisconsin

SOUTH REGION
Alabama
Arkansas
Florida
Georgia
Kentucky
Louisiana
Mississippi
North Carolina
Oklahoma
South Carolina
Tennessee
Texas

WEST REGION
Alaska   Wyoming
Arizona
California
Colorado
Hawaii
Idaho
Montana
Nevada
New Mexico
Oregon
Utah
Washington

The Board of Governors should include among its voting members reasonable representation for males and females and individuals who are actively engaged in amateur athletic competition in Archery, or who have represented the United States in international amateur athletic competition in Archery within the preceding ten (10) years. The Board membership and voting power held by the archer athletes must not be less than twenty percent (20%) of the Board of Governors.

Members of the Board of Governors (except the athlete member of the Board) elected at an Annual Meeting shall hold office for four (4) years and shall serve consecutively no more than two (2) terms of four (4) years each, but may, after a one-year absence from the Board, be re-appointed or re-elected. The athlete member of the Board of Governors shall be elected to serve a two (2) year term at the Annual Meeting in every odd numbered year and shall serve consecutively no more than two (2) terms of two (2) years, but may after a one-year absence from the Board be re-appointed or re-elected.

2. In every even numbered year, the Chairman of the Board of Governors within thirty days after election to office shall, upon approval of the Board of Governors, appoint a nominating committee of four NAA members one from each Region. It shall be the duty of this committee to prepare a slate of two candidates for each of the impending vacancies on the Board of Governors and this work shall be completed and the Executive Director notified by January 31 of the odd numbered year in which the election is to be held.

When requested by the Nominating Committee, the Executive Director shall solicit recommendations by mail from the affiliated NAA clubs in each of the respective Regions, or the solicitation may be by published notices in representative archery magazines or bulletins, and the Executive Director shall report the names and other information so received to the Chairman of the Nominating Committee for the committee's guidance in preparing the slate. Names of additional candidates other than those on the nominating committee's slate may be placed on the ballot by petition signed by at least five members from the Region for which the candidate is being proposed (except that, in the case of additional candidates for the athlete member of the Board, such candidates' names may be placed on the ballot by at least five members from any Region or Regions), provided the petition is in the hands of the Executive Director and the Nominating Committee at least forty-five days before the Annual Meeting. No other nominations shall be received and all candidates shall have agreed in writing of their willingness to serve and shall meet such other requirements as have been set forth by the Board of Governors.

The Chairman of the Nominating Committee shall present the nominees for election by a majority of the members from the nominees' region voting by proxy or by mail at the next Annual Meeting at which the election is held. The athlete member shall be elected by a majority vote of all members entitled to vote on this position at the Annual Meeting in person, by proxy or by mail. The members of the Nominating Committee may also serve as election tellers.

A nominee elected from a region must have been a legal resident of the region from which he/she serves on the Board of Governors for not less than ninety (90) days at the time of his/her nomination by the Nominating Committee and must remain a resident of that region throughout his/her term of office, or be replaced by appointment.

3. The Tournament Director shall be appointed by the President of the NAA and approved by the Board of Governors. The Tournament Director shall continue

in office until the conclusion of the tournament for which he was selected. If the location of the next tournament is not decided upon at the annual meeting, then the Tournament Director shall be selected as soon as possible by the Board of Governors. The Tournament Director shall appoint a tournament committee, with the approval of the Chairman of the Board, and shall serve as its Chairman. The Tournament Director shall have charge of the annual target tournament of the NAA subject to such rules and regulations as may be prescribed by the Board of Governors. The Tournament Director shall present the championship medals, awards, and prizes after the tournament; and perform such other duties as may be assigned by the Board of Governors.

4. The Executive Director and Treasurer, shall be selected by the Board of Governors and shall continue in office until resignation or removal by the Board of Governors. The Board of Governors may set remuneration to be paid to the Executive Director and Treasurer for their services.

5. The representative to the Athlete's Advisory Council of the United States Olympic Committee shall be nominated from and elected by only those archers who have represented the NAA in USOC recognized international competition within the ten-year period preceding the election. The election shall take place by mail at least ninety days prior to the end of each quadrennium. The representative so elected shall serve a four-year term. An alternate representative shall be elected to serve should the representative be unable to perform his/her duties. The individual of the opposite sex receiving the next highest number of votes shall be the alternate representative.

6. The fiscal year of the NAA shall be from January 1 to December 31, and the terms of office of the elected and appointed members, shall be from September 1 to August 31.

ARTICLE VII – VOTING BY MAIL

The By-Laws of the NAA may provide for voting by mail by members in the election of members to the Board of Governors at the direction of the Board of Governors, but, in the event mail voting is allowed in the election of Board members, in such cases at least a majority of all votes that members are entitled to cast in the election must be cast for the election to be effective. The By-Laws may also provide for voting by mail by members at the direction of the Board of Governors on an amendment to the Constitution of the NAA or on a proposed merger, consolidation, or dissolution, but, in the event mail voting is allowed in such matters, in such case the affirmative vote of at least two-thirds of all votes that members are entitled to cast on the question shall be required for the action to be effective. Mail voting shall not otherwise be allowed in any other matters except as otherwise permitted by applicable law and as may be provided in the By-Laws of the NAA. Whenever a matter is submitted to the membership for mail voting, the mail votes shall be sent to and counted by the Executive Director. In the event the mail voting is allowed in connection with action to be taken at a meeting of the membership, the mail votes must be received by the Executive Director at least one week prior to the meeting in order to be counted. If the mail voting occurs other than in conjunction with a meeting of the membership, the question submitted for voting by mail shall be decided by the majority of the votes cast by mail as determined by a count of the mail votes received by the Executive Director three weeks after the date ballots are mailed to the membership.

ARTICLE VIII – FEES AND DUES

1. Annual dues for membership shall be fixed by By-Law.

2. Fees for sponsored Tournaments, or for participation in such tournaments, shall be established by the Board of Governors. Insofar as possible, tournament expenses shall be kept within the tournament income.

ARTICLE IX – ANNUAL MEETING

1. The NAA shall hold its Annual Meeting in connection with the Annual Target Tournament, at a time and place designated by the Board of Governors.

2. Special meetings of the members for any purpose or purposes may be called by the President/Chairman of the Board of Governors or by action of the Board of Governors. Notice of any special meeting so called shall be given in the manner prescribed as applicable law.

3. At each meeting of the members, a member entitled to vote thereat may vote by proxy executed in writing by the member or by such member's duly authorized attorney-in-fact. Such proxy shall be filed with the Executive Director (or with the secretary of the meeting) before or at the time of the meeting. No proxy shall be valid after eleven months from the date of its execution unless otherwise provided in the proxy.

ARTICLE X – ELIGIBILITY

The NAA will be governed by the Eligibility Rules of the International Archery Federation (FITA) and the International Olympic Committee (IOC), as specified by FITA Constitution and Rules:

For Eligibility, see F.I.T.A. Constitution and Rules or IOC Code as it pertains to IOC sanctioned events.

ARTICLE XI – BOARD OF JUSTICE

1. The Executive Director shall solicit the membership for a list of possible candidates for the Board of Justice. Members present at the Annual Meeting shall elect a Board of Justice for a three-year term to investigate alleged breaches of the NAA Constitution and Rules by Regional Associations or members.

2. One member shall be elected each year to serve a three year term on a staggered basis.

3. No two members of the Board of Justice can belong to the same Region.

4. Members of the Board of Justice cannot belong to the NAA Board of Governors or be an officer of a Regional Association.

5. This three member Board shall elect its own Chairperson.

6. Cases can be submitted to the Board of Justice through the Executive Director by a) the President; b) the Board of Governors; c) Regional Associations; d) Judges or Juries of Appeal for cases arising in tournaments under their supervision.

7. Examination of a case shall include a fair hearing of all parties involved.

ARTICLE XII – SANCTIONS

1. The Board of Justice shall submit on each case examined a detailed report that shall also propose: a) dismissal of the case as irrelevant, or b) acquittal, or c) sanctions to be imposed.

2. Sanctions can be: a) public reproach, b) withdrawal of record recognition, c) withdrawal of awards and prizes, d) temporary suspension of up to one year, e) expulsion from the NAA.

3. An expelled Regional Association can apply again for membership after one year has elapsed.

4. Refund of costs sustained by the NAA for the investigation of the case may be claimed from a party found guilty.

5. Board of Justice proposals of sanction shall be ratified by the NAA Board of Governors except for cases brought against elected officers for alleged misuse of office or if expulsion of a Regional Association is proposed, in which cases the proposal shall be circulated to all members and submitted for ratification by the members present at the next Annual Meeting.

6. Ratification by the Board of Governors or membership is a final determination by the NAA.

ARTICLE XIII – APPEALS

1. If, after a final determination by the NAA as provided in Article XII, a party feels aggrieved by the decision of the Board of Governors, then said party may appeal the Board of Governors' decision. Such an appeal shall be made to the United States Olympic Committee (USOC) according to the Constitution of the USOC if the matter is within the jurisdiction of the USOC.

2. If the matter is not within the jurisdiction of the USOC and the aggrieved party wishes to appeal the decision of the NAA Board of Governors or membership, then said party shall submit the matter not later than six months following such decision to any regional office of the American Arbitration Association for binding arbitration.

3. Parties submitting to arbitration as provided for in this section agree to be bound by the arbitral award, unless the award is inconsistent with the Constitution and By-Laws of the NAA.

ARTICLE XIV – ALTERATIONS AND AMENDMENTS TO THE CONSTITUTION

This Constitution may be altered or amended in the manner prescribed by applicable law.

By-Laws
of the
National Archery
Association
of the
United States, Inc.

Adopted March 1990

ARTICLE I – ANNUAL MEETING

1. The Annual Meeting may be called to order by the President at any time after the opening of the annual target tournament if no competitive shooting is then in progress and reasonable notice has been given to all contestants. Except as herein provided, it shall not adjourn finally until after the banquet and award presentation.

2. The order of business at the Annual Meeting shall be:
   - Reading of the Minutes of the last meeting.
   - Announcement by the President of the place for holding the next annual target tournament and the selection of the Tournament Director.
   - Report of the Board of Governors.
   - Report of the Executive Director.
   - Report of the Treasurer.
   - Report of the Nominating Committee.
   - Election of members of the Board of Governors.
   - Old Business.
   - New Business.**
   - Announcement and giving of awards by the Tournament Director.
   - Adjournment.

** All new business to be brought before the meeting must be by resolution signed by at least five members and filed with the Executive Director at least forty-five days before the meeting.

The President shall have authority to limit or end debate on any matter.

3. If it is impossible to determine all awards in time to announce them at the Annual Meeting, the Executive Director shall announce the results by mail to the participants of the tournament.

ARTICLE II – COMMITTEES

1. The President shall, upon approval of the Board of Governors, appoint such Committee Chairpersons as may be deemed advisable, to hold office until such time the new Chairperson is appointed, whose duties shall be to make investigations, recommendations, proposals, and reports to the President on all matters falling within the field of their assignment.

2. The Tournament Committee shall be appointed by the Tournament Director with the approval of the President.

3. Any member of the NAA may serve on more than one committee with the exception of the President. He/She may serve as Chairperson of the Executive Committee.

4. The Chairman of any committee may, upon approval of the Board of Governors, appoint all of the members of the committee.

ARTICLE III – MEMBERSHIP DUES

1. The annual dues for Active Membership shall be: $23 for one year or $60 for three years; spouse and dependent children (under 18 and living at the same address) an additional $7.50 per year (maximum of four), per person. Youth (under 18) $10, full-time student $13, and Associate Member $10 per year. Club membership including Collegiate, JOAD and local $30 per year; State or Regional Association $50 per year; Life membership $300. All of these memberships (except Associate Membership) are to include a subscription to the official magazine of the NAA.

2. The annual dues for Sustaining or other national association membership shall be an amount as may be offered but not less than $100 per annum, and shall include a subscription to an archery magazine. Sustaining or other national association membership shall be non-voting.

3. Upon payment of annual dues, membership shall be granted for one or more years from the first day of the month in which dues were paid.

4. Any member who is more than one month in arrears in the payment of dues shall be dropped from the rolls and may be reinstated again only as a new member.

5. With the exception of Associate Member, a voting member is any member 18 years of age or over and a United States citizen (except in the case of the Athlete's Advisory Council representative election, Article VI, (5) of the Constitution) and a U.S. citizen in the following classes of membership: Active, Life and Honorary.

ARTICLE IV– ANNUAL TARGET TOURNAMENT: DATE, PLACE AND MANAGEMENT

1. An Annual Target Tournament, to determine the NAA Archery Championships of the United States and for other appropriate competition in archery, shall be held between July 15th and September 1st.

2. The Annual Target Tournament will be held at Miami University in Oxford, Ohio.

3. The Board of Governors may decide, from time to time, because of special considerations, to hold the Annual Target Tournament elsewhere than Miami University. The place for the next Tournament shall be announced at the annual business meeting, if possible.

4. The Tournament Committee, appointed by the Tournament Director, shall, subject to the guidance and approval of the Board of Governors, arrange and manage all details of the Annual Target Tournament and submit a proposed budget and complete final financial report within 90 days after completion of the tournament.

5. The Annual Target Tournament shall, in general, follow the rules and regulations as approved by the Board of Governors for the preceding tournament. The same rounds, events, and archery activities shall be held, and any change

in the regular program shall have received the prior approval of the Board of Governors.

6. Only members of the NAA who have paid their dues and who are not obligated for shooting fees or rotating trophies, to the NAA in any way, may participate in any competitive events in the NAA. All non U.S. citizens shall compete in the guest division.

ARTICLE V— TOURNAMENT RULES

1. All tournament competition shall be in accordance with FITA Shooting rules.

ARTICLE VI — ANNUAL TARGET TOURNAMENT: PRIZES AND TROPHIES

1. The Executive Director shall be the custodian of all prizes and trophies of the NAA and shall keep a record of them, including the names of the donors, the conditions of competition governing their award and the names and scores of those who win them.

2. Archers awarded the temporary custody of prizes and trophies shall give a written receipt for them and shall be responsible for their return, in good order, to the local awards chairman of the sponsoring organization for the coming tournament, at least four weeks before the tournament.

3. The Cyrus E. Dallin medal, usually called the Dallin Medal, shall be the championship medal of the NAA. It shall be awarded only to those in the Senior Division. In gold, it shall be awarded, as a gift of the NAA, to the man and woman champions and to no one else. In silver, it may be given to the intermediate boy and girl champions and to the winners of the second places in the championship standings for men and women. In bronze, it may be given to the winners of second places for intermediate boys and girls and of third places for men and women. No Dallin Medals shall be given or awarded other than the above.

4. Except as set forth in Section 3 of this Article, the Board of Governors may authorize or provide such trophies or awards as they deem proper for all divisions of the NAA, or they may change or retire at any time any awards which they feel should be discontinued.

ARTICLE VII — CHAMPIONSHIPS AND TITLES

1. All titles shall be recorded and dated as of the year in which they are won, but they shall be held until the next Annual Target Tournament, even though that may be more than one year later.

2. The Champion Archers shall be decided on the highest combined scores of all regular target rounds in the respective divisions. Only United States citizens are eligible for Champion Titles.

ARTICLE VIII — AFFILIATED CLUBS AND ASSOCIATIONS

1. Any regular organized Archery Club whose members live geographically near each other so that they meet together reasonably often for practice, may apply to the Executive Director of the NAA for affiliation and may be accepted by the approval of the Executive Director and President, on payment of annual dues.

2. Membership in an affiliated Club does not convey individual membership in the NAA.

3. Any State, Regional, or National Association may affiliate with the NAA upon approval of the Executive Director and the President, provided its membership is representative of the archers of the territory over which it has jurisdiction.

Each state and region may have one association affiliated with the NAA providing there is evidence that they promote NAA programs. This membership will be granted upon approval of the Board of Governors. Criteria for approval would include evidence of commitment to NAA programs, including sponsorship, within a calendar year, of a state or regional championship held under FITA Shooting rules in each: indoor, field and target. If these criteria cannot be met, then application from other organizations may be considered.

4. To qualify for NAA awards for tournament shooting, tournaments of affiliated Associations and Clubs must be conducted in accordance with FITA Shooting Rules and, if required, satisfactory evidence to this effect must be furnished to the Executive Director of the NAA.

ARTICLE IX—MEMBERSHIP VOTING BY MAIL

1. At the direction of the Board of Governors, mail voting by members may be allowed in the election of members to the Board of Governors in connection with any Annual Meeting at which members to the Board of Governors are to be elected. If the Board so directs that such voting by mail shall be allowed, the Executive Director shall prepare and mail to every member entitled to vote at the Annual Meeting a ballot for such mail voting. Such ballots shall be sent out by the Executive Director within such period of time prior to the Annual Meeting as the Board may prescribe (but in all events such ballots shall be sent out at least thirty days prior to the Annual Meeting).

2. At the direction of the Board of Governors, mail voting by members may also be allowed on proposed amendments to the Constitution of the NAA and on any proposed merger, consolidation or dissolution in such manner and under such time limitations as may be prescribed by the Board consistent with the provisions of the Constitution and the requirements of applicable law.

ARTICLE X—ALTERATIONS AND AMENDMENTS TO THE BY-LAWS

These By-Laws may be altered or amended by action of the Board of Governors, provided such alteration shall not be effective until approved by action taken by a two-thirds vote of the members present at an Annual Meeting or at a special meeting of the members called for the purpose. Additionally, proposed changes to these By-Laws may be submitted by any member for adoption by the membership at any Annual Meeting provided they are first presented to the Board of Governors and the Board feels that the proposed changes warrant a vote of the membership at the Annual Meeting; and provided further that such proposed changes must be mailed to every member by the Executive Director at the direction of the Board at least thirty days before the Annual Meeting at which they are to be voted upon and shall be adopted only by the affirmative votes of two-thirds of the members present at the Annual Meeting.

Appendix II

CONSTITUTION OF THE NATIONAL FIELD ARCHERY ASSOCIATION OF THE UNITED STATES, INC.

ARTICLE I. NAME
The name of this Association shall be "National Field Archery Association of the United States, Incorporated," indicated in the abbreviations as NFAA.

ARTICLE II. PURPOSE
A. To unite field archery associations of states into one organized unit that will work uniformly and effectively in providing for the development of the sport of archery in conformance with the will of a majority of the membership.
B. To provide the basic plan by which individual archers can organize into clubs that join together to form an Association within a state, in order to regulate and administer the sport within the described region.
C. To provide a basic plan by which such field archery associations may become affiliated with the National Field Archery Association.
D. To foster, expand, promote and perpetuate the practice of field archery and any other archery games as the Association may adopt and enforce uniform rules, regulations, procedures, conditions, and methods of playing such games.
E. To encourage the use of the bow in the hunting of all legal game birds and animals, and to protect, improve, and increase the sport of hunting with a bow and arrow.
F. To conduct a continuous educational program designed to acquaint the public and the archer with the use of the bow as a recreation and a weapon suitable for the hunting of legal game.

G. To conduct tournaments to determine national championships in all archery games adopted by the Association and to provide sanctions for tournaments.
H. To develop programs dedicated to the conservation and preservation of game and its natural habitat, and to cooperate with the federal and state agencies and sportsman and conservation organizations also dedicated to this purpose.
I. To cooperate with other archery associations to foster and perpetuate the use of the bow in accordance with its ancient and honorable traditions.
J. To foster and perpetuate a spirit of good fellowship and sportsmanship among all archers.
K. To evolve and conduct programs that will give recognition to archers for proficiency with the bow and arrow in all sanctioned competition and hunting accomplishments.
L. To regularly inform each member, in good standing, as to the major problems and issues affecting the sport of archery and hunting with bow and arrow, and/or to the action proposed or taken in order that the membership may make its will known to their duly elected representatives.

ARTICLE III. MEMBERSHIP

A. Individual Memberships:
   1. Honorary Membership, with exemption from regular fees and dues:, may be granted for exceptional merit and service, upon recommendation of the Board of Directors Council and submitted to the Board of Directors 60 days prior to the annual meeting. Such recommendations must be approved by a majority vote of the Board of Directors at the annual meeting.
   2. Life Membership with exemptions from regular fees and dues may be granted to head of household, wives and children under 18 upon payment per following schedule:
      a) Life Membership shall entitle an individual to all services provided by NFAA except tournament competition privileges and any other services that must be supplied by or through the resident state association as defined in paragraph 3 of this section.
      b) Life members who are 55 years of age and older will be exempted from paying registration fees at National and Sectional tournaments.
      c) All Past Presidents of the NFAA will be made Life Members with all its privileges.
   3. Adult Membership shall be granted to any individual 18 years of age or older upon application and payment of regular fees and dues through the affiliated state or foreign association of his residence. In the event no such affiliated association exists, membership may be granted by application and payment of dues:
      a) Directly to NFAA Headquarters, or
      b) Through an affiliated state association whose boundary is contiguous to the state of residence.
      c) In order to compete in any sectional tournament, an archer must be a member of a state affiliate within that section.
   4. Cub, Youth or Young Adult Membership shall be granted to individuals under 18 years of age in the same manner as for the adult membership except a date of birth must accompany the individuals membership.

5. Adult Patron Membership may be granted to an individual 18 years of age, or older, as the result of his/her contribution of $500 or more to the NFAA, upon a majority approval of the NFAA Board of Directors. Said patron or patroness shall be exempt for life from NFAA dues and fees only.

6. NFAA Bowhunter Membership, noncompetitive, shall be granted to any individual upon application and payment of applicable fees and dues directly to NFAA Headquarters. Membership benefits shall include one year's subscription to the official NFAA publication, Big & Small Game awards program, landowners guarantee, and eligibility for all hunting award contests sponsored by the NFAA. The NFAA Bowhunter Membership shall count on the weighted ballot.

7. Professional Membership: Archers eighteen years of age and over who are NFAA members in good standing shall be eligible for membership.

8. Action of a club or state association of the NFAA resulting in suspension of membership will result in temporary revocation of all rights and privileges.

   a) In any cause for action the member must be notified in writing of the alleged violation and afforded a period of not less than 30 days to correct the violation or present a defense.

   b) If, during this period of time the violation has been corrected, all membership privileges will be reinstated.

   c) If the violation has not been corrected and no defense is offered within the period specified the suspension will become permanent.

   d) Upon notice that a defense is being prepared the state association will schedule a hearing within 30 days from the date such notice of intent is received.

   e) The decision rendered may be appealed to the Board of Directors Council.

   f) Copies of the charges and all actions and notices thereafter must be properly documented and sent to the club, the state association, the NFAA Director and the Executive Secretary of the NFAA.

9. Adjacent NFAA affiliated states shall be authorized to arrive at unilateral or reciprocal non-resident membership arrangements with approval of the Sectional Councilman(men) when an individual or club's major archery activities are in other than his resident state. Agreements between state associations must be fully documented and filed with the respective Sectional Councilman(men) and NFAA Headquarters.

10. Problems arising from such agreements or proposed agreements shall be resolved by a Board of Arbitration comprised of three (3) or more Directors of the states within the section(s) not directly involved in the dispute. Members of the Arbitration Board shall be appointed by the Councilman(men) of the section(s) involved.

11. Any individual member of the NFAA may; be removed from NFAA office or barred or suspended from NFAA membership for cause by majority vote of the NFAA Board of Directors when in session or by majority of the Board of Directors Council when the Board of Directors are not in session. Any member so removed, barred or suspended shall have full opportunity to present his/her defense to the charges. When provisions of the NFAA Constitution and/or By-Laws provide for removal or suspen-

sion as concerns specific individuals or offices, this paragraph shall be superseded in areas of conflict.

B. Association membership:

1. Association Membership shall be granted to one association of any state, foreign country or countries that supports the principals of, and abides by the rules, regulations, procedures and policies adopted by the National Field Archery Association upon payment of proper fees and dues established by the NFAA. That association shall be the governing association for NFAA activities within its respective area and may promote individual programs to create more archers and members.

2. Conditions of Association Membership: In order to be granted membership in the NFAA, the state or foreign country must:

   a) Have a Constitution and By-Laws consistent with NFAA rules, regulations, procedures and policies, approved by the Board of Directors Council; and must file a copy of this document with the NFAA office which may be reviewed by the NFAA Board of Directors at the annual meeting.

   b) Must require all its elected and appointed officers be members of good standing in the NFAA. (Effective January 1, 1988)

   c) Pay Association fees and dues set by the NFAA within the deadline limits for such payment, as listed under Constitution Article XII.

   d) Require membership in the NFAA and the state association as essential for competition in all official NFAA rounds as listed under By-Laws Article VI.

   e) Recognize NFAA approved handicap cards, and do not issue any association membership card(s) that can be used as substitutes for the NFAA handicap card.

   f) NFAA membership will not be mandatory below the state level.

   g) NFAA membership requirements may be waived at State level only in:

      1) Special events conducted for the sole purpose of membership promotion.

      2) Special events conducted in conjunction with Bowhunter Jamborees and Bowhunter Education programs.

      3) The issuance of non-competitive state association memberships.

      4) In guest divisions not shooting for awards.

   h) The special events as listed in paragraphs 1, 2, and 4 above shall be limited to one such event per year.

   i) Send a representative to an annual meeting empowered to act for the state association on any and all issues before the NFAA Board of Directors while in session or in mail session.

   j) Enforce all rules, regulations and policies of the NFAA.

   k) Refer all instances of questionable interpretation to the NFAA Rules Interpretation Committee.

3. Compliance Affidavit:

   On or before November 30th of each year, each authorized state association shall submit a compliance affidavit. The affidavit form shall be approved by the Board of Directors Council and provided by NFAA Headquarters. The affidavit, accompanied by a listing of the state association officers for the following year, the current amended state constitution and bylaws, and the required affiliation fee, shall be forwarded to the Sectional Councilman for review. By affixing his signature and forwarding the file to NFAA Headquarters, the Councilman provides authority for the NFAA Executive Secretary to issue continuance of association membership for the next calendar year.

4. Approval/Denial of Association Membership:
   A state or foreign association shall be granted membership in the NFAA upon submission of affiliation papers and compliance affidavit at which time the Board of Directors Council, after review of the documents, shall by physical meeting or mail ballot, approve or deny said association.

5. Loss of Association Membership:
   a) Failure to pay membership fees and dues within the deadline established by the NFAA.
   b) Failure to abide by, or enforce, the rules, regulations and policies of the NFAA.
   c) Failure to properly supervise and/or administer handicap.
   d) Failure to collect NFAA membership fees in the issuance of handicap cards.
   e) Failure to promptly remit fees and reports to NFAA.
   f) Failure to submit the required compliance affidavit.

6. Expulsion or Suspension of Association Membership:
   a) Expulsion or suspension of association membership may occur as a result of any of the failures as listed in subsection 5 of this section.
   b) If expulsion or suspension is required, the following steps will be taken:
      1) Upon presentation of evidence of cause for action the Board of Directors Council will present specific charges against the state association to the association and the Sectional Councilman.
      2) The association will have 30 days to prepare a defense or to correct the deficiency.
      3) At the end of the 30 day period, the Board of Directors Council will reexamine the case. If the evidence was not valid or the deficiency is being corrected, the matter will be dropped. If the evidence was valid and no steps to correct the deficiency have been initiated, the charge along with the evidence and the defense (if submitted by the state association) will be immediately presented to the Board of Directors along with a motion for expulsion or suspension. The motion must be presented to the Board of Directors within 90 days of the time the evidence was first presented to any member of the Board of Directors Council.

7. Reinstatement of Association Membership:
   Action to reinstate membership lost through expulsion or suspension shall be sustained upon approval by a 2/3 vote of the Board of Directors.

C. Affiliate Membership:
   1. Shall be granted to all manufacturers of archery or related equipment for a yearly sum of $1,000.00.
   2. Shall be granted to all wholesalers of archery or related equipment for a yearly sum of $200.00.
   3. Shall be granted to all distributors or retailers of archery or related equipment for a yearly sum of $50.00.

BY-LAWS

ARTICLE I. GENERAL RULES
FOR FIELD ARCHERY GAMES

A. Terms:
1. Unit – A 14 target course, including all official shots.
2. Round – Two such units, or twice around one.
3. Double Round – Two complete rounds.
4. Out – First unit to be shot in a round.
5. In – Second unit to be shot in a round.
6. Stake – Shooting position.
7. Face – Target face.
8. Butt – Any object against which the face is placed.
9. Shot – This term in connection with the stake number, i.e., "4th shot", shall be used in referring to the different shots on any course.
10. Spot – Aiming center.
11. Timber – Warning call to other archers who may be in danger zone, announcing that you are ready to shoot.

B. Definitions:
1. Style – Refers to the type of shooting equipment used by the archer, i.e., Freestyle, Freestyle Limited, Barebow, Competitive Bowhunter, Bowhunter Freestyle or Bowhunter Freestyle Limited.
2. Division – Refers to the separation of competitive archers by category, i.e., Adult, Junior or Professional.
3. Age and Sex – Refers to the division of competitive archers according to age and sex, i.e., adult, young adult, youth or cub; and male or female.
4. Class and/or Flight – Refers to the division of competitive archers according to skill level.
5. Scratch Score – Refers to an archer's score before it has been adjusted by his/her handicap.
6. Net Score – Refers to an archer's score after his/her scratch score has been adjusted by his/her handicap.
7. Handicap – Refers to the number of artificial points an archer receives to adjust his/her scoring ability to the common level of perfect.
8. Handicap Differential – Refers to the difference between an archer's scratch score and perfect.

C. Targets:
1. They shall not be placed over any other larger targets nor shall there be any marks on the butt or foreground that could be used as points of aim.
2. All butts must be so placed that the full face is exposed to the shooter.
3. In all National and Sectional tournaments using official NFAA rounds, sixteen 20 cm target faces shall be used for the 20, 25, 30, 35 feet and the 11 yard shot. The butt shall be so constructed so as to encompass the targets in a 4 by 4 configuration. Where 35 cm target faces are specified four 35 cm target faces will be used. The butt shall be so constructed as to encompass the targets in a 2 by 2 configuration.
4. An archer shall not deface his/her target in any manner to include punching a hole, enhancing the X or any other portion of the target in an effort to gain sighting/aiming advantage. Any target so defaced shall be re-

moved by the tournament chairman. Repeated offense shall be grounds for removal of the offender from the tournament. Note: The tournament chairman may have the archer's name placed on the target, as in indoor tournaments, however, the name will not be on or in the scoring area of the target.

D.   Shooting Positions:
1.   All shooting position stakes shall be numbered, but the yardage given may be optional.
2.   It shall be permissible to use two or more shooting position stakes at any or all one-position targets, provided the stakes are equidistant from the target.
3.   All shooting positions shall be plainly visible. When ground level markers are used in place of traditional stakes, a sign shall be posted listing the various positions for each round.

ARTICLE II. NFAA SHOOTING STYLES AND EQUIPMENT RULES

A.   General:
1.   A conventional bow of any type may be used provided it subscribes to the accepted principal and meaning of the word "bow" as used in archery competition, i.e., an instrument consisting of a handle (grip) riser and two flexible limbs, each ending in a tip with string nock. The bow is braced for use by a single bowstring attached directly between the two string nocks only. In operation it is held in one hand by the handle (grip) riser while the fingers of the other hand draw, hold back and release the string.
2.   Compound bows may be used, provided:
   a)   Basic design includes a handle riser (grip) and flexible limbs.
   b)   Total arrow propelling energy is developed from a flexing of the materials employed in limb construction.
   c)   Weight reduction factor is of no consequence.
   d)   Bows which develop any portion of arrow propelling energy from sources "other than the limbs" shall not be allowed. This is not to be construed to mean that compound bows which employ other sources of arrow propelling energy, not specifically listed in this paragraph, will be allowed.
   e)   The cables of the compound bow shall be considered as part of the string and all applicable string rules except color requirements shall apply.
3.   This Paragraph Is Applicable Only To Competition On Unmarked Distance Tournaments: The use of a range finder is prohibited. At no time shall any device be allowed that would in any manner be an aid in establishing the distance of any shot. No archer may refer to any written memoranda that would aid in determining the distance to the target.
4.   Any device that would allow the mass weight, or the draw weight of the bow to be relieved from either or both arms, at full draw, shall be declared illegal.
5.   All overdraws shall be designed in such a fashion as to prevent the arrow from falling off the rest, endangering other competitors.

6. All Equipment rulings must be accompanied by an example of the item in question; to the assigned committee and for examination by the Board of Directors prior to voting.

B. Barebow:
1. Archers shooting Barebow style will use bow, arrows, strings and accessories free from any sights, marks or blemishes.
   a) String will be made of one or more strands. Strands will be of one consistent color of the archer's choice. The center serving on the string will be served with one layer of any material suitable to use, but material will be of one consistent size and one consistent color. Placement of a nock locator on the serving will be permitted.
   b) No written memoranda shall be allowed.
2. An adjustable arrow plate may be used to control the space between the arrow and the face of the sight window.
3. The use of stabilizers shall be permitted.
4. One consistent nocking point only is permitted.
   a) Nocking point shall be held by one or two nock locators, which shall be snap on type, shrink tubing, thread or dental floss, tied or served on the serving. Nocking point locators shall not extend more than one half inch (1/2″) above or below the arrow nock when at full draw.
5. No mechanical device will be permitted other than one non-adjustable draw check and level mounted on the bow, neither of which may extend above the arrow. "Note: Mechanical type arrow rests and cushion plungers are legal."
6. Releases other than gloves, tabs, or fingers shall be deemed illegal.
7. All arrows shall be identical in length, weight, diameter and fletching, with allowance for wear and tear.
8. The ends or edges of laminated pieces appearing on the inside of the upper limb shall be considered a sighting mechanism.
9. No device of any type, including arrow rest, that may be used for sighting, may be used or attached to the archer's equipment.
10. The pylon (string clearance bar) will be allowed in this style if it is not located in the sight window.
11. Any part of the arrow rest extending more than 1/4 inch above the arrow is deemed illegal in the Barebow style.
12. An arrow plate extending more than 1/4 inch above the arrow is deemed illegal in the Barebow style.

C. Freestyle:
1. Any type of sight and its written memorandum may be used.
2. Any release aid may be used provided it is hand operated and supports the draw weight of the bow.

D. Freestyle Limited:
1. Any type of sight and its written memorandum may be used.
2. Release aids shall be limited to gloves, tabs and fingers.

E. Competitive Bowhunter:
1. This style of shooting is for those with heavy tackle equipment used during hunting activities. Junior Bowhunters shall not be recognized.
2. No device of any type (including arrow rest), that may be used for sighting, may be used or attached to the archer's equipment.
3. There shall be no device, mechanical or otherwise, in the sight window except the arrow rest and/or cushion plungers.

4. Any part of the arrow rest extending more than 1/4 inch above the arrow is deemed illegal in the Competitive Bowhunter style.

5. An arrow plate extending more than 1/4 inch above the arrow is deemed illegal in the Competitive Bowhunter style.

6. No clickers, drawchecks, or levels will be allowed. No laminations, marks, or blemishes may appear in the sight window or upper limb.

7. String shall be one color only. End serving and center serving may be of different colors than the string, but center serving must be of one color only. One consistent nocking point only is permitted. Nocking point locators shall not extend more than one half inch (1/2") above or below the arrow nock when at full draw. Any marks, ties or string attachment to the string (except brush buttons and silencers properly located) shall invalidate its use in this division.

8. One anchor point only is permitted.

9. An Archer shall touch the arrow when nocked with the index finger against the nock. Finger position may not be changed during competition. In cases of physical deformity or handicap, special dispensation shall be made.

10. Releases other than gloves, tabs, or fingers shall be deemed illegal.

11. Each time an archer shoots a round, all arrows shall be identical in length, weight, diameter and fletching with allowances for wear and tear.

12. The Field Captain, or his counterpart, shall be the final authority regarding equipment and style eligibility, and may reclassify at his discretion.

13. Brush buttons, string silencer, no less than 12 inches above or below the nocking point, and bow quiver installed on the opposite side of the sight window, with no part of the quiver or attachments visible in the sight window, are legal. One straight stabilizer, coupling device included if used, which cannot exceed 12 inches at any time, as measured from the back of the bow may be used in the Competitive Bowhunter style. No forked stabilizer or any counter balance will be legal.

14. The following broadhead standard will be followed whenever broadheads are authorized for tournaments:
    a) Male — 7/8 inch cutting edge width (minimum).
    b) Female — 3/4 inch cutting edge width (minimum).

15. There shall be no restrictions on the bow draw weight. Arrows must be equipped with a minimum of 125 grain points for men and a minimum of 100 grain points for women.

16. Any device for lengthening or shortening the draw length of an archer shall be prohibited.

17. An archer will not be permitted to change the draw weight of the bow during a round.

18. The pylon (string clearance bar) will be allowed in this shooting style if it is not located in the sight window.

19. No written memoranda shall be allowed.

20. All official NFAA rounds shall be considered official rounds for the Bowhunter style of shooting, and further all classification shall be based upon the Field and Hunter rounds.

F. Freestyle Bowhunter:

1. A sight with a maximum of 5 fixed reference points that must not be moved during a round. Pin sights are to be of straight stock from point of

anchor to sighting point, with only one sighting reference possible from each pin. Hooded pins or scopes cannot be used. The maximum sight extension measurement shall be 5″, measured from the back of the bow at the center of attachment to the foremost part of the sight assembly, as measured on a horizontal plane. Lighted or illuminated sights (pins) are illegal.

2. Release aids will be permitted.
3. A kisser button or string peep sight will be permitted, but not both. Whichever is installed must be secured so as not to be movable between shots of different distances.
4. It will not be mandatory in this style of shooting to provide for other than one division for men and one division for women.
5. All rules of the Competitive Bowhunter shooting style, except those excluded by this section, shall also apply to the Freestyle Bowhunter shooting style.

G. Freestyle Limited Bowhunter:
1. A sight with a maximum of 5 fixed reference points that must not be moved during a round. Pin sights are to be of straight stock from point of anchor to sighting point, with only one sighting reference possible from each pin or reference point. Hooded pins or scopes cannot be used. The maximum sight extension measurement shall be 5″, measured from the back of the bow at the center of attachment to the foremost part of the sight assembly, as measured on a horizontal plane. Lighted or illuminated sights (pins) are illegal.
2. Release aids will not be permitted.
3. A kisser button or string peep will be permitted, but not both. Whichever is installed must be secured so as not to be movable between shots of different distances.
4. It will not be mandatory in this style of shooting to provide for other than one division for men and one division for women.
5. All rules of the Competitive Bowhunter shooting style, except those excluded by this section, shall also apply to the Freestyle Limited Bowhunter shooting style.

H. Traditional:
1. Adults shooting traditional style will use recurve or long bows.
2. No sights, stabilizers or counter balance.
3. Arrow shafts with 125 grain points for men and 100 grain for women. The points must be commercially manufactured.
4. Arrows shall be identical in length, weight, color except for normal wear.
5. String will have single color middle serving.
6. One single nocking point only is permitted.
7. One or two nock locaters, which may be snap-on type shrink tubing, thread or dental floss tied or served on the serving.
8. Arrow rest no more than 1/4 inch above arrow.
9. One anchor point only is permitted.
10. An archer shall touch the arrow when nocked with the index finger against the nock. Finger position may not be changed during competition.
11. If it is not covered in this statement, it is deemed illegal.

ARTICLE III. DIVISIONS OF COMPETITION

A. Divisions are recognized as follows:
   1. Adult:
      Is provided for male and female archers. Archers who wish to retain their
      amateur status are responsible to comply with I.O.C. Rule 26 (refer to
      Addendum Article II).
   2. Junior:
      Is provided for male and female archers in age groups of young adult,
      youth and cub. Junior archers are considered amateurs and it is their
      responsibility to comply with I.O.C. Rule 26 (refer to Addendum Article
      II).
      a) General:
         1) No archer may compete with or against archers of another junior
            division in any official National or Sectional championship
            tournament.
         2) Archers may elect to compete in any higher division, junior or
            adult, with written parental consent. An NFAA form in triplicate
            shall be provided for parental or guardian signature. One copy
            must be filed with NFAA Headquarters and one copy with the
            state association Secretary. Once this option has been exercised
            the archer may not revert back.
         3) The youth and young adult archers only are eligible for 20 pins
            and other awards in the same manner as adult division.
         4) Archer's date of birth must appear on his/her official membership
            card.
         5) Freestyle, Freestyle Limited, and Barebow shall be the only recog-
            nized shooting styles for Junior Division archers.
      b) Cub:
         1) This classification is established for archers under 12 years of age
            at National and Sectional tournaments but is optional at state
            level and below.
         2) Cub shooting positions shall be marked with black stakes.
         3) The cub's handicap must be established entirely on the cub course
            and is not applicable to or from any other course.
         4) Cub official target units shall consist of:

Yardage	Field	Hunter	Animal Group	International
20 Ft	20 cm	20 cm	4	—
10	35 cm	35 cm	4	—
10	35 cm	35 cm	4	35 cm
10	35 cm	35 cm	4	35 cm
10	35 cm	35 cm	3	35 cm
15	50 cm	35 cm	3	50 cm
18	50 cm	50 cm	3	50 cm
20	50 cm	50 cm	3	50 cm
20	50 cm	50 cm	2	50 cm
20	50 cm	50 cm	2	65 cm

20	65 cm	50 cm	2	65 cm
25	65 cm	65 cm	1	65 cm
30	65 cm	65 cm	1	—
30	65 cm	65 cm	1	—

(For the 15 target round, add one more yardage which would be 10 yds. 35 cm Field, 35 cm Hunter and Group 4 Animal.)

5) The cub archers shall receive distinctive 50 point progressive merit patches. They shall be awarded on official 28 target rounds for one consecutive score of one 50 point increment between 50 and 550. Applications for cub merit patches shall be made to the state association secretary. Patches are furnished free of charge by the NFAA.

6) Cub members of the NFAA are eligible for patches for a perfect 20 score on their distances shot — 10, 15, 18, 20, 25 and 30 Yards. Patches would have designated distances on face. Application for patch should be submitted within 30 days by the eligible archer for the award, accompanied by the proper fee, to the State Secretary or Chairman.

c) Youth:
1) The youth classification is established for archers age 12 through 14.
2) The handicap must be established entirely on the youth (50 yard maximum) course and is not applicable to or from any other course.
3) Any and all official NFAA units or rounds shall not contain shots over 50 yards. Group 1 animal faces shall be shot from the closest walkup animal stake only.
4) Youth official target units shall consist of and be the same as the adult rounds with the following exceptions:

Field Round	Youth Yardage	Face Centimeters
55 Yards	40	65
60 Yards	45	65
65 Yards	50	65
80, 70, 60, 50 Yds.	50	65
Hunter		
70, 65, 61, 58, Yds.	50	65
64, 59, 55, 52 Yds.	50	65
58, 53, 48, 45 Yds.	45	65
53, 48, 44, 41 Yds.	41	50
International Round		
55 Yds.	50	65
60 Yds.	50	65
65 Yds.	50	65

5) The youth archers shall receive distinctive 50 point progressive merit patches. They shall be awarded on official 28 target rounds for one consecutive score of one 50 point increment between 50 and 550. Applications for youth merit patches shall be made to the state association secretary. Patches are furnished free of charge by the NFAA.

6) The shooting positions for youth archers shall be marked blue.

d) Young Adult:

1) The young adult classification is provided for archers 15 through 17 years of age and for those younger who have waived into this division.

2) The young adult must establish his handicap entirely on the 80 yard (adult length) course and it is not applicable to or from any other course.

3. Professional:

a) Membership:

1) Archers eighteen years of age and over who are NFAA members in good standing shall be eligible for membership.

2) Members of other National Professional Archery Organizations must pay NFAA pro dues and compete in the NFAA Professional Division, at Sectional and National tournaments.

b) Code of Ethics:

1) The professional archer should conduct himself at all times in a manner that will bring respect and honor to himself, archery, and the NFAA.

2) A professional archer shall make every effort to comply with all tournament rules and regulations both published and intended.

3) A professional archer shall not allow his name or likeness to be used in such a manner as to misrepresent any product, nor shall he make claims that tend to misrepresent any product and mislead purchasers as to the actual value or quality of such products.

4) A professional archer shall make every effort to protect the amateur standing of amateur archers.

5) NFAA Pro Division will consider the disciplinary action taken for a violation of the Code of Ethics by another Professional organization.

c) Dress Code:

1) General.
The professional archer shall present himself in clean, neat attire, acceptable to public view.

2) Recommended.
Men: Slacks or mid thigh shorts, shirt with collar and appropriate footwear.
Women: Slacks, skirt or mid thigh shorts with blouse and appropriate footwear.

3) Not acceptable.
Swimming suits, cut offs and obscene or vulgar slogans or pictures on clothing.

d) Disciplinary Action:

1) Action may be taken by any current NFAA member through the tournament chairman. The following items are subject to immedi-

ate disqualification from the tournament and may be subject to further disciplinary action.

    a. Obvious witnessed intoxication while shooting on the range is in progress.

    b. Verified cheating.

    c. Blatant violation of code of ethics or dress code.

2) Protests must be in writing, signed and submitted to the tournament chairman within one hour of completion of shooting for that day's round.

3) A Pro Division member having paid annual dues shall not alter his competitive status for that calendar year.

4) All professional archers not renewing annual dues will be ineligible to compete for NFAA awards for one calendar year.

e) Tournament Sanction:

1) Tournament sponsors wishing sanction of their tournament by this division shall furnish the NFAA Executive Secretary a letter of guarantee verifying an obligation to make payment of the advertised purse. Sanction fee would be $50.00; $40.00 of which will be added to the Pro Division tournament guarantee fund and $10.00 to the NFAA treasury. This division may furnish a consultant for advisory assistance for said sanction fee if requested.

2) Must be negotiated with NFAA 6 months prior to shoot date.

3) Upon sanction, a notice will be sent to the Pro Division membership.

4) The decision to negotiate a "sanction tournament" will be at the discretion of the Executive Secretary, the Pro Division Chairman and the NFAA President.

f) Equipment Rules:

1) Participants in tournaments sanctioned by the Pro Division will abide by the equipment rules of the NFAA.

g) Tournament Competition:

1) Members of this division will not compete for awards other than money and/or merchandise in tournaments below the state level. At the state championship they will be required to compete in the Pro Division, if one is available. However, members are encouraged to support all types of tournaments by purchasing a score card for the regular registration fee.

    a. A NFAA Pro may compete for trophy awards at the state level with the adult shooters, providing there is no pro division recognized at that tournament.

    b. The NFAA Pro Division recognizes only the Freestyle and Freestyle Limited styles of shooting.

h) Pro Chairman:

1) The Chairman of the Pro Division will be nominated by the Pro Division members present at Indoor Nationals. The chairman shall be elected by a mail ballot of all NFAA Pro members. His/her term of office will be two years beginning July 1 of the election year. The mail ballots will be sent by NFAA Headquarters to the Pro members within 30 days of the nominations and sent back to NFAA headquarters by return mail within 60 days of the nominations. All Ballots not returned will be treated as abstentions.

    2) The Chairman of the Pro Division may be removed for cause, from office by a majority vote of the NFAA Council.

    3) The Pro Chairman will attend the Annual Board of Directors meeting where he/she serves as chairman of the Pro Agenda committee. His/Her travel will be paid by the Pro Division.

    4) Duties:

        a. To chair and conduct a Pro Division meeting at the Outdoor National tournament.

        b. To coordinate the Pro tournament schedule.

        c. To enforce the professional code of dress and ethics.

        d. Assist the tournament chairman at the National Championship tournaments on pro division matters.

        e. Compute awards for the National Championships and provide a list of pro winners to the tournament chairman and forward one to NFAA headquarters.

i) Sectional Representatives:

    1) The Sectional Pro Representative will be nominated and elected by the sectional pros at the indoor sectional championship. The term of office shall be two (2) years. The Sectional Pro Representative will serve as Pro Advisor to the Councilman.

        a. The Sectional Councilman will conduct the election at the indoor sectional championship. Nominations will be made, in writing, to the Sectional Councilman no later than one (1) week prior to the sectional indoor championship. The Councilman may also take further nominations from the pros present.

        b. The election of the Sectional Pro Representative will be the first order of business at the indoor sectional championship. Immediately following the election, the elected Sectional Pro Representative will chair and conduct that Pro meeting.

    2) Duties:

        a. To chair and conduct a Pro Meeting at the sectional indoor and outdoor tournament.

        b. To present, in writing, to the sectional councilman all proposals, pro agenda items, etc., for consideration by the sectional council at their annual sectional meeting. Such proposals/agenda items to be in the councilman's hands no later than three (3) weeks prior to the annual sectional meeting.

        c. To enforce the professional code of dress and ethics in the section.

        d. Assist the tournament chairman at the sectional championship on pro division matters as requested.

        e. Compute awards for the sectional pros.

            1) Give list of pro winners to Sectional Councilman to be forwarded to NFAA Headquarters.

            2) The sectional pro purse shall consist of $25.00 pro purse fee plus $5.00 forwarded from headquarters for each pro member of that section.

        f. Act as a mediator for pro division problems in his section working closely with the Sectional Councilman.

g. Should a problem arise, the sectional pro representative will contact the sectional councilman, who in turn will contact the NFAA Director(s) of the involved state(s) to resolve the problem.

j) Purse Allocation:

1) By shooting style

a. The total purse for each shooting style shall be determined by the registration of that style at a sanctioned event unless decreed otherwise by tournament sponsor. Example: Should Pro Freestyle registration equal 12% of the total Pro registration, then 12% of the total purse would be assigned to that division.

b. Should only 1 archer register in a given style, he/she will be awarded their percentage of the purse providing he/she finishes the tournament.

k) Purse Division:

1) General Guidelines

a. Note: These guidelines are made available as a reasonable and acceptable method to distribute winnings. They are not mandatory.

Shooters	Place	Distribution in %
1-3	1	100%
4-6	2	65-35%
7-9	3	50-30-20%
10-12	4	50-25-15-10%
13-15	5	45-25-15-10-5%
16-18	6	40-20-15-12-8-5%
19 or over	1 place for every 3 shooters	

2) All outside prize money offered by the Pro Division shall be distributed to the entire division.

l) National Ranking:

1) Each period will last for one year and commence on January 1.

2) Pro points can be earned only at NFAA Professional Division sanctioned events.

3) The National, Sectional, and State Championships are automatically sanctioned events. (Points may be earned only at a state field and/or state indoor championship tournament.)

4) In the event that a state championship tournament does not recognize a pro division, pro members will earn the point value applied to the position finished in the adult division.

5) No tournament will be awarded a greater number of points than assigned to the National Championships.

6) A pro member may earn no more than 25 pro points in "5 point" tournaments in a ranking period.

7) The following schedule of point values shall apply.

a. NATIONAL CHAMPIONSHIP—200 possible points. Points distributed to the first 40 places. Decrements of five (200-195-190-185 etc.).

b. SECTIONAL CHAMPIONSHIP—50 possible points. Points distributed to the first 10 places. Decrements of five (50-45-40-35 etc.).

c. STATE CHAMPIONSHIP—25 possible points. Points distributed to the first 5 places. Decrements of five (25-20-15-10-5).

d. OTHER NFAA PRO SANCTIONED TOURNAMENTS— points will be awarded based upon the cash awards available for members of the pro division "as determined by the NFAA Council."

Cash	Points	Places	Distribution
$100 to 999	5	1	5
1,000 to 1,999	10	2	10-5
2,000 to 2,999	15	3	15-10-5
3,000 to 3,999	20	4	20-15-10-5
4,000 to 4,999	25	5	25-20-15-10-5
5,000 to 5,999	30	6	30-25-20-15-10-5
6,000 to 6,999	35	7	35-30-25-20-15-10-5
7,000 to 7,999	40	8	40-35-30-25-20-15-10-5
8,000 to 8,999	45	9	45-40-35-30-25-20-15-10-5
9,000 to 9,999	50	10	50-45-40-35-30-25-20-15-10-5

$10,000 and above   Point values will be negotiated.

m) Guarantee Fund/Pro Bonus:

1) Funds are accrued in the NFAA Professional Division guarantee fund to stimulate professional archery competition.

2) Tournament sponsors wishing support from this fund shall contact the NFAA Councilman, Pro Chairman or NFAA Executive Secretary at least 6 months prior to the event.

3) The fund will guarantee for prize money at a sanctioned event in the form of a NFAA Pro Bonus. The amount of this Bonus will be based on past performance by established tournaments or will be set by the Council on all new tournaments. The Pro Bonus at these tournaments will be for NFAA Pros only.

4) A minimum purse of $6000 for the National Indoor Tournament and a minimum of $6000 for the National Outdoor Tournament, will be guaranteed by the NFAA Pro Division and funded from the Pro Guarantee fund only.

n) Tournament Default:

In the event of a default of a sanctioned event, the fund shall guarantee payment of NFAA Pro Bonus Money only.

o) Professional Dues:

The NFAA Professional fees being $50.00 per member for the calendar year. The following guidelines will be used in disbursing membership dues:

National Indoor Championship Prize Fund	$10.00
National Field Championship Prize Fund	10.00
Sectional Indoor Championship Prize Fund	5.00

Sectional Field Championship Prize Fund	5.00
Tournament Guarantee Fund	15.00
NFAA Administration Cost	2.50
Emergency, Patch and Expense Fund	2.50
Total	$50.00

ARTICLE IV. TOURNAMENTS

A. National Tournaments:

1. A National Outdoor championship tournament shall be provided annually, at a time and place to be determined by a 2/3 majority vote of the Board of Directors Council. All bids submitted for National tournaments will be sent to the host state Director at least 15 days before contracts are signed, and copies must be available at NFAA Headquarters for inspection.

2. The Board of Directors Council shall also establish entry fees, awards, and any or all other conditions.

3. At the National Outdoor championship tournament all flight awards will be presented at the tournament site immediately upon completion and tabulation of scores.

4. A National Indoor championship tournament may be provided annually by the same procedure.

5. All unused targets ordered by hosting clubs for National tournaments must be purchased by the host club at cost price, or returned postage paid to NFAA Headquarters. The Chairman's report for National tournaments shall include an accounting of targets ordered, targets used, and targets unused.

6. Disputes and or Protests arising at this tournament will be discussed and ruled upon by a committee consisting of the Tournament Director, NFAA President, One (1) Councilman, and two (2) Directors, available at the tournament. The Councilman and Directors will be chosen at random by the Tournament Director. (To become effective immediately 2/15/91.)

7. The Range Inspection and approval will be conducted by the NFAA Director of the Hosting State. (To become effective immediately 2/15/91.)

B. Sectional Tournaments:

1. A Sectional Outdoor championship tournament shall be provided annually in each section, with the time, place and rounds to be determined by members of the Board of Directors within the section. All bids submitted for Sectional tournaments will be sent to the host state Director at least 15 days before contracts are signed, and copies must be available at NFAA Headquarters for inspection.

2. The entry fees, awards, and any or all other conditions for these tournaments, except late registration, shall be established by NFAA.

    a) Late registration will be at the discretion of the NFAA directors of that section.

    b) Host club may keep up to ten (10) percent of registration fee as processing fee for archers who do not show.

3. A Sectional Indoor championship tournament may be provided annually by the same procedure.

4. Sectional tournaments shall consist of official NFAA rounds.

5. An archer may choose to shoot in several Indoor and Outdoor Sectional Tournaments of his choice, but only may compete for awards in that section of his residence.

C. State Association Approved Tournaments:
The NFAA affiliated states may provide any number of outdoor and indoor tournaments, up to and including the state championship level.

D. Definitions:
1. NFAA Official Round: The NFAA recognizes as official those rounds described in By-Laws Article VI, which are: Field Round, Expert Field Round, Hunter Round, Animal Round, "300" Field Round, "300" Hunter Round, International Outdoor Round, NFAA Indoor Round, NFAA Indoor Championship Round, Freeman Round, Flint Bowmen Indoor Round, 810 and 900 Target rounds and the 300 Animal round.
2. NFAA Sanctioned Round: The NFAA shall grant official sanction to any of the above NFAA Official Rounds when said round is conducted by the NFAA or through its recognized state affiliate; when said round is held on an NFAA approved facility using official NFAA targets; and when said round conforms to By-Laws Articles I, IV, and VI.
3. NFAA Handicap Round: The NFAA recognizes as official for recording on the NFAA handicap card any Field or Hunter round or 14/14 combination of same; and any "300" Field or "300" Hunter round, which fulfills the requirements of NFAA sanction.

E. Shooting Equipment Styles:
The divisions of competition and styles of shooting provided at National and Sectional tournaments shall be those designated by the Board of Directors at an annual meeting. Said established styles of shooting and divisions of competition are not mandatory below the Sectional level. National and Sectional tournaments shall provide for the recognized styles of shooting in the Adult, Junior and Professional divisions.

F. National and Sectional Divisions of Competition:
1. Divisions of competition and styles of shooting to be recognized at National and Sectional tournaments:
a) Professional, Adult, Young Adult, Youth and Cub.
(*) Refer to Article III, Section A, para 3 item a) 2).
2. Styles of shooting to be recognized shall be:
PRO: Freestyle,
Freestyle Limited
ADULT: Freestyle,
Freestyle Limited,
Barebow,
Bowhunter,
Bowhunter Freestyle,
Bowhunter Freestyle Limited,
Traditional

YOUNG ADULT	YOUTH	CUB
(Ages 15–17)	(ages 12–14)	(under 12)
	Freestyle	
	Freestyle Limited	
	Barebow	

3. In addition, a complimentary Senior Division for archers ages 55 and over shall be provided at National and Sectional tournaments and is optional at State level and below. Any member competing in the Senior Division will compete also in the flight in which he/she is placed with other archers in their style of shooting and will be eligible for both awards.
   a) Styles of shooting for men and women shall be as listed in paragraph 2 above.
   b) Awards shall be medals only.
G. Flighting for National and Sectional tournaments:
   The method of determining flights at National and Sectional tournaments shall be printed in the contracts and on the registration forms.
   1. The NFAA flight system will be used at National and Sectional tournaments.
      a) Flights will be provided in each division and shooting style as follows: 1 to 15 shooters, one flight; 16 to 30 shooters, two flights; 31 to 45 shooters, three flights; 46 to 60 shooters, four flights; 61 or more shooters, five flights; and so forth.
      b) An optional alternate flight system for the sectional level tournaments with 200 shooters or less. (Located in policy section).
   2. For Outdoor Nationals and Sectionals, archers may be arranged in flights by their handicaps at the start of the tournament. Archers without established handicaps may be placed into flights at the end of the first handicap round (or at the discretion of the tournament chairman).
   3. For Indoor Nationals and Sectionals, archers shall be arranged in flights according to score shot in the first round.
   4. Equal division of the number of archers in each flight will be maintained, except that the last flight will record a lesser number (for two flights) or an unequal number (for three or more flights) as may be required. When two or more tie scores appear at the flight break, the archers tied will be placed at the top of the lower flight, without disturbing the remaining flights as originally established.
   5. The flight system does not apply to the Professional Division.
H. Awards:
   1. For purpose of awards individual groups listed in 'E' above shall decide individually what awards shall be given. The unit system may be used by any of the above groups. The unit rule is defined as follows: One award for one through three archers in a class. Two awards for four through six archers in a class. Three awards for seven or more archers in a class.
   2. Archers awarded the temporary custody of prizes and trophies shall be responsible for their return in good order to the Executive Secretary at least two weeks before the next annual tournament.
I. Use of Handicaps:
   1. All handicaps as provided under "Handicapping" shall be recognized.
   2. The NFAA shall issue official NFAA handicap cards.
J. Tournament Officials:
   1. Tournament Chairman
      a) At all NFAA sanctioned tournaments a Tournament Chairman shall be appointed and it shall be his duty to:
         1) See that the requirements of NFAA sanction are fulfilled, through the NFAA Director, NFAA Councilman, or designated NFAA administrator.

2) See that a target captain and two scorers are appointed for each group.
3) Designate the order in which groups are to shoot or assign the stakes from which each group is to start, depending on which system is used.
4) Have the option to set a time limit, either by target or by round, when such tournament must be completed.
5) Be the final authority in settling disputes which arise over rules or conduct of the tournament, unless notice of intent to protest is given and followed by submission of a written protest within one hour after leaving the range on the day of the protested incident. A $25.00 National and $15.00 Sectional protest fee must accompany the written protest at National and Sectional tournaments, which will be refunded if the protest is upheld.
6) Inspect or designate an official of the tournament to inspect any Barebow, Bowhunter, Freestyle Bowhunter and Freestyle Bowhunter Limited equipment at any time during an NFAA sanctioned event that they feel necessary.

2. Target Captain.
   a) At all NFAA sanctioned tournaments a Target Captain shall be appointed for each group and it shall be his duty to:
      1) Report any archer in his group violating the rules set forth in the NFAA By-Laws.
      2) Be the final judge of all disputed arrows in his group.
      3) Verify equipment failure for any archer in his group.

K. Shooting Rules:
   1. Archers shall shoot in groups of not less than 3, or more than 6; 4 shall be the preferred number. No group of less than three shall turn in an official score.
   2. For shooting position at the shooting stake the foursome, by mutual agreement, shall decide which two shall shoot from which side of the shooting stake.
      a) At the conclusion of each 14-target unit the archers shall change their order of shooting. Those who shot first shall shoot last and those who shot last shall shoot first.
      b) Starting with the first target an archer shall shoot from the same side of the shooting stake for fourteen targets. At the conclusion of each 14 target unit those archers who have been shooting from the right side shall shoot the remainder of the course from the left side; those on the left shall shoot from the right side.
      c) The archer must straddle an imaginary shooting line, which is marked by the distance stake and parallel to the target face, while shooting the required arrows. No archer may advance to the target until all arrows have been shot by the group, except for yardages that are 19 yards or less and when there are more than four archers in a group on 35 cm targets or smaller. Archers may elect to shoot at a clean target after all previous shooters in the group have shot and had their arrows scored.
      d) Any arrow(s) shot from other than a predesignated position in the designated shooting order shall be considered "lost" and may not be scored.

3. When shooting at butts with multiple target faces, the first 2 shooters will shoot the bottom target faces. When target faces are placed side by side (i.e. 50 cm) the archer on the left will shoot the left target face; the archer on the right will shoot the right target face. On fan positions the same applies, except each archer will shoot two arrows at each target. Any arrow striking the wrong target shall be considered a miss and may not be re-shot.
   a) 20 cm targets will be shot vertically. The shooter may elect to shoot top to bottom or bottom to top.
4. One group shall not hold up the following groups while looking for lost arrows. Enough arrows shall be carried so that each archer may continue shooting, and return later to find missing arrows. If one or more open targets in front and two or more groups back up, the delaying group shall allow backed up groups to shoot through.
5. No archer may practice on any shot of a course to be used for tournament shooting later the same day. Special practice targets should be supplied. The first target of each round may be used as practice at the discretion of the tournament chairman. The maximum number of arrows allowable will be determined by the round being shot.
6. An archer leaving the range for any reason other than an equipment failure may be privileged to return to his group and complete unfinished round or subsequent rounds. He will not be privileged to make up any missed in the interim.
7. In the case of an equipment failure verified by the target captain, the archer may have the needed time, with a maximum of 45 minutes, as granted by a tournament official for equipment repair or replacement and a maximum of four (4) practice arrows. Then, in the presence of the tournament official, be allowed to shoot the targets missed. This occurrence of repair or replacement may not happen more than once in any tournament day.
8. No archer may shoot (compete) in any one tournament more than one time unless advertised as a multiple registration tournament.
9. In case of inclement weather, the tournament shall continue unless a prearranged signal is given by the tournament chairman. Any archer leaving the range shall be automatically disqualified.
10. No alcoholic beverages may be carried or consumed on any range or practice area during shooting hours at National or Sectional tournaments.
11. Tripods for spotting scopes and tripods for binoculars shall not be permitted during outdoor competition at National or Sectional Tournaments.

L. Scoring:
   1. Arrows must remain in the target face until all arrows are scored. In all NFAA Rounds, an arrow shaft cutting two rings must cut completely through the line to be counted in the area of next higher value. They may then be withdrawn.
   2. The status of doubtful arrows shall be determined before drawing any arrows from the target, and such arrows may not be touched until after being recorded.
   3. The target captain shall be the final judge of all disputed arrows.

4. Offground skids or glances into the target shall not be counted. Arrows striking objects over the shooting lane may be re-shot.

5. Arrows passing through the face, but still in the butt, may be pushed back and scored as hits in the circles through which they went. This does not mean that they may be withdrawn and then stuck back through the target.

6. Arrows believed to have passed through the target may be re-shot with marked arrows, which will not be scored if the doubtful arrows are found in the butt.

7. Unsuspected pass throughs: in any instance where arrows are found to have obviously passed through in such a manner they cannot be properly scored and their location and the condition of the butt convince the target captain that the arrows did indeed pass through a scoring area, the archer may return and reshoot from the obvious distances or furthest distances involved.

8. Witnessed bounce outs, believed to have hit the target in the scoring area, will be re-shot.

9. In any tournament where the method of shooting of a tie is not decided in advance, ties shall be decided by shooting the first three (3) targets. In any tournament where field faces are involved, field faces shall be used. If a tie still exists after three targets, continue from target to target until the tie is broken.

10. An archer who shoots arrows at the target in excess of the prescribed number shall lose the arrow or arrows of higher value in all NFAA rounds. A penalty of one point will be assessed for each arrow shot over the prescribed numbers.

11. A dropped arrow is one which falls while being transferred from the quiver to be nocked on the string, or in preparation for a shot; or which falls from the string during a controlled letdown. (A dropped arrow may be re-shot.)

12. Scorecards must be signed as correct by scorekeeper and archer. Once submitted a scorecard cannot be retrieved for purposes of changing totals. An Archer who has signed and submitted a scorecard as correct which has incorrect total(s) shall immediately be disqualified.

ARTICLE V. THE NFAA HANDICAP

A. General:

1. Essence of NFAA Handicap System. Handicapping is the great equalizer among sportsmen of differing abilities. The National Field Archery Association presents this archery handicap system in the conviction that, when faithfully operated, it results in equitable handicaps no matter where archers live and play. The handicap system does not exclude the use of both handicap and/or scratch shooting in the same tournament. The national system of handicapping must meet two main requirements, which are:

   a) Simple enough for operation by the small, modestly equipped club as well as the largest state association.

   b) Thorough enough to produce fair, uniform handicapping the country over.

2. Handicap Name:

The handicap produced by this system is termed a "NFAA Handicap". Such a handicap should be identified on a card or elsewhere as a "NFAA Handicap" or as "Computed under NFAA Handicap System".

3. Purposes:

   a) Provide fair handicaps for all archers, regardless of ability.
   b) Reflect the archer's inherent ability as well as his recent scoring trends.
   c) Automatically adjust his handicap down or up as his game changes.
   d) Disregard freak low scores that bear little relation to the archer's normal ability.
   e) Make it difficult for the archer to obtain an unfairly large handicap increase at any revision period.
   f) Make a handicap continuous from one shooting season to the next without need of adjustment.
   g) Encourage the archer to keep his game near its peak.
   h) Establish handicaps useful for all archers, from championship eligibility to informal games.
   i) Make handicap work as easy as possible for the handicapper.

B. Establishing a Handicap:

   1. An archer's handicap shall be computed on the official NFAA field and/or hunter round, and shall be computed by the following table:

   Best score of 2, scores 80% of avg. differential.

   2 best scores of 5, scores 80% of avg. differential.

   3 best scores of last 7, scores 80% of avg. differential.

   The first and second methods shall be computed only for those archers who have not recorded the minimum of seven scores needed for a full handicap.

   2. An archer's handicap shall be derived only from those scores shot within the last twelve (12) month period.

   3. All handicaps must be established during a tournament held on official NFAA targets, approved NFAA 2-Star Ranges or higher, and where official NFAA field or hunter rounds are shot.

   4. The differential is the difference between the actual average and perfect. (Example: Last 7 scores are 430, 415, 440, 440, 450, 460 and 410. The best 3 scores are 440, 450 and 460. Average = 450. 560 minus 450 = 110. 80% of 110 equals 88, which is the handicap.)

C. Handicap Procedure:

   1. A new archer, or one who holds an expired handicap card, shall be issued a handicap card in the most expedient manner upon the payment of established fees, and must shoot two official scores to establish handicap.

   2. No archer shall be permitted to compete in an NFAA registered tournament in which any official NFAA rounds are shot unless he holds a valid handicap card, or has made proper application, except as specified in Constitution Article III, Section B, paragraph 2g).

   3. No archer shall be issued a handicap card unless the archer is a member in good standing of the NFAA and a state association chartered and recognized by the NFAA.

   4. Each person will be responsible for keeping a current handicap in the proper place on the handicap card.

     5. If a person shoots more than one style, he must be handicapped in each style.

D. Handicap Cards:
1. All official handicap cards shall be printed by the NFAA and shall be made available, free of charge, to affiliated state associations. The card shall have provisions to indicate NFAA state and club membership, all styles of shooting, and shall provide space for recording scores for all recognized styles of shooting.
2. Handicap cards shall be issued by the association which has granted membership as provided under Constitution Article III.
3. Handicap shall be concurrent with membership, i.e., expiration of membership in the NFAA shall void handicap.
4. No handicap card shall be issued by the NFAA in conjunction with direct NFAA membership applications, provided an affiliated state association exists in the area where the archer resides with the exception to those states that are taking advantage of the NFAA membership billing program.
5. The handicap and membership card shall carry the full name, address, date of birth (if under the age of 18) and affiliated state of the archer.
6. Handicap and membership cards of military personnel in transit or on temporary duty shall be recognized.
7. A handicap chart for the NFAA field and hunter rounds will accompany all handicap cards.

E. Scores to be Recorded on Handicap Cards:
1. All scores recorded on the handicap cards shall be the actual scores for the field and/or hunter rounds.
2. All scores shot in tournaments using field and/or hunter rounds shall be recorded.
3. All recordings on the handicap card shall be on the basis of each 28 targets, i.e., a tournament of 28 targets field and 28 targets hunter . . . each score is to be recorded. If a 14 field and 14 hunter . . . the combined total shall be recorded. If a 28 field and 14 hunter . . . the round that is completed shall be recorded. No fractional round shall be recorded.

F. Lost or Misplaced Handicap Cards:
1. An archer who has been handicapped but cannot submit a handicap card or statement from his club secretary showing his/her true handicap is required to compete without handicap for that tournament.
2. An archer may not submit club secretary evidence of handicap to the state handicap officer or NFAA board member for more than 14 consecutive days. The archer must apply for a replacement handicap and membership card. The application must be accompanied by the fees established by the NFAA and the state association. The replacement card shall run concurrent with his/her previous card as recorded in the records of the state association and/or records of the NFAA.

G. Administration of Handicaps:
1. Handicap shall be administered through the state association chartered and recognized by the NFAA. If no chartered or recognized association exists, the NFAA shall administer the system.
2. The state association shall maintain a satisfactory control to insure that handicap is properly administered.

3. The state associations shall agree no archer is denied a handicap card upon proper application and payment of fees, regardless of race, creed or color.
4. The state association shall agree that no member in good standing with the NFAA is denied a handicap card.
5. State associations may not impose additional requirements for handicap.
6. The state association shall furnish the NFAA with a duplicate of current handicap card holders in a form satisfactory to NFAA. This information will be furnished at the same time as membership handicap cards are forwarded to the archer.
7. Non-compliance with these requirements shall be grounds for immediate suspension of recognition by the NFAA. The state association must submit within 30 days a brief, showing cause why the offending association's charter and recognition should not be revoked by the NFAA Board of Directors Council.
8. The use of non-official targets shall not be construed as a permissive to negate the provisions of the handicap article.

ARTICLE VI. OFFICIAL NFAA ROUNDS

A. Field Round:
   1. Standard Unit:
      A standard unit shall consist of the following 14 shots:
      15, 20, 25, 30 yards at a 35 cm face
      40, 45, 50 yards at a 50 cm face
      55, 60, 65 yards at a 65 cm face
      (for these distances — 4 arrows at each)
      And the following four position shots, each arrow to be shot from a different position or at a different target: 35 yards at a 50 cm target, all from the same distance, but from different positions of different targets:
      45, 40, 35, 30 yards at a 50 cm target.
      80, 70, 60, 50 yards at a 65 cm target.
      35, 30, 25, 20 feet at a 20 cm target.
   2. Targets:
      Four face sizes shall be used. The outer ring diameter shall be 65 cm, 50 cm, 35 cm, & 20 cm. The spot shall be two black rings with white X in center ring, two white rings and two outside black rings, (X-ring used for tie breakers only). The rings have the following diameters:

Target Diameter	65 cm	50 cm	35 cm	20 cm
Outer Black Ring:	65 cm	50 cm	35 cm	20 cm
Inner Black Ring:	52 cm	40 cm	28 cm	16 cm
Outer White Ring:	39 cm	30 cm	21 cm	12 cm
Inner White Ring:	25 cm	20 cm	14 cm	8 cm
Outer Black Spot:	13 cm	10 cm	7 cm	4 cm
X-Ring:	6.5 cm	5 cm	3.5 cm	2 cm

   a) Multiple target faces may be used at all distances.

3. Shooting Positions: The prescribed distances in this section are to be adhered to without variation. Each NFAA chartered club with an approved field course shall have the option of marking the distances on the shooting stakes of the following NFAA Rounds: Field, Hunter and Animal. In laying out the course any order may be used as the official shooting order on any four position shot.

4. Shooting Rules: Each archer shall shoot 4 arrows at each of the 14-target layouts in a unit. In 10 cases this shall mean shooting the 4 arrows from a single stake at a single face. In the other 4 it may mean either shooting 1 arrow from each of four stakes at a single face, or it may mean shooting all four arrows from a single stake but at four separate faces or one arrow from each of four stakes at either two (2) faces or four (4) faces.

5. Scoring:
   a) The scoring is 5 points for the spot, 4 for 2 white circles and 3 for outside black rings.
   b) An arrow shaft cutting two rings shall be scored as being in the ring of the greater value. The outer line of the Field target is outside the scoring field. For that reason the arrow shaft must cut the line so that no color of the line can be seen between arrow shaft and scoring field before a hit may be counted. The same is true for the inner line between the 2 circles.
   c) The X-Ring is used for tie breakers only.

B. NFAA Expert Field Round:
   1. Standard Unit:
   A standard unit shall consist of the following 14 shots:
   15, 20, 25, 30 yards at a 35 cm face
   (4 arrows at each distance)
   40, 45, 50 yards at a 50 cm face
   (4 arrows at each distance)
   55, 60, 65 yards at a 65 cm face
   (4 arrows at each distance)
   And the following four-position shots, each arrow to be shot from a different position or at a different target:
   35 yards at a 50 cm target, all from the same distance, but from different positions of different targets:
   45, 40, 35, 30 yards at a 50 cm target.
   80, 70, 60, 50 yards at a 65 cm target.
   35, 30, 25, 20 feet at a 20 cm target.

   2. Targets:
   a) Four face sizes shall be used:
      1) 65 cm face with a 6.5 cm X-ring
      2) 50 cm face with a 5 cm X-ring
      3) 35 cm face with a 3.5 cm X-ring
      4) 20 cm face with a 2 cm X-ring
   The spot shall be two black rings with white X-ring in center ring, two white rings and two outside black rings (X-ring is used for tie-breakers only).

   3. Shooting Positions:
   The prescribed distances in subsection 1 of this by-law are to be adhered to without variation. Each NFAA chartered club with an approved field

course shall have the option of marking the distances on the shooting stakes.

4. Shooting Rules:

Each archer shall shoot 4 arrows at each of the 14-target layouts in a unit. In 10 cases this shall mean shooting the four arrows from a single stake at a single face. In the other four it may mean either shooting one arrow from each of the four stakes at a single face, or it may mean shooting all four arrows from a single stake but at four separate faces, or one arrow from each of four stakes at either two (2) faces or four (4) faces.

5. Scoring:

a) The scoring is 5 points for the spot, 4 for 2nd circle, 3 points for the 3rd circle, 2 points for the 4th circle and 1 point for the 5th circle. The X-ring is used for tie breakers only.

b) An arrow shaft cutting two rings shall be scored as being in the ring of the greater value. The outer line of the field archery target is outside the scoring field. For that reason the arrow shaft must cut the line so that no color of the line can be seen between arrow shaft and scoring field before a hit may be counted. The same is true for the inner line between the two circles.

C. Hunter Round:

1. Standard Unit:

The 14 targets form a unit. Twice around the unit makes a round, or two such units laid out make a round.

2. Targets:

The Hunter Round target has two white rings with black X in center ring, and two outside black rings. (X-ring used for tie breakers only). 20 cm targets will be shot two ways, from bottom to top or top to bottom. The rings have the following diameters:

Target Diameter	65 cm	50 cm	35 cm	20 cm
Outer Black Ring:	65 cm	50 cm	35 cm	20 cm
Inner Black Ring:	39 cm	30 cm	21 cm	12 cm
Outer White Spot:	13 cm	10 cm	7 cm	4 cm
X-Ring:	6.5 cm	5 cm	3.5 cm	2 cm

The following shows the target face size and aiming spot, with the yardage distances that are to be used.

Target Size: 65 cm target, with 13 cm white spot.

70-65-61-58
64-59-55-52
58-53-48-45

Target Size: 50 cm target, with 10 cm white spot.

53-48-44-41
48
44
40
36-36-36-36

Target Size: 35 cm target, with 7 cm white spot.

32-32-32-32

28-28-28-28

23-20

19-17

15-14

Target Size: 20 cm target, with 4 cm white spot.

11

    a)   Multiple target faces may be used at all distances.

  3. Shooting Positions:

One feature of this round is that it takes a lot of stakes. Where one stake is used, a stake at least 18 inches above ground is recommended. On the two-stake shots use stakes that extend 12 inches above ground and stakes that are not over 6 inches above ground for the four-stake shots. Such an arrangement will help eliminate a lot of confusion.

  4. Shooting Rules:

In shooting the Hunter Round the archer will observe the following shooting positions:

    a)   1 stake — shoot 4 arrows from the same stake.

    b)   2 stakes — shoot 2 arrows from each stake.

    c)   4 stakes — shoot 1 arrow from each stake.

  5. Scoring:

Scoring is 5 points for the spot, 4 for center ring, and 3 for the outer ring. The X-ring is used for tie breakers only. An arrow shaft cutting two rings must cut completely through the line to be counted in the area of next higher value.

D. Animal Round:

  1. Standard Unit:

The 14 targets form a unit. Twice around the unit makes a round, or two such units laid out differently make a round. The one basic 14 target unit may be varied to make any number of courses that would all be different. It is simple and easy to lay out and change. Once the maximum and minimum distances are known, then the target distance can be laid out anywhere within these distances and be according to NFAA rules. This round, its animal targets and its sliding scale system of scoring is more of a measure of the hunting archer's shooting skill than the standard Field Round.

  2. Targets:

    a)   The targets for this round are animal targets with the scoring area divided into two parts. The high scoring area is oblong while the low scoring area is the area between the high scoring area and the "hide and hair" line or "feathers", as the case may be. The area between the "hide and hair" line (including the line) to the outside of the carcass is considered a non-scoring area.

    b)   The high scoring area of Group No. 1 is 9 inches wide by 14¼ inches long with rounded ends. Targets in this group are the black bear, grizzly bear, deer, moose, elk, and caribou.

    c)   The high scoring area of Group No. 2 is 7 inches wide by 10½ inches long with rounded ends. Targets in this group are the small black bear, antelope, small deer, wolf, mountain lion.

    d) The high scoring area of Group No. 3 is 4½ inches wide by 7 inches long with rounded ends. Targets in this group are the coyote, raccoon, javelina, turkey, fox, goose, wildcat, and pheasant.

    e) The high scoring area of Group No. 4 is 2½ inches wide by 3⅝ inches long with rounded ends. Targets in this group are the turtle, duck, grouse, crow, skunk, woodchuck, jack rabbit and rockchuck.

    f) In the above target groups the animals mentioned are for a general description and not to be construed as confined to the particular species. Any animal or bird which is legal game and consistent in size with a particular group may be used.

3. Shooting Positions:

    a) The following chart gives distances and target groups:

Positions	Group	Targets	Max Yds	Min Yds	Spread Yds
3 walk-up shots	1	3	60	40	20
3 walk-up shots	2	3	45	30	15
4 one position shots	3	4	35	20	15
4 one position shots	4	4	20	10	10

    b) The shooting distance shall be marked its exact distance, but in the spread defined, in paragraph a) above for the National and Sectional level tournament and may be marked at tournaments below that level.

    c) Each target in Group 1 faces is a five yard walk-up. There are three targets in the group. Select your distances between 60 and 40 yards for the first stake, move up five yards for the next stake and five more yards for the third stake.

    d) Each target in Group 2 faces is a three yard walk-up. There are three targets in Group 2. Select your distance between 45 and 30 yards for the first stake, move up three yards for the next stake and three more yards for last stake.

    e) Each target in Group 3 faces is one distance. There are four targets in this group. Shoot all arrows from each stake as selected between 35 and 20 yards.

    f) Each target in Group 4 is one distance. There are four targets in Group 4. All arrows shall be shot from each of the four stakes from distances selected between 20 yards and 10 yards. If the faces posted are different, the archer may shoot any face presented, even including a target that has been shot by another member of the group. In this instance the archer must declare his choice.

4. Shooting Rules:

A maximum of three marked arrows may be shot, in successive order, and the highest scoring arrow will count. In the case of walk-up targets the first arrow must be shot from the farthest stake, the second arrow from the middle stake, and the third arrow from the nearest stake, in order to be scored. No Archer shall advance to the target and then return to the stake to shoot again in the event of a missed arrow.

5. Scoring:
   a) 20 or 18 for the first arrow
      16 or 14 for the second arrow
      12 or 10 for the third arrow
   b) The arrow shaft must cut through the line to score. If an arrow shaft touches the outside edge of an animal target it does not score. If it hits the target and cuts into, but not through, the "hair and hide" line, it does not score. It must cut through this line to score a shot of lower value. To score, an arrow shaft must cut through this line.

E. 15 Target "300" Field Round:
   1. Standard Unit:
      A Standard Unit shall consist of the following 15 shots:
      15, 20, 25, 30 yards at a 35 cm face
      (4 arrows at each distance)
      40, 45, 50 yards at a 50 cm face
      (4 arrows at each distance)
      55, 60, 65 yards at a 65 cm face
      (4 arrows at each distance)
      And the following four position shots, each arrow to be shot from a different position or at a different target: 35 yards at a 50 cm target, all from the same distance; but from different positions or different targets:
      45, 40, 35, 30 yards at a 50 cm target.
      65, 60, 55, 50 yards at a 65 cm target.
      30, 25, 20, 15 yards at a 35 cm target.
      35, 30, 25, 20 feet at a 20 cm target.
   2. Targets:
      a) Four face sizes shall be used:
         1) A 65 cm face with 6.5 cm X-ring.
         2) A 50 cm face with 5 cm X-ring.
         3) A 35 cm face with 3.5 cm X-ring.
         4) A 20 cm face with a 2 cm X-ring.
         The spot shall be two black rings with white X in center ring, two white rings, and two outside black rings. (X-ring used for tie breakers only). The rings have the following diameters:

Target Diameter	65 cm	50 cm	35 cm	20 cm
Outer Black Ring:	65 cm	50 cm	35 cm	20 cm
Inner Black Ring:	52 cm	40 cm	28 cm	16 cm
Outer White Ring:	39 cm	30 cm	21 cm	12 cm
Inner White Ring:	25 cm	20 cm	14 cm	8 cm
Outer Black Spot:	13 cm	10 cm	7 cm	4 cm
X-Ring:	6.5 cm	5 cm	3.5 cm	2 cm

Animal targets bearing these official round faces may be used, in which case the faces need not be painted, only outlined, but aiming center or spot must be plainly visible. Spot must be painted some color sharply contrasting with the target color. This same spot and ring target is official without animal silhouette.

3. Shooting positions:

The prescribed distance in subsection 1 of this By-law is to be adhered to without variation. Each NFAA Chartered club with an approved field course shall have the option of marking the distances on the shooting stakes of the following NFAA rounds: Field, Hunter, Animal, and International. In laying out the course any order may be used as the official shooting order on any four position shot.

4. Shooting Rules:

Each archer shall shoot 4 arrows at each of the 15 target layouts in a unit. In 10 cases this shall mean shooting the four arrows from a single stake at a single face. In the other five it may mean either shooting one arrow from each of four stakes at a single face, or it may mean shooting all four arrows from a single stake but at four separate faces.

5. Scoring:

   a) The scoring is 5 points for the spot, 4 for 2 white circles and 3 for the outside black rings. The X-ring is used for tie-breakers only.

   b) An arrow shaft cutting two rings shall be scored as being in the ring of the greater value. The outer line of the field archery target is outside the scoring field. For that reason the arrow shafts must cut the line so that no color of the line can be seen between arrow shaft and scoring field before a hit may be counted. The same is true for the inner line between the two circles.

F. 15 Target "300" Hunter Round:

1. Standard Unit:

The 15 targets form a unit. Twice around the unit makes a round or two such units laid out make a round.

2. Targets:

The Hunter Round target has two white rings with black X in center ring, and two outside black rings. (X-ring is used for tie-breakers only). 20 cm targets will be shot two ways, from bottom to top or top to bottom. The rings have the following diameters:

Target Diameter	65 cm	50 cm	35 cm	20 cm
Outer Black Ring:	65 cm	50 cm	35 cm	20 cm
Inner Black Ring:	39 cm	30 cm	21 cm	12 cm
Outer White Spot:	13 cm	10 cm	7 cm	4 cm
X-Ring:	6.5 cm	5 cm	3.5 cm	2 cm

The following shows the target face sizes and aiming spot, with the yardage distances that are to be used.

Target Size: 65 cm with 13 cm white spot

64-59-55-52

58-53-48-45

58

Target Size: 50 cm target, 10 cm white spot

53-48-44-41

48

44

40

36-36-36-36

Target Size: 35 cm target, 7 cm white spot

32-32-32-32
32-28-24-20
28-28-28-28
23-20
19-17
15-14

Target Size: 20 cm target, 4 cm white spot
11

3. Shooting Positions:

One feature of this round is that it takes a lot of stakes. Where one stake is used, a stake at least 18 inches above ground is recommended. On the two-stake shots use stakes that extend 12 inches above ground, and stakes that are not over 6 inches above ground for the four-stake shots. Such an arrangement will help eliminate a lot of confusion.

4. Shooting Rules:

In shooting the Hunter Round the archer will observe the following shooting positions:

a) 1 stake — shoot 4 arrows from the same stake.

b) 2 stakes — shoot 2 arrows from each stake.

c) 4 stakes — shoot 1 arrow from each stake.

5. Scoring:

Scoring is 5 points for the spot, 4 for center ring, and 3 for the outer ring. The X-ring is used for tie breakers only. An arrow shaft cutting two rings must cut completely through the line to be counted in the area of next higher value.

G. 15 Target "300" Animal Round:

No classification can be made on this round.

1. Standard Unit:

The 15 targets form a unit. Twice around the unit makes a round, or two such units laid out differently make a round. The one basic 15 target unit may be varied to make any number of courses that would all be different. It is simple and easy to lay out and change. Once the maximum and minimum distances are known, then the target distance can be laid out anywhere within these distances and be according to NFAA rules. This round, its animal targets and its sliding scale system of scoring is more of a measure of the hunting archer's shooting skill than the standard Field Round.

2. Targets:

a) The targets for this round are animal targets with the scoring area divided into two parts. The high scoring area is oblong while the low scoring area is the area between the high scoring area and the "hide and hair" line or "feathers", as the case may be. The area between the "hide and hair" line (including the line) to the outside of the carcass is considered a non-scoring area.

b) The high scoring area of Group No. 1 is 9 inches wide by 14¼ inches long with rounded ends. Targets in this group are the black bear, grizzly bear, deer, moose, elk and caribou.

c) The high scoring area of Group No. 2 is 7 inches wide by 10½ inches long with rounded ends. Targets in this group are the small black bear, antelope, small deer, wolf and mountain lion.

d) The high scoring area of Group No. 3 is 4½ inches wide by 7 inches long with rounded ends. Targets in this group are the coyote, raccoon, javelina, turkey, fox, goose, wildcat and pheasant.
e) The high scoring area of Group No. 4 is 2½ inches wide by 3⅝ inches long with rounded ends. Targets in this group are the turtle, duck, grouse, crow, skunk, woodchuck, jack rabbit, and rockchuck.
f) In the above target groups the animals mentioned are for a general description and not to be construed as confined to the particular species. Any animal or bird which is legal game and consistent in size with a particular group may be used.
3. Shooting Positions:
   a) The following chart gives distances and target groups:

Position	Group	Targets	Max Yds	Min Yds	Spread Yds
3 walk-up shots	1	3	60	40	20
3 walk-up shots	2	3	45	30	15
4 one position shots	3	4	35	20	15
5 one position shots	4	5	20	10	10

   b) The shooting distance shall be marked its exact distance but in the spread defined in paragraph a) above for National and Sectional level tournaments and may be marked at tournaments below that level.
   c) Each target in Group No. 1 faces is a five yard walk-up. There are three targets in the group. Select your distances between 60 and 40 yards for the first stake, move up five yards for the next stake and five more for the third stake.
   d) Each target in Group No. 2 faces is a three yard walk-up. There are three targets in Group No. 2. Select your distance between 45 and 30 yards for the first stake, move up three yards for the next stake and three more yards for last stake.
   e) Each target in Group No. 3 faces is one distance. There are four targets in this group. Shoot all arrows from each stake as selected between 35 and 20 yards.
   f) Each target in Group No. 4 is one distance. There are five targets in Group No. 4. All arrows shall be shot from each of the five stakes from distances selected between 20 and 10 yards.
4. Shooting Rules:
   A maximum of three marked arrows may be shot, in successive order, and the highest scoring arrow will count. In the case of walk-up targets the first arrow must be shot from the farthest stake, the second arrow from the middle stake, and the third arrow from the nearest stake, in order to be scored.
5. Scoring:
   a) 20 or 16 for the first arrow; 14 or 10 for the second arrow; 8 or 4 for the third arrow.
   b) The arrow shaft must cut through the line to score. If an arrow shaft touches the outside edge of an animal target it does not score. If it hits the target and cuts into, but not through, the "hair and hide" line,

it does not score. It must cut through this line to score a shot of lower value. To score, an arrow shaft must cut through this line.

H. NFAA International Round:
  1. Standard Unit:
     a) The NFAA International Round is a 20-target (ten targets per unit) variable distance round designed for use in areas where the availability of land is restricted or limited. The round is ideally suited for public parks and recreational facilities. The NFAA International Round course requires a minimum of space and can be readily constructed on any level or gently rolling plot of ground. A 20-target course will adequately handle up to 80 participants at one time. The International Round may be laid out on a roving type range, or on an established "Field Round" course. However, whenever possible it is recommended that it be laid out in a progressive order, 20 yards through 65 yards.
     b) Permanent type roving ranges are subject to course approval by the NFAA Director. Non-permanent park type ranges shall not be subject to approval by the NFAA Director.
  2. Targets:
     a) Target faces shall conform to the specifications of the NFAA Hunter Round.
     b) Each target position shall have one target butt.
        1) There shall be one or more target faces used on each butt.
        2) In the use of the International Round, the required number of faces used for camps and schools shall be left to the discretion of the coaches or teachers.
     c) Distance:
        1) The distances and corresponding target sizes for the International Round are as follows:

Distances Yard	Target Size Centimeters
20	35
25	35
30	35
35	50
40	50
45	50
50	50
55	65
60	65
65	65

     d) All distances must be measured to the exact yardage.
  3. Shooting Position:
     a) Each target shall have two shooting positions.
     b) The two shooting positions shall be parallel to the target face.
     c) The two shooting positions shall be the same distance from the target and shall be separated by not less than 4 feet.
     d) The distances shall be written on markers which are visible to the archer.

    e) Each distance marker shall show the number of the target and the distance to be shot.

    f) If more than one unit is needed, the shooting positions for the targets shall be numbered from 1 to 20.

4. Shooting rules:

    a) Three arrows are shot at each distance.

    b) All other rules for shooting the official Field Round shall apply to the International Round.

    c) The maximum distance for youth in the International Round shall be 50 yards.

5. Scoring:

    a) The scoring on the targets shall be:

        1) 5 points for each arrow in the center white spot.

        2) 4 points for each arrow in the inner black ring.

        3) 3 points for each arrow in the outer black ring.

        4) No points for arrows striking the background.

    b) An arrow shaft cutting two rings shall be scored as being in the ring of higher value.

I. NFAA Indoor Round:

1. Standard Unit:

Shall consist of 60 arrows, shot as 3 games, at a distance of 20 yards. Each game shall consist of 4 ends of 5 arrows per end or as an alternate, 5 ends of 4 arrows per end.

2. Targets:

    a) The target face shall be 40 cm in diameter and shall be of a dull blue color. The spot shall be two white rings with blue X in center ring. All inscribed scoring rings shall be white.

    b) The bullseye shall be 8 cm in diameter with a 4 cm X-ring.

    c) The Tournament Director may allow the archer to use the Indoor Championship target.

3. Shooting Positions:

Shooting positions will provide sufficient area to enable two archers to shoot simultaneously at one target butt.

4. Shooting Rules:

    a) An archer shall stand so that he has one foot on either side of the shooting line.

    b) The time limit shall be 5 minutes when shooting 5 arrows per end and 4 minutes when shooting 4 arrows per end.

    c) The method of breaking ties will be at the discretion of the tournament director.

    d) In the event of equipment failure, the archer will have 15 minutes repair time without holding up the tournament. One practice end will be allowed. The archer shall be allowed to shoot any arrows he or she did not shoot during the 15 minutes repair time, after the final end.

    e) Two ends of practice will be allowed at all Indoor National and Sectional Tournaments and be optional at State Level and below. (To be effective immediately 2/15/91).

5. Scoring:

    a) The scoring is 5, 4, 3, 2. 1 from the spot out.

    b) X-Rings shall be counted and used as tie breakers.

    c) All arrows will be scored and recorded before touching or drawing any arrows from the target.

d) An arrow cutting two rings shall be scored in the ring of greater value. Scoring is determined by the position of the shaft. The shaft must cut through the line and touch the area of higher value in order to be scored as the higher value.

e) Witnessed bounce outs or arrows passing completely through the target will be reshot.

f) Hits on the wrong target will be scored as misses.

g) When an arrow is dropped while the archer is in the act of shooting, he may shoot another arrow in place of the dropped arrow if the dropped arrow is within 10 feet of the shooting line.

h) If an archer shoots more than the prescribed number of arrows in an end, only the prescribed arrows of lower value will be scored. A penalty of one point will be assessed for each arrow shot over the prescribed number.

i) If an archer shoots less than the prescribed number of arrows in one end he may shoot his remaining arrows if the omission is discovered before the end is officially completed; otherwise they shall be scored as misses.

j) When using the NFAA Indoor Championship Target:

    1) Scoring shall be 5 points for the combined 4 cm X-ring and 8 cm white ring and 4 points for the combined 12 cm and 16 cm blue rings.

    2) One arrow shall be shot at each of the four or five targets during each round. If more than 1 arrow is shot into a target, the arrow of higher scoring value is lost.

J.   NFAA Indoor Championship Round:

    1. Standard Unit:

      a) The standard unit shall consist of 5 ends of 4 arrows or 4 ends of 5 arrows per end shot at 20 yards.

      b) The number of units shot on this round is recommended as 3, but is left to the discretion of the host.

    2. Targets:

      a) The target face shall contain either four or five 16 cm targets on a screened blue surface.

      b) The inner scoring ring (X-ring) shall be 4 cm in diameter and white in color.

      c) The second scoring ring shall be 8 cm in diameter and white in color.

      d) The third scoring ring shall be 12 cm in diameter and shall be dull blue in color. The fourth scoring ring shall be 16 cm in diameter and dull blue in color.

    3. Scoring:

      a) The scoring is 5 points for the X-ring, 4 points for the white 8 cm ring, 3 points for the blue 12 cm ring and 2 points for the blue 16 cm ring.

    4. Shooting:

      a) One arrow shall be shot at each of the 16 cm targets of the championship target face.

      b) If more than one (1) arrow is shot into a target, the arrow of the lowest value will be scored. A penalty of one (1) point will be assessed for each arrow shot over the number."

c) The method of breaking ties will be at the discretion of the tournament director.

K. NFAA Freeman Round:
1. The standard unit shall consist of 60 arrows, shot as 3 games at distances of 10, 15, and 20 yards. Each game will include 4 ends of 5 arrows per end.
   a) The first game shall be 3 ends at 10 yards and 1 end at 15 yards.
   b) The second game shall be 3 ends at 15 yards and 1 end at 20 yards.
   c) The third game shall be 4 ends at 20 yards.
2. Targets, shooting rules, and scoring shall be same as listed for the NFAA Indoor Round.

L. Freeman Bowhunter Indoor Round:
1. Distance and amount of arrows: same as for the NFAA Freeman Round.
2. Targets: same as for the NFAA Freeman Round, or may be Group 4 Animal targets at 10 and 15 yards and Group 3 Animal targets at 20 yards.
3. Scoring: Circle targets 5-4-3-2-1 (refer to Article VI, Section H, paragraph 5a). Animal targets 5 for kill and 4 for non-vital.
4. Leagues: Made up of teams based on handicapping of two scores. Each team to be made as equal in shooting as possible. Each shooter to declare which type of target he will shoot at. Type of target can be changed only at the halfway point of league competition. Preformed teams are not allowed.
5. Handicap: Based on two scores using the NFAA 300 handicap system.
6. Awards: Regular Freeman Indoor patches.
7. Fees: Current NFAA league sanction fees.

M. Flint Bowman Indoor Round
1. Standard Unit:

Target Number	Distance	No. of Arrows	Target Size
1	25 yards	4	35 cm
2	20 feet	4	20 cm
3	30 yards	4	35 cm
4	15 yards	4	20 cm
5	20 yards	4	35 cm
6	10 yards	4	20 cm
7	30, 25, 20, 15, yds	1 each	35 cm

   a) 56 arrows shall be considered one round.
   b) Top row target centers shall be spaced 48 inches from the floor. Bottom row target centers shall be spaced 30 inches from the floor.
2. Targets:
The targets are standard 20 cm and 35 cm field target faces placed in two rows on each boss. The center of the upper row shall be 48 inches from the floor. The center of the lower row shall be 30 inches from the floor and directly below the upper targets.

3. Shooting Positions:
   a) This round is to be shot on a 30 yard range with shooting lines marked parallel to the target line at distances of 20 feet, 10, 15, 20, 25, & 30 yards.
   b) Starting at the 30 yard line, and proceeding toward the target line, the shooting lines are to be numbered 3, 1, 5, 4, 6 and 2.
   c) There shall be a separate lane for each boss and the archer shall go from one shooting line to his next shooting line in the lane for the boss on which his two targets are placed.
   d) The targets on the boss in the second lane shall be reversed from those in the first lane. Those in the third lane shall be exactly as those in the second lane.
4. Shooting Rules:
   If an archer starts out on a high target, as in lane one, he shoots his second end on the low target in the same lane. The archer continues to shoot at the targets in this lane until he has shot as seven targets. For his second seven target score, he should go to another lane in which the targets are in reverse from the one he started out on.
5. Scoring:
   Scoring shall be the same as the Field Round.
6. 20-Yard Flint Round:
   a) Because of the inability of many clubs to obtain the necessary space for a 30-yard indoor round, the NFAA has provided rules for a 20-yard round as follows:

Target Number	Distance	No. of Arrows	Target Size
1	50 ft.	4	35 cm
2	20 ft.	4	20 cm
3	60 ft.	4	35 cm
4	45 ft.	4	20 cm
5	40 ft.	4	35 cm
6	30 ft.	4	20 cm
7	60, 50, 40, 30, ft.	1 each	35 cm

   b) Rules:
      Rules for the 20 yard round are the same as for the Flint Indoor Round.
N. NFAA 810 Target Round
   1. Standard Unit
      A. Adults
         1) 30 arrows at 60 yards
         2) 30 arrows at 50 yards
         3) 30 arrows at 40 yards
      B. Young Adult/Youth
         1) 30 arrows at 50 yards
         2) 30 arrows at 40 yards
         3) 30 arrows at 30 yards

C. Cubs
1) 30 arrows at 40 yards
2) 30 arrows at 30 yards
3) 30 arrows at 20 yards

2. Targets
   a) The target face may be of any suitable material that will not damage arrows and that will retain stability of size, shape, and color under adverse weather conditions.
   b) The scoring area of the target face shall be forty-eight (48) inches in diameter. The target face is divided into 5 concentric color zones arranged from the center outwards as follows: Gold (Yellow), Red, Blue, Black and White.
   c) A scoring line, not more than one-tenth inch in width shall be provided between scoring rings. An arrow must break the inside edge of the scoring line of the face to score the higher color.
   d) Target face colors should be reasonably "dull" and "non-glaring" and conform as closely as possible to the following color code, as specified in the Munsell Color Charts. Colors are listed from the center out.

Color	Hue	Value	Chroma	Notation
Gold	6.5Y	8.1	10.7	5.OY-8.0-12.0
Red	8.5R	4.9	12.6	5.OR-4.0-14.0
Blue	5.OB	6.5	8.0	5.OB-7.0-6.0
Black	1.5RP	2.9	0.3	None-2.0-0.0
White	0.5GY	8.94	0.6	None-9.0-0.0

3. The Target Range
   a) The target field shall be laid out so that shooting is from South to North. A maximum deviation of 45% is allowed for local tournaments if required by terrain available.
   b) The targets shall be equally spaced 5, plus or minus 1, yards (4 to 6 yards) apart, measured from the center of the gold to the center of the gold of the adjacent target.
   c) The center of the gold on the target face shall be mounted 51 inches from the ground. The target face shall be inclined away from the shooting line at an angle from 12 to 18 degrees from the vertical.
   d) Range distances shall be accurately measured from a point on the ground perpendicular to the center of the gold on the target face to the shooting point.
   e) Target lines and shooting lines, or range lines shall be plainly and accurately marked on the ground, and shall be not more than 6 inches in width. Target lines or shooting lines may be arranged to require the shooters to move forward from the longest range to lesser distances while the targets remain stationary, or to require the targets to be brought forward from longer to lesser distances while the shooter uses a stationary line.

f) Individual target lanes shall be suitably and plainly marked either by center lines, or by lines designating the side boundaries of each lane. Pegs, chalk lines, trenches, or mowed strips are suitable markings. Local tournaments may deviate from this rule.

g) There shall be a minimum of 20 yards clear space behind the targets, which may be reduced by a suitable bunker or backstop. Spectators, participants or pedestrians shall not be allowed behind the targets while shooting is in progress, or even beyond 20 yards if there is the slightest possibility of being struck by the wildest arrow.

h) There shall be a clear area of at least 20 yards on each side of the field as a safety lane.

i) Bow racks, tackle boxes, or other objects which protrude above the ground shall not be allowed within six feet of the shooting line.

j) At least every third target should have a small wind flag, of a size and color easily visible from the 60 yard line, mounted at least two feet above the top of the target. Local tournaments may deviate from this rule.

k) Staggered shooting lines, wherein one group of archers shoot from a position forward of another group, are considered unsafe. In emergency, they may be used provided an unused lateral safety lane of at least 20 yards is maintained as a buffer.

4. The Target Butt and Target Backstop
   a) The target backstop shall be of any suitable material that will not damage arrows or allow them to pass through or bounce out frequently.
   b) The target backstop shall not be less than 50 inches in diameter.
   c) Target backstops shall be securely anchored to the ground to prevent accidental toppling.
   d) Target identification shall be by means of numerals, at least 8 inches high, on soft cardboard or other suitable material, so as to be easily visible at 60 yards and should be mounted near the base of the target.

5. Shooting Positions
   a) The shooting area is an area starting at the shooting line and extending 6 feet to the rear, and which runs parallel to and adjacent to the shooting lines.
   b) An archer shall stand so that he has one foot on each side of the shooting line. He shall also stand 18 inches from the center of the target lane or 18 inches from the boundaries.
   c) Any archer may retire from the shooting line to avoid proximity to tackle or a shooting practice that he considers unsafe, and may resume shooting when safe conditions prevail.
   d) Archers may not shoot at varying distances from different shooting lines, nor engage in unauthorized practice, unless separated laterally by the width of at least four target lanes.

6. Shooting Rules
   a) An END consists of six arrows shot in two groups of three.
   b) A COMPLETED END is that condition when all six arrows have been shot. A Field Official shall signal the finish of each end. Unless this signal is immediately challenged by those archers who have not

released 6 arrows, the end shall be considered complete, and the archer shall have no recourse to shooting additional arrows.

c) A PERFECT END is six arrows shot consecutively in the gold during one end.

d) Any kind of a bow may be used, providing it is shot by holding it in one hand and the string in the other, without mechanical assistance of support which in the opinion of the tournament officials would give undue advantage over other competitors.

e) Any kind of arrows may be used provided that it does not, in the opinion of the tournament officials, damage the targets unreasonably.

f) Any type of a sight or aiming device attached to the bow may be used. Any type of point-of-aim may be used which does not protrude more than six inches above the ground and does not interfere with shooting or scoring.

g) Any type of artificial spotting aid may be used, provided it be restricted for use behind the shooting area. An archer may not interrupt his shooting turn to use a spotting aid.

h) Foot markers may be left on the shooting line during the round provided they are embedded in the turf and do not extend more than one-half (½) inch above the ground.

i) Ground quivers may be placed on the shooting line while the archer is in the process of shooting but must be removed to the tackle area while others are shooting and during the scoring interval.

j) Initial target assignments may be made according to any system designated by the tournament officials. There shall not be less than three nor more than five archers assigned to each target in use, and four is customary.

k) Archers shall be re-assigned targets after each round on the basis of their total score for rounds completed.

l) There shall be at least three uninterrupted practice ends, at the longest distance, followed without interruption by the beginning of scoring for the round.

m) There shall be no practice permitted after a postponement or delay unless such postponement or delay exceeds thirty (30) minutes. In such cases the amount of practice shall be according to the following schedule:
1) Thirty (30) to sixty (60) minute delay — one practice end.
2) Sixty (60) minutes or more delay, unless interrupted by a scheduled lunch period or night fall — two practice ends.

n) A blast of the whistle shall be the signal to commence or cease shooting for each end. Two or more signal blasts, an immediate interruption for all shooting.

o) If an archer shoots less than six arrows in one end, he may shoot the remaining arrows if the omission is discovered before the end is officially completed, otherwise they shall score as misses.

p) If an archer shoots more than six arrows in one end, only the lowest six shall score.

q) Archers may not make up lost rounds, ends, or arrows except as specified.

r) If a target falls before an end is scored, that end shall be reshot by all archers on that target.

s) Equipment failures, mishaps, or other occurrences not specifically covered in other rules shall not entitle an archer to repeat a shot unless the mis-shot arrow can be reached by the bow from the archer's position on the shooting line.

t) If an arrow should hand from the target face, shooting shall be interrupted and a Field Official shall immediately reinsert the arrow in its proper place in the scoring face.

u) Any archer should call to the attention of the Field Officials any rule infractions, unsportsman-like or unseemly conduct, or ANY SAFETY HAZARDS. The Field Officials are empowered to take such steps as their judgment indicates to correct the situation, including warning, scoring penalties, and even expulsion from the tournament in severe cases.

v) In all official 6-Gold shoots, ends shall be shot "three and three". Half (or the closest possible number to half) of the archers assigned to each target shall take position and shoot three arrows each. They shall then retire and the remaining archers assigned shall shoot three arrows. Then the first group shall shoot their remaining arrows. Finally the second group on each target shall shoot their remaining three arrows. The Field Captain may require shooting six arrows at a time only in an emergency where the time saved is necessary to complete the schedule.

w) Tie scores shall be resolved in favor of the archer shooting the highest score at the longest distance, then the next longest distances, in decoding order. If still tied through all distances, then ties shall be resolved in favor of the archer with the greatest total number of Golds, then Red, then Blues, then Blacks. If still tied, the tie shall be resolved in favor of the archer with the greatest number of perfect ends. If still tied, it shall be so recorded.

x) Coaching an archer on the shooting line by means of inaudible and inconspicuous signs or symbols is permitted, providing that such coaching is not distracting to other contestants. If a contestant on the same target or adjacent targets complains that such activity is personally distracting, such coaching must be terminated immediately. Audible coaching of archers on the shooting line is not permitted.

7. Scoring

a) Arrows in the standard target face shall be evaluated as follows: Gold-9, Red-7, Blue-5, Black-3, White-1.

b) If an arrow in the target touches two colors, breaking the inside edge of the black scoring line, the higher color shall count. Doubtful arrows must be determined for each end before the arrows or target face have been touched, otherwise the lower value must be taken.

c) An arrow that has passed through the scoring face so that it is not visible from the front shall count 7 at 60 yards or less, and 5 for ranges beyond 60 yards. Arrows passing completely through the target, if witnessed, are scored in the same manner.

d) An arrow which rebounds from the scoring face, if witnessed, shall score the same as a pass-through.

e) An arrow embedded in another arrow on the scoring face shall score the same as the arrow in which it is embedded.

f) Hits on the wrong target shall score as misses.

g) The archer chosen to pull the arrows from the target, normally the first in order of assignment, shall be the Target Captain and shall rule all questions on his target subject to appeal to the Field Officials.

h) The Target Captain shall call the value of each arrow as he pulls it from the target and it shall then be recorded independently by two contestants acting as scorers, normally the next two assigned to the target. Scorers should check results after each end to avoid errors.

i) Each archer is individually responsible for seeing that his arrows are called correctly and properly entered on the score cards, and that his score cards are turned in to the proper officials.

8. Field Officials

a) Field Officials shall be appointed by the tournament officials and shall rank in authority as follows: Field Captain, Lady Paramount, Assistants to the Field Captain, Assistants to Lady Paramount.

b) The Field Officials shall have the responsibility and authority to organize, supervise and regulate all practice, shooting and competition in accordance with regulations and customs; to interpret and to decide questions of rules; TO MAINTAIN SAFETY CONDITIONS; to enforce sportsmanlike behavior; to score doubtful arrows; to signify the start, interruptions, delays, postponements and finish of competition.

c) Repeated infractions or discourteous or unsportsmanlike conduct, not sufficiently grave as to require expulsion, shall be penalized by the Field Officials after an appropriate warning as follows: For the first repetition after warning, the loss of the highest arrow of that end: for the second repetition, expulsion from the tournament without refund.

d) Decisions of the lesser field officials shall be final unless immediately appealed to Field Captain.

e) Decisions of the Field Captain shall be final unless verbal notice of intent to protest is given to the Field Captain, and unless this is followed by the submission of a written protest to the Tournament Chairman prior to the determination of the winners.

O. NFAA 900 TARGET ROUND:

The only difference between the 810 round and the 900 round is the method of scoring.

Item 7a listed above in the 810 Target Round will change to read as follows: Arrows in the standard target face shall be evaluated as follows: Inner Gold-10, Outer Gold-9, Inner Red-8, Outer Red-7, Inner Blue-6, Outer Blue-5, Inner Black-4, Outer Black-3, Inner White-2, Outer White-1.

ARTICLE VII. THE NFAA INDOOR LEAGUE PROGRAM

A. Terms:

1. Round—A type of game; Freeman, NFAA Indoor Round.

2. End — Five arrows shot consecutively by an archer during his/her turn to score.
3. Game — The divisions of a round; 4 ends of 5 arrows.
4. Series — Three games shot in a round.
5. League — A number of teams competing against one another in match play.
6. Team — The basic unit of a league composed of two or more archers and a permissible limit of alternate members.
7. League Period — Total number of weeks a league will be in competition.
8. Scratch Score — An archer's actual score before it has been adjusted by a handicap.
9. Average — An archer's average is computed from the average of scores of the last six games.
10. Handicap or Match Score — An archer's score after it has been adjusted by his handicap.
11. Absentee Score — A score shot prior to a league match to an anticipated absence. Absentee scores may not exceed the archer's average.
12. Blind Score — A score used for a missing member(s). Blind scores are computed by subtracting 5 points from the archer's average score.
13. Team Average — The combined averages of all archers on a team.
14. Team Points — Points a team earns by game and series wins. In league play a team earns one point for each game won. In addition, one point is awarded the team having the highest series total score.

B. League Sanction:
　　1. Any NFAA chartered association, club or archery lane may apply for the Indoor Archery League Program.
　　2. League sanction will be granted provided:
　　　　a) The league sessions will be conducted on a NFAA approved range.
　　　　b) Official NFAA targets are used in official NFAA rounds.
　　　　c) A league sanction fee of $5.00 per archer is submitted to NFAA Headquarters.
　　3. The NFAA, in granting league sanction, will furnish:
　　　　a) League Sanction Certificate.
　　　　b) League Secretary instruction guide.
　　　　c) League forms including team score sheets, team standing forms, team shooting schedules and individual archer handicap or game record cards.
　　　　d) Individual progression awards.

C. League Formation, Officers and Duties:
　　1. A temporary chairman should be appointed by the association, club or manager of a commercial archery lane desiring to establish the Indoor Archery League. This chairman will conduct an election of league officers at the initial meeting of league archers. After the election of officers, decisions must be made regarding:
　　　　a) Number of archers on a team.
　　　　b) Type of round, NFAA Indoor or Freeman.
　　　　c) Type of handicap, Team or Individual.
　　　　d) Substitution rules, Absentee and Blind Scoring.

    e) Awards, trophies, point money, etc.

    f) Shooting fees, sanction fees and manner of payment.

2. Management of the league shall be vested in a Board of Directors, composed of team captains chosen by the respective members of their teams, and the elected officers of President, Vice-President, and Secretary. The Board shall decide any disputes or protests occurring between individuals or teams in league play, and shall render final decisions in regard to interpretation of league regulations.

3. President:

The President shall preside at all meetings and shall act as Range Captain during league sessions. He/She shall have the authority to regulate practice shooting and competition in accordance with official rules and customs, and to maintain safety conditions. He/She will be the final authority in scoring doubtful arrows when requested by a target captain.

4. Vice-President:

The Vice-President will act in the absence of the President.

5. Secretary:

The Secretary is responsible for the proper conduct of the league and shall guarantee league functions in the manner as required by the NFAA; shall collect team shooting fees and keep complete records of league finances; shall compile individual and team scores and compute averages and/or handicaps as required; shall post a record of team standings; shall administer the NFAA awards program; shall post team schedules and make lane and target assignments for each session; shall collect and remit sanction fees to the NFAA; and shall perform such other duties as may be requested of him/her by the President or required by the rules governing the league.

D. League Regulations:

1. League Sanction: Is provided for a continuous league period. Individual archers or teams may be added after the league has started, provided applicable forms and sanction fees are submitted.

2. Eligibility: League shooting will be open to all archers. Individual membership requirements may be imposed by the host organization in accordance with regulations of the state association to which it is affiliated.

3. Targets: The official NFAA Indoor League target shall be used in all league sessions.

4. Teams: The number of archers on a team will be decided by the league membership at the initial league meeting. An archer may transfer to another team with approval of both team captains and the Board of Directors.

5. Late Joining Teams: If necessary, teams may be added. However, in team standing, new teams will be scored as losing all previous series.

6. Handicap Systems: Either team or individual handicap may be selected by preference of the league membership.

    a) Team handicap will be computed at 80% of the difference in the average scores of any two teams that will compete against each other in a league series. These handicap points will be given to the lower scoring team before the series begins.

    b) Individual handicap will be computed at 80% of the difference between an archer's average scratch score and perfect. These handicap points will be given to each individual before a series begins.

7. Team Points: In league play there are 4 possible points to be won in a 3 game series. One point is earned for each game won and one point is won by a team having the higher series total. When two teams have tie scores for a game, ½ point is won by each team.

8. Average: An archer's average will be computed weekly from the average of the last six games shot. During the initial league series each archer's high game and low game will be discarded and the remaining score used as the average in determining team points. The same procedure will be used during the second league series, but thereafter will revert to a six game average.

9. Late Joiners Or Alternates: Averages for late joiners or alternates without established averages will be computed in the same manner as described in paragraph 8, above.

10. Handicap: An archer's handicap will be computed weekly from the average of the last six games shot. 80% of the difference between 100 and the six game average will be the handicap. During the initial league series the high game and low game will be discarded and the remaining score will be used as the average in computing the handicap. The same procedure will be used during the second league series and for averages for late joiners or alternates without established handicaps.

11. Absent Team Members: A certain number of team members must be present to compete. Having fewer than the minimum required will result in forfeiting the series. The minimum of archers present for four member teams will be two; for 3 member teams, one; and for two member teams, one.

12. League Alternates: Several alternate or substitute archer procedures may be employed. The system selected is left to the preference of the league membership. Once a system has been adopted by the league there must be no variation unless a change has been voted by the league Board of Directors.

    a) A list of league alternates may be on file with the league secretary. Any archer so listed will be eligible to fill in vacancies on any team in the league.

    b) Each team may carry an additional team member as an alternate. In this instance, the alternate may shoot only if vacancies exist on his team.

    c) A league may elect not to allow any type of alternate rule.

13. Absentee Score: A league may elect to allow absentee scores in lieu of or in addition to its alternate rule. An absentee score must be witnessed and may not exceed the archer's average. Points above his average will be dropped.

14. Blind Scores: A blind score may be used for a missing archer. It will be determined by subtracting 5 points from the archer's average score. This blind score will be used for each game in the current series. Blind scores should not be used for computing future averages.

15. Late Arrival: A team member arriving before the second game has started may participate in the balance of the game but their score for the first

game will revert to blind score procedure. Arrival after the second game has started will disqualify them and blind score procedure will be used for his series.

16. Divisions Of A League: The league period will be divided into first and second halves. All teams will start the second half with zero wins and losses. Individual averages and/or handicaps will be carried into the second half.

17. League Championship: A shootoff, one 3-game series, between the winner of the first half and the winner of the second half shall decide the League Championship.

18. Final Event Ties: Teams which are tied at the end of the last night of the league, and first and second half winner teams will shoot off the tie in a normal four end game of 20 arrows. If the tie is not broken, shooting will continue until one team shoots a better end (5 arrows) in sudden death. Averages and/or handicaps will not be recomputed for the purpose of shooting off ties.

E. Shooting Rules:

1. Team Captain: Each team will select a team captain from its members. The team captain shall be responsible for the attendance of the members of their team and for their behavior at all league sessions. They will collect all shooting fees, including those of tardy members, and submit them to the league secretary. They will direct the shooting order of their team, appoint an archer to score and pull the opposing team's arrows and another to record the scores. They shall check and initial score sheets at the end of each session and submit them to the league secretary.

2. Target Order: The score sheets will indicate which butt and lane (left or right) where each team will shoot. The first two left lane archers will shoot the top left targets and the last two will shoot the lower left targets. The first two right lane shooters will shoot the top right targets and the last two, the lower right targets. Lane assignments will be changed each week to insure a fair rotation.

3. Alternation of Shooters: After the completion of six ends, teams shall change lanes and targets: Archers who shot top targets on one side will shoot bottom targets on the other side, etc.

4. Target Captain: Team captains shall each act as a target captain on the opposing team's shooting lane and score all doubtful arrows. Their decision will be final unless immediately appealed to the Range Captain.

F. Awards:

1. Individual Achievement Awards: All archers who shoot in a sanctioned NFAA Indoor League will be eligible for individual achievement awards as follows:

120 patch	240 patch
140 patch	260 patch
160 patch	270 patch
180 patch	280 patch
200 patch	290 patch
220 patch	300 patch

The first three individual achievement awards won by an archer during a league period will be presented by the NFAA free of charge. Additional awards may be won but a charge to cover the cost of the awards will be assumed by the league sponsor or recipient of the award.

2. A League Championship Pin will be presented to each member of a league championship team.
3. Individual achievement awards are available for presentation to all state association sanctioned indoor tournaments. A charge to cover the cost of the awards will be assumed by the tournament host.

ARTICLE VIII. THE NFAA OUTDOOR LEAGUE PROGRAM

A. Terms:
  1. Round — A type of game: Field, Hunter or International Round.
  2. End — Four arrows in Field or Hunter, 3 arrows in International Round.
  3. Game — The divisions of a round; 14 Field, 14 Hunter, 10 International.
  4. Series — Two games shot in a round.
  5. League — A number of teams competing against another in match play.
  6. Team — The basic unit of a league composed of two or more archers and a permissible limit of alternate members.
  7. League Period — Total number of weeks a league will be in competition.
  8. Scratch Score — An archer's actual score before it has been adjusted by a handicap.
  9. Average — Use regular outdoor field handicap system.
  10. Absentee Score — A score shot prior to a league match due to an anticipated absence. Absentee scores may not exceed the archer's average.
  11. Blind Score — A score used for a missing member(s). Blind scores are computed by subtracting 5 points from the archer's average score.
  12. Team Average — The combined averages of all archers on a team.
  13. Team Points — Points a team earns by game and series wins. In league play a team earns one point for each game won. In addition, one point is awarded the team having the highest series total score.
B. League Sanction:
  1. Any NFAA chartered association, club or archery lane may apply for the Outdoor Archery League Program.
  2. League Sanction will be granted provided:
     a) The league sessions will be conducted on a NFAA approved range.
     b) Official NFAA targets are used in official NFAA rounds.
     c) A league sanction fee of $5.00 per archer is submitted to NFAA Headquarters.
  3. The NFAA, in granting league sanction, will furnish:
     a) League Sanction Certificate.
     b) League Secretary instruction guide.
     c) League forms, including team score sheets, team standing forms, team shooting schedules and individual archer handicap or game record cards.
     d) Individual progression awards.
C. League Formation, Officers and Duties:
  1. A temporary chairman should be appointed by the association, club or manager of a commercial archery lane desiring to establish the Outdoor

Archery League. This chairman will conduct an election of league officers at the initial meeting of league archers. After the election of officers, decisions must be made regarding:

a) Number of archers on a team.

b) Type of Rounds, NFAA Field, Hunter or International.

c) Type of handicap, Team or Individual.

d) Substitution rules, Absentee and Blind Scoring.

e) Awards, trophies, point money, etc.

f) Shooting fees and sanction fees and manner of payment.

2. Management of the league shall be vested in a Board of Directors, composed of team captains chosen by the respective members of their teams, and the elected officers of President, Vice-president and Secretary. The Board shall decide any disputes or protests occurring between individuals or teams in league play, and shall render final decisions in regard to interpretation of league regulations.

3. President:

The President shall preside at all meetings and shall act as Range Captain during league sessions. He/She shall have the authority to regulate practice shooting and competition in accordance with official rules and customs, and to maintain safety conditions. He/She will be the final authority in scoring doubtful arrows when requested by a target captain.

4. Vice-President:

The Vice-President will act in the absence of the President.

5. Secretary:

The Secretary is responsible for the proper conduct of the league and shall guarantee league functions in the manner as required by the NFAA; shall collect team shooting fees and keep complete records of league finances; shall compile individual and team scores and compute averages and/or handicaps as required; shall post a record of team standings; shall administer the NFAA awards program; shall post team schedules and make lane and target assignments for each session; shall collect and remit sanction fees to the NFAA, and shall perform such other duties as may be requested of him/her by the President or required by the rules governing the league.

D. League Regulations:

1. League Sanction: Is provided for a continuous league period. Individual archers or teams may be added after the league has started, provided applicable forms and sanction fees are submitted.

2. Eligibility: League shooting will be open to all archers. Individual membership requirements may be imposed by the host organization in accordance with regulations of the state association to which it is affiliated.

3. Targets: The official NFAA Outdoor League target shall be used in all league sessions.

4. Teams: The number of archers on a team will be decided by the league membership at the initial league meeting. An archer may transfer to another team with approval of both team captains and the Board of Directors.

5. Late Joining Teams: If necessary, teams may be added. However, in team standing, new teams will be scored as losing all previous series.

6. Handicap Systems: Regular NFAA outdoor handicap system.
7. Absent Team Members: A certain number of team members must be present to compete. Having fewer than the minimum required will result in forfeiting the series. The minimum of archers present for four member teams will be two; for three member teams, one; and for two member teams, one.
8. League Alternates: Several alternate or substitute archer procedures may be employed. The system selected is left to the preference of the league membership. Once a system has been adopted by the league there must be no variation unless a change has been voted by the League Board of Directors.
   a) A list of league alternates may be on file with the league secretary. Any archer so listed will be eligible to fill in vacancies on any team in the league.
   b) Each team may carry an additional team member as an alternate. In this instance the alternate may shoot only if vacancies exist on his team.
   c) A league may elect not to allow any type of alternate rule.
9. Absentee Score: A league may elect to allow absentee scores in lieu of or in addition to its alternate rule. An absentee score must be witnessed and may not exceed the archer's average. Points above his average will be dropped.
10. Blind Scores: A blind score may be used for a missing archer. It will be determined by subtracting 5 points from the archer's average score. This blind score will be used for each game in the current series. Blind scores should not be used for computing future averages.
11. Late Arrivals: A team member arriving before the second game has started may participate in the balance of the game but their score for the first game will revert to blind score procedure. Arrival after the second game has started will disqualify them, and blind score procedure will be used for their series.
12. Divisions Of A League: The league period will be divided into first and second halves. All teams will start the second half with zero wins and losses. Individual averages and/or handicaps will be carried into the second half.
13. League Championship: A shootoff, one 2-game series, between the winner of the first half and the winner of the second half shall decide the League Championship.
14. Final Event Ties: Will be handled the same as ties are broken on outdoor Field rounds.
E. Shooting Rules:
   1. Team Captain: Each team will select a team captain from its members. The team captain shall be responsible for the attendance of the members of their team and for their behavior at all league sessions. They will collect all shooting fees, including those of tardy members, and submit them to the league secretary. They will direct the shooting order of their team, appoint an archer to score and pull the opposing team's arrows and another to record the scores. They shall check and initial score sheets at the end of each session and submit them to the league secretary.
   2. Target Order: Round will be shot according to outdoor shooting, as per round shot.

3. Target Captain: Team captains shall each act as target captains on the opposing teams and score all doubtful arrows. Their decision will be final unless immediately appealed to the Range Captain.

F. Awards:

1. Individual Achievement Awards: All archers who shoot in a sanctioned NFAA Outdoor League will be eligible for individual achievement awards as follows:

120 patch	240 patch
140 patch	260 patch
160 patch	270 patch
180 patch	280 patch
200 patch	Perfect Patch
220 patch	

The first three individual achievement awards won by an archer during a league period will be presented by the NFAA free of charge. Additional awards may be won but a charge to cover the cost of the awards will be assumed by the league sponsor or recipient of the award.

2. A League Championship Pin: Will be presented to each member of a league championship team.

3. Individual achievement awards are available for presentation to all state association sanctioned outdoor tournaments. A charge to cover the cost of the awards will be assumed by the tournament host.

ARTICLE IX. RULES GOVERNING THE 20 AND 15 PIN AWARDS

A. These awards may be won in the NFAA Field, Hunter or International round, or portions thereof, with a distinctive pin and set of bars for each round.

B. An archer shall become eligible for these awards upon shooting a 20 score on any field or hunter target or upon shooting a 15 on any International target on any officially approved NFAA course using official NFAA targets while competing in any of the following tournaments:

1. The National Field Archery Association Annual Tournament.
2. Any National Field Archery Association mail tournament.
3. Any Chartered club or association tournament.

C. Only clubs and associations chartered with NFAA shall be permitted to register tournaments as 20/15 Pin Tournaments.

D. Only adult, young adult and youth members of the NFAA are eligible and the archer must have his score card signed by two witnesses. Application for the 20/15 bar shall be submitted within 30 days, by the archer eligible for the award, accompanied by a fee, sent to the state association secretary or awards chairman. The same procedure is followed for the 20/15 pin award, accompanied by the appropriate fee.

E. Adult, young adult and youth members of NFAA may earn yardage bars to attach to the 20 Pin Award for scoring 20 on the 20, 35, 50 and 65 centimeter targets and under the rules set up for the 20 Pin Award. The bars shall have the distance shot marked on the bar.

F. Adult, young adult and youth members of NFAA may earn yardage bars to attach to the 15 Pin Award for scoring a 15 on the 35, 50 and 65 centimeter targets and under the rules set up for the 20 Pin Award. The bars shall have the distance shot marked on the bar.

G. Upon receiving the pin and entire series of bars in any one style of shooting, the NFAA Perfect Pin shall be awarded an archer upon application and verification of achievements through the state association secretary. Perfect pins are available for the Field, Hunter and International rounds. No fee is involved in this award.

H. Adult and young adult members of NFAA may earn an Animal Perfect Pin by shooting a 280 on a 14-target unit at a registered tournament. The cost of the pin shall be paid for by the archer.

ARTICLE X. 500 CLUB AND/OR PERFECT CLUB

A. Any member who records a score of 500 or more, from the adult stakes, on a NFAA Field round or NFAA Hunter round or combination of 14 Field–14 Hunter, shall be eligible to join the NFAA 500 Club. The feat must be accomplished on a NFAA approved course.

B. Any member who records a perfect score from the adult stakes on a NFAA Field Round or NFAA Hunter Round, or combination of 14/15 Field–14/15 Hunter, or the International Round, shall be eligible to join the NFAA Perfect Club: The feat must be accomplished on a NFAA approved course, at a registered tournament.

C. Any member who records a perfect score on any NFAA official indoor round shall be eligible to join the NFAA Perfect Club. The feat must be accomplished at a registered tournament.

D. These awards shall consist of appropriate certificates. Embroidered 500 Club patches or Perfect Club patches are also available, for a fee.

E. Application for membership in the 500 Club or Perfect Club shall be made to NFAA Headquarters.
   1. Application shall be accompanied by the applicant's score card. The date, location of the course and signatures of two witnesses shall appear on the card.
   2. Application blanks shall be supplied by the NFAA Headquarters upon request.

ARTICLE XI. NFAA SERVICE PINS

A. Cumulative membership in the NFAA shall be recognized by the awarding of an appropriate lapel pin.

B. Periods of membership indicated shall be 10, 15, 20, 25, 30, 35, 40, 45 and 50 years.

C. The pins shall be awarded by NFAA Headquarters upon application through the state association secretary, or directly to NFAA Headquarters.

D. Eligibility for service pins shall be determined on the basis of available membership records at NFAA Headquarters and/or those of the affiliated state association, or any other proof of cumulative membership.

ARTICLE XII. ART YOUNG AWARDS

A. Game Awards Of The National Field Archery Assn.
   1. There shall be two: The "Art Young Big Game Awards" and "Art Young Small Game Awards".

2. The purpose of the Art Young awards is to promote interest in hunting with the bow and arrow, to encourage good sportsmanship and to give recognition by the organized field archers to their members who obtain game with the bow.

3. Rules:
   a) All animals must be taken in accordance with the laws of the state, territory, province, or county, whichever is appropriate, and in accordance with the rules of fair chase.
   b) In order to be eligible for awards, all animals must be reported within (1) one year of the date taken. A handling fee, to be established at the beginning of each year by the Executive Secretary, shall accompany each application.
   c) The hunter must have taken possession of the animal to receive credit for the award.
   d) It shall be the responsibility of the hunter to know the legal status of species hunted.
   e) Animals specified as big game by the NFAA are not eligible for credit in the Art Young Small Game awards system.
   f) Members who willfully take game out of season, take protected animals or otherwise violate game laws, falsify a claim or deliberately witness a falsified claim shall be expelled from the NFAA and all its programs. An expelled member may petition the NFAA for reinstatement after one year. The Bowhunting and Conservation Committee shall rule on the petition.
   g) An additional award shall not be given for game previously accepted under a prior awards system. (Persons who have amassed a combination of seven or more pins under the original program as of July 1, 1973, and have so requested by January 1, 1974, shall be allowed to continue the original program. The same animals used in claiming any portion of the original Master Bowhunter award may not be used again for awards in another program).
   h) Any game taken from areas where they are officially designated as "rare" or "endangered" shall be ineligible for awards.

B. Art Young Big Game Awards:
   1. Definition of Big Game:
      All species that are recognized as Big Game by responsible conservation department within accordance with State, territory, province, country, whichever is appropriate. Reference material such as the "Audubon Society's series on birds and mammals" may be used. Master species list available from Headquarters: recommendations for additions or deletions to the master list shall be reviewed by the Bowhunting and Conservation Committee at each annual N.F.A.A. meeting.
   2. Eligibility: "Art Young Big Game Awards" is limited to members of the NFAA at the time of the kill. There shall be no geographical restrictions, either as to residence of the claimant or to the location in which the game is secured.
   3. Claim of Award: Any member of the NFAA wishing to claim the Art Young Big Game pin, or the subsequent awards will apply to the NFAA Headquarters for an application blank, supply the information and evidence called for, and mail it to NFAA Headquarters.

4. Awards: An Art Young Big Game pin and a NFAA Big Game patch shall be given for the first example of each species taken with bow and arrow according to the NFAA rules, for a processing fee. Duplicate NFAA Big Game patches can be obtained by sending in the Big Game application form and appropriate fee.

C. Art Young Small Game Awards:

1. Definition of Small Game: "All legal game shall be recognized for the Small Game Program, including subspecies. Reference materials such as the "Audubon Society's series on Birds and mammals may be used". Recommendation for additions or deletions to the master list shall be reviewed by the Bowhunting and Conservation Committee at each annual NFAA meeting.

2. Eligibility: This shall be the same as for the "Art Young Big Game Award". If several species are taken within such a (1) one year period, they may be held and reported at one time. However, no species may be reported more than (1) one year after taking.

3. Awards:
   a) The Art Young Small Game Arrowhead Pin shall be given upon taking the first six species of small game. In addition, an Art Young Small Game program patch shall be available.
   b) For each additional four species taken by a member an additional award in the form of a bar with the number 4 shall be presented to the hunter. There shall be no limit to the number of bars which may be earned, but all game must be legally taken.
   c) A particular species may not be claimed more than once by any bowhunter participating in the Art Young Small Game program, except in states which have fewer than 3 species designed legal small game for bowhunting. At least one of the animals claimed must be considered "game" by the local conservation department.

D. Bowhunter Awards:

1. There shall be three classes of Bowhunter Awards:
   a) Bowhunter Pin
   b) Expert Bowhunter Pin
   c) Master Bowhunter Pin
   d) Grandmaster Pin
   e) A cloth patch corresponding to the above bowhunter awards will be available for an additional fee. Master Bowhunter Patch will be accompanied by a chevron for 1st degree and/or 2nd degree.

2. Eligibility:
   a) A person may be awarded the Bowhunter Pin when he/she has earned the Art Young Small Game arrowhead pin and one four bar, and two Big Game arrowhead pins.
   b) A person may be awarded the Expert Bowhunter Pin when he/she has earned the Bowhunter Pin plus one additional four bar and one additional Big Game arrowhead pin.
   c) A person may be awarded the Master Bowhunter Medal when he/she has earned the Expert Bowhunter Pin plus three additional four bars and three additional Big Game arrowhead pins.
   d) A person may be awarded the Grand Master Bowhunter Pin when he/she has earned the Master Bowhunter Pin two additional times.

He/She will earn one degree each time he/she completed the Master Bowhunter pin requirements; i.e. 1st degree master, 2nd degree master, Grand Master on 3rd degree.

3. Claim of Awards:
    a) All applications must be made to the NFAA Headquarters. Verification that all species, to the best of his knowledge, were legally taken must be made by another NFAA member. No application will be accepted by NFAA without such verification.

E. Bowfisher Program and Awards:
   1. NFAA Bowfisher of the Year. This program would have four winners. These winners would be determined by the largest fish in each of the four categories. These species would be shark, carp, gar and ray.
      Rules are as follows:
      a) Must be a member of NFAA.
      b) There will be four awards. One for shark, gar, carp and ray.
      c) There will be no charge for entering a fish.
      d) Entry deadline will be December 31.
      e) The entrant will furnish NFAA with a picture of the fish next to a measurable object and a signed affidavit by two witnesses stating that they were present at the time of the weighing. Winners will be determined by weight.
      f) All entries will be inspected by the NFAA to determine the winner. The winners will then be notified by mail.
      g) The winners will receive an engraved plaque.
      h) Application shall be available from Headquarters and sectional officers of the NFAA in charge of bowhunting.
   2. NFAA Bowfisher Records.
      This is a program whereby NFAA keeps records of who holds the distinction of having taken the biggest fish of any certain species by means of bow and arrow.
      Rules are as follows:
      a) Must be a member of NFAA.
      b) There will be no charge for entering a fish.
      c) These records will stand for one year, at which time the NFAA will review all entries and make all necessary change to update the records list. If no records are beaten, they remain on the list for the next year. These changes will be done by the NFAA.
      d) Entry deadline will be December 31.
      e) The entrant must furnish NFAA with a picture of the fish next to a measurable object, and a signed affidavit by two witnesses stating that they were present at the time of weighing.
      f) New entrants that make the top ten list will receive a certificate.
   3. Patch Program.
      This program will consist of two different types of patches. One would be a regular shoulder patch denoting that you are a NFAA Bowfisher. The second patch would be a bar type patch that would denote what types of fish you have taken.

F. Diamond Buck Award:
   1. The Diamond Buck Award will be given for the largest example of mule deer, whitetail deer and blacktail deer based on antler measurements. The

antlers must be scored by Pope and Young Club or Boone and Crockett methods and verified by one of these club's official measurers. Applications shall be available from NFAA Headquarters and from sectional officers of the NFAA in charge of bowhunting.

   2. The Diamond Buck Award will be limited to NFAA members in good standing at time of harvest.

G. Application Disapproval:
   1. In the event an application is disapproved the hunter has the right to petition the NFAA Bowhunting and Conservation Committee. The petition must be in writing and must state the facts of the claim. It shall be the responsibility of the review committee to study the applicable game laws and the petition and make a recommendation to the Bowhunting and Conservation Committee. The chairman shall appoint the 3 man committee to rule on the claim and act on the claim within 60 days.
   2. The results of the petition shall be kept confidential, but the ruling shall be sent in writing to each member of the committee, the NFAA Headquarters and the petitioner.

ARTICLE XIII. RULES FOR COMPTON MEDAL OF HONOR

A. The NFAA medal of honor shall be known as the Compton Medal of Honor, and it shall be bestowed sparingly and only in recognition of outstanding and unselfish contributions to archery in any of its phases.

B. To the end that the Compton Medal of Honor shall for all time retain its place as the most highly esteemed award in all archery, the safeguarding of its future will be entrusted to a committee of three NFAA members who must have been members for ten years and one former Compton Medal of Honor recipient selected by the President. The members will be appointed to 3-year terms on a rotation basis, with one new member being appointed each year.

C. The Medal of Honor committee shall be free of all restrictions as to their choice of recipients except:
   1. That the Compton Medal of Honor shall not be bestowed upon any elected officer of the association during his tenure of office, and
   2. That their deliberations will be held in strict confidence which shall not be violated.

D. The President of NFAA shall be the honorary chairman of the committee, with the following duties and authority:
   1. He shall appoint from among the committee members an acting chairman to serve in that capacity for one year, thus providing for rotation of the acting chairmanship.
   2. He shall have the sole authority to decide for, or against, such candidate only as may be reported to him by the acting chairman as having a majority, though less than unanimous support of the members of the committee.
   3. He shall accept a unanimous recommendation by the committee as mandatory upon him to order the bestowal of the Compton Medal of Honor.
   4. He shall prepare, or have prepared, a citation in accordance with the committee's unanimous choice, or with his affirmation of the committee's majority recommendations, as the case may be.

E. In conjunction with receiving the Compton Medal of Honor the recipient will automatically be awarded an Honorary Lifetime Membership.

F. The Executive Secretary shall be responsible for the custody of the dies for the Compton Medal of Honor and shall pay out of the treasury the costs of the striking and engraving of such replicas of the medal when directed by the President.

G. A copy of these regulations shall appear in each issue of the NFAA Constitution and By-Laws booklet.

ARTICLE XIV. RULES GOVERNING THE AWARD OF THE MEDAL OF MERIT

A. The NFAA Medal of Merit shall be bestowed sparingly in recognition of unselfish contributions to field archery and its closely allied activities. The inscription, "Opera, Artes, Honor" (Works, Skills, Honor) which appears on the medal, shall serve as the measure.

B. To each of the states and each of the sections comprising the NFAA is given the privilege of nominating worthy members of the NFAA as candidates for the award. The state through its NFAA Director; the section through its Councilman shall, after receiving instructions from their respective memberships, submit nominations to the NFAA Executive Secretary. Qualifications and endorsements shall accompany every nomination.

C. An individual may be awarded only one Medal of Merit for all time.

D. The NFAA Executive Secretary shall furnish all available information on all nominations to the Board of Directors Council, which, after discussion and investigation, may vote on the issue. A two-thirds yea vote shall be required to affirm the award. The Executive Secretary shall forward the medal to the state or section for presentation.

E. The NFAA Executive Secretary shall be the custodian of the dies for the medal and the archives of the award. The initial cost of design, striking and engraving shall be paid out of the treasury of the NFAA. The unit bestowing the award (state or section) shall pay a suitable fee to the NFAA for the medal.

F. The name of the unit (state or section) making the award shall be engraved on the medal.

G. A copy of these regulations shall appear in each issue of the NFAA Constitution and By-Laws book.

ARTICLE XV. THE ORDER OF THE BONE

A. Members of this order shall receive an award pin and a membership card.

B. Members shall be chosen by a committee to be appointed by the President of the NFAA.

C. Requirements for membership:
   1. Be a member in good standing of the NFAA.
   2. Pull a conspicuous "boner" pertaining to archery hunting.
   3. Write or cause to be written a full account of events leading up to and following said "boner" in publishable story form. Whenever possible, articles will be selected to appear in the official publication, although you may win the award and not have your article published due to lack of space. Stories should be mailed to NFAA Headquarters and should include the date the boner was committed.

ARTICLE XVI. FELLOWSHIP OF ROBINHOOD

A. Any member who telescopes an arrow, previously lodged in the highest scoring area of a target during an NFAA sanctioned event, shall be eligible for recognition in the Fellowship of Robinhood.
B. The award shall consist of a certificate in old English text.
C. Applications shall be made to NFAA Headquarters.
   1. Applicants shall describe the general circumstances of the shot, including the date and the signature of one witness on the scorecard which must be submitted with the application.
   2. Application blanks shall be supplied by NFAA Headquarters upon request.

ARTICLE XVII. CLUB/SHOP CHARTER AND COURSE APPROVAL

A. Club/Shop Charter Procedures:
   1. NFAA charter and continued affiliation authorizes automatic sanction of state association tournaments for all official NFAA rounds conducted by the club, provided such rounds are held on an approved NFAA indoor or outdoor facility and provided they conform to Articles I, II, III, IV, and VI of these By-Laws. Sanction shall mean that said round is conducted by the NFAA or through its recognized state affiliate; when said round is held on a NFAA approved facility using official NFAA targets; and when said round conforms to Articles I, II, III, IV and VI of these By-Laws.
   2. An archery club having a minimum of five (5) Head of Household members, meeting requirements in NFAA Constitution Article III, Section A, Paragraph 2 or 3, may be chartered with the NFAA upon approval of the state association and the NFAA Director who has jurisdiction. A Shop whose Owner or Lane Manager is a current member of NFAA may be chartered with the NFAA upon approval of the state association and the NFAA Director who has jurisdiction. A club/shop charter may be granted by the NFAA only after prior approval of the state association and NFAA Director. No state association shall approve an application for charter unless the club/shop meets minimum state requirements.
   3. Application for charter will be made in triplicate, and along with the proper fees, shall be forwarded to the state association secretary. After approval by the state association all three copies will be forwarded to the NFAA Director for review. Upon granting his approval the NFAA Director will affix his signature, forward one copy to NFAA Headquarters, return the second copy to the state association secretary, and retain the third copy for his records. Upon receipt of properly executed application and charter fee at NFAA Headquarters the Executive Secretary is authorized to issue the charter. Effective date of the charter will be shown as the date of approval by the NFAA Director.
   4. A newly chartered club will pay a $20.00 fee to charter with the NFAA and have a Constitution and By-Laws that is in compliance with the State requirements. A newly chartered Shop will pay a $20.00 fee to charter with the NFAA. After establishing charter, continued affiliation will be maintained through the state association and the NFAA Director.
   5. Sixty days prior to expiration of club/shop affiliation, the NFAA shall provide the club/shop with an affiliation renewal form in triplicate and a

list of these clubs/shops will be sent to the state secretary and director. Upon successful renewal of state NFAA affiliation, the state secretary will forward one copy to NFAA Headquarters of the completed form with a $10.00 renewal fee, one copy to the NFAA Director and retain the third copy. Upon receipt of the approved renewal form and renewal fee at NFAA Headquarters, affiliation will be extended for an additional year. If a Club/Shop changes their Constitution and By-Laws within the year they will send a copy along with the charter renewal to the State Secretary and the NFAA Director. Failure to renew affiliation by the last day of the month in which the club/shop charter expires, shall result in the club/shop being dropped from the active rolls of NFAA.

6. A club/shop dropped from the NFAA due to lapse of affiliation shall forfeit its right to hold NFAA sanctioned tournaments. Its NFAA course approval, and its NFAA club liability insurance shall be suspended until the Club/Shop Charter has been reinstated.

B. Course Approval Procedure:

1. The NFAA recognizes as official only tournaments held on NFAA approved courses and makes no awards for competition on any other course. Courses must be inspected by the NFAA Director, or his designated representative. Any one that is designated to represent the Director must be a member in good standing of the NFAA.

2. Any NFAA chartered club/shop having a range will have it inspected for safety by the NFAA State Director or his designated representative every two years. When inspecting a Bowhunter range the NFAA Director will use the course layout regulations and the safety regulations that pertains to a marked or unmarked Bowhunter range.

3. To get a course approved, indoor or outdoor, the club secretary/shop manager, must contact the NFAA Director for that geographical area. The Director will provide the necessary forms and arrange for inspection. The inspection must be conducted by the Director or his designated representative. Inspection forms shall be made in triplicate, with one copy being retained by the club, one retained by the Director, and one forwarded to NFAA Headquarters.

4. The NFAA Director or his delegate shall be paid .21 per mile by a club/shop or association for travel incurred to inspect their course/range.

5. After inspection has been made, the NFAA Director or his delegate has been reimbursed for travel incurred and the completed forms have been reviewed and signed by the NFAA Director or his designated representative, they shall be forwarded to NFAA Headquarters, together with the $15.00 course approval fee. This fee covers either an outdoor range approval or an indoor range approval or a combination of both outdoor, indoor ranges, if approval is completed at the same time. The club/shop shall then be issued the appropriate course rating certificate(s).

6. If course approval is completed within a 4 month period from the effective date of charter, no fee will be required for the initial approval.

7. Course approval shall expire two years from the date of issue except when a change is made in the course, or a higher rating is desired. In each instance, a new course approval must be obtained. Procedures as outlined in subsections 3 and 4 of this section must be followed. The $15.00 course approval fee will apply.

8. The Club secretary, Association secretaries or Shop Owner/Manager, shall be notified by NFAA Headquarters four (4) months prior to expiration of their course approval. If successful inspection and approval has not been completed prior to the date of expiration, the NFAA Executive Secretary shall notify the Club Secretary, Shop Owner/Manager, the State Association Secretary and the NFAA Director that the range is no longer an approved range.

9. Course approval may be withdrawn at any time when, in the opinion of the NFAA Director, a condition falls below the standards for the rating awarded.

10. Revocation or expiration of course approval shall mean that no NFAA sanctioned events may be conducted on the course.

11. NFAA Star Rating: To receive a rating of ONE STAR, a course must meet all the requirements listed in 13 below. A one star course rating represents compliance with minimum requirements. A one star course rating is not considered satisfactory for tournament competition. No tournaments can be registered and no NFAA awards allowed for any scores shot on a one star course.

   A TWO STAR COURSE rating will require compliance with 12 and 13 below, plus the requirements of 70 BONUS points from 14 below.

   A THREE STAR COURSE rating will require compliance with 12 and 13 below, plus the requirements of 190 BONUS points from 14 below.

   A FOUR STAR COURSE rating will require compliance with 12 and 13 below, plus the added requirements of 250 BONUS points from 14 below.

   A FIVE STAR COURSE rating will be granted to any four star course provided there is at least one 14 target unit which readily lends itself to TV filming, plus the added requirements of 300 bonus points from paragraph 14 below.

   A TV range should be more than a regular roving range. It should lend itself to TV filming in a manner which would allow the cameraman to cover more than one group or target at a time. It should be at least one 14 target unit. Several recommended configurations of a TV range would include:

   1) Target shot off of a road, trail or field where the shooter shoots the target and returns to the road/trail/field.

   2) Targets set in a semi-circle, straight line or "V" configuration in a field.

   The TV portion of the range may be the complete range or, if part of a larger range (such as 14 or 28 targets) should be an integral part recognizable as such.

   Course rating of TWO, THREE, FOUR and FIVE stars makes the course eligible for tournament competition, registration, and NFAA awards. The optional Cub and Animal Round shooting positions as well as Youth shooting positions, when present, must be up to standards and become a regular requirement of the inspection program.

12. Course Layout Requirements:
   a) Distances used shall be those given in the current edition of the NFAA By-Laws.

b) All distances shall be correct and no deviation is permitted. Inspectors will check any distance in question with a tape or other means. The clubs shall tape all targets from shooting position to target butts.

c) All butts must be stable so there is no danger of tipping. If such a chance exists, then they must be braced or anchored.

d) Shooting lanes must be cleared so that the lightest bows can shoot an arrow to the target without being deflected.

e) Any person, regardless of height, must have a clear view of the full face of the target.

f) If the target is not back-stopped, one-half the target distance shall be cleared behind the butt. If back stopped, or ditched, then the area to such back-stop shall be cleared so that arrows may easily be found.

g) Area one-fourth the shooting distance shall be cleared in front of the butts.

h) Paths between targets should be clearly marked and clear enough for easy walking with no obstruction, preferably so that archers can walk two abreast. If the inspector has any difficulty finding his way, this must be remedied. Paths should preferably be at the side of the shooting lane.

i) Shooting position shall be marked with target numbers, or separate target number marker shall be present and shooting stake color uniformity; Field-White, Hunter-Red, Animal-Yellow, Cub-Black, Youth-Blue.

j) Bales or butts must not leak arrows. They shall not be reinforced with any material which will damage arrows.

k) The course shall provide appropriate rest room facilities. It is most desirable that these rest rooms should meet the minimum requirements provided by the laws of their state or townships. Such requirements can be obtained from the local county Board of Health. Due to the condition of many of these facilities, city or county Board of Health affidavits should be required. A privy law is on the books of every state of the nation. Each city, county and township also has its own requirements and very often are more strict than the state's.

13. Safety Requirements:

a) No course shall receive approval until all safety hazards, in the opinion of the inspector, are removed.

b) No paths leaving targets shall go directly behind butts.

c) If target butt is situated so that any path, target, road or building are behind at any reasonable distance, then the target must be provided with an adequate backstop.

d) Practice area must be placed so that no paths or roads pass a reasonable distance behind practice butts. Practice area shall be treated as a giant sized target, and so cleared and backed.

e) A minimum ranging from 25 feet to 50 feet must be provided between any paths or shooting lanes paralleling another shooting lane. This minimum range permits tolerance to be used, depending upon terrain, length of shot, and any distance used must preserve absolute safety.

f) Distance on either side of a target to be free from archers shall range (depending upon conditions and length of shot) from 15 to 30 degrees from the shooting position. Example: For a 40 yard target; 120 feet, tangent 30 degrees, equals 120 X (0.57735) equals 68 feet clear distance on each side of the butt (about 23 yards). (If 30 degrees is used, then factor is always 0.57735). This does not mean all clear, but only that no shooting positions, waiting areas, etc., be located in this area.

g) No target shall be situated on top of a hill where a miss becomes virtually a flight arrow.

h) SAFETY REQUIREMENTS FOR INDOOR ARCHERY RANGES.

1) All pillars or structural parts of the building, including automatic equipment, which in the eyes of the inspector would present an undue hazard shall be properly protected so as not to damage arrows and to prevent rebound to the shooting lines.

2) The area behind the target butt shall be protected so as not to damage overshot or sideshot arrows. The backstop material shall extend to a minimum height of 8 feet from the floor.

3) Bow racks and other accessories shall be of a design and position so as not to create a hazard to either equipment or personnel.

4) Automatic butts returning with arrows imbedded shall stop without creating a hazard to archers on the shooting line (between 30 to 36 inches from the line.)

5) Ranges with movable equipment shall have a warning system in the event anyone should advance to the target. Once a participant has passed the shooting line in the direction of the target, the alarm system will activate. Alarm systems may be bells or horns audible to the entire range.

6) Walk-up ranges shall be a sign posted stating that no one shall advance to the targets until an appropriate signal is given. The signal may be a switch-operated device or a manual signal. The sign shall be conspicuous from the shooting stake. No size required.

i) STANDARDS FOR INDOOR ARCHERY RANGES:

1) Target butts may be made of straw, excelsior or any other material which in the eyes of the inspector would be damaging to the arrows and yet provide suitable stoppage.

2) Butts shall not be made of material which in a short time will allow the passage of arrows.

3) At any time butts begin to allow pass-through arrows, the condition shall be corrected at once.

4) Each butt shall be large enough to carry the needed target faces for the round being shot. Each shall have sufficient backing without overlapping one another. The minimum size shall be 40" square or 48" in diameter. A deviation in minimum size will be permitted in those club-type operations where each archer is assigned his own butt providing it is large enough to fully support a 40 cm. target face.

5) There shall be at least one face (or set) on the butt for each archer shooting on that line.

6) The distance from the floor to the bottom of the butt shall be 16" minimum.

7) Ceiling to floor distance shall be a minimum of 8′6″. Each shooting lane shall be 24″ minimum.

8) Movable equipment shall be capable of stopping the target at the following distances, plus or minus 4″, 20, 15 and 10 yards. 55, 50, 40, 35, 25 and 20 feet.

j) LIGHTING FOR INDOOR ARCHERY RANGES.

1) The illumination on the targets shall be situated and placed so as not to allow the light rays to be directed toward the shooting line. At no time will direct light rays be allowed to be in view of the archers so as to disturb his/her shooting.

2) The acceptable amount of light on the targets has been established at 30 foot candles. Indoor ranges should maintain a 30 foot candle lighting illumination.

The Executive Secretary of the NFAA may allow deviations to certain rules listed herein except those listed under safety on the recommendation of the inspector. Any such deviations allowed shall be stated on the approval certificate on display.

14. Bonus Points: Clubs having more than one 14 target field range meeting the requirements of paragraphs 12 and 13 will receive additional bonus points of 5 points for 2-14's, 10 points for 3-14's, 15 points for 4-14's, and 20 points for 5-14's or more 14's.

a) GROUP I:

1) Cleanliness: If range and all facilities are clean and neat, and provided with trash disposal cans, fresh paint, etc. — 10 points.

2) If range paths are wide, cleared and mowed — 5 points.

3) Road: Passable the year round — 5 points.

4) Practice Area: Balanced to size of club, especially set-up, cared for, and provided with good shootable bales and backing — 5 points.

5) Camping Area: Specially set up and designated — 5 points.

6) Parking Area: Specially arranged so that it is more than just open area (leveled, signs, etc) — 5 points.

7) Picnic Area: A picnic area shall consist of mowed area, 1 picnic table, 1 grill or fireplace, and trash can — 10 points. (Two points for each additional picnic table and/or grill).

8) Extra directional signals, signs, etc., on range and ground — 5 points.

9) Club entrance sign — 10 points.

10) 50% of club archery membership NFAA members — 15 points.

11) 100% of club archery membership NFAA members (10 members or more) — 20 points.

12) Shooting stake color uniformity — 10 points. (Field–White; Hunter–Red; Animal–Yellow; Cub–Black; Youth–Blue).

13) Shooting lanes wide enough to accommodate 4 shooting positions, so 4 archers may shoot at one time on all targets — 20 points.

b) GROUP II:

1) Childrens play area separated by fence, etc. — 5 points. Swings, 2 points each; Sandboxes, 2 points each; Slides, 2 points each.

2) Club bulletin regularly published — 10 points.

3) Club signs and decorations at the entrance—5 points.
4) Safe drinking water—15 points.
5) PA System—5 points.
6) NFAA approved instructor—10 points.
7) Club or dealer arrangement for selling equipment—5 points.
8) Regularly scheduled club events, shoots, parties, picnics, etc. Allow one point per activity with a maximum of 10 points.
9) Regularly scheduled Junior Program (Junior Olympics, etc.)—5 points.
10) Club owned land—20 points (1 point for every two acres).
11) NFAA Liability Insurance—10 points.

c) GROUP III:
1) Kitchen facilities (building)—10 points.
2) Separate broadhead range, sand banked—20 points.
3) Bow racks on range and general area—5 points.
4) Benches and seats on range. ¼ point per target—7 points.
5) Double toilet facilities, over and above the minimum requirements: neat, clean and sanitary—10 points.
6) Paid caretaker—15 points.

d) GROUP IV:
1) Storeroom: Building for supplies—5 points.
2) Running water in facilities—5 points.
3) Club house at range—20 points.
4) Club house heated—10 points.
5) Electricity to facilities—10 points.
6) Extra shooting facilities: Short course (childrens course or practice course)—5 points.
7) Electrically lighted: Practice area—5 points; one 14 target unit—15 points; parking, picnic area, etc.—5 points.

ARTICLE XVIII. NFAA HALL OF FAME

The NFAA Archery Hall of Fame will consist of those persons bestowed the Compton Medal of Honor. Their pictures and a description of their achievements will be displayed at NFAA Headquarters. Further, a plaque listing all Medal of Merit recipients will be on display.

ARTICLE XIX. AMENDMENTS

The By-Laws may be amended or revised by a two-thirds vote of the Board of Directors, as voted at the annual meeting or by mail ballot.

ADDENDUM

I. Opinions and Interpretations

NFAA CONSTITUTION AND BY-LAWS

Interpretation and opinions from either the chairman or parliamentarian during the Annual Meeting will appear in a reference section of the minutes of the Annual Meeting.

II. National Archery Association

For information on Amateurism and the rounds shot by the NAA contact them at the address below:

NATIONAL ARCHERY ASSOCIATION
1750 EAST BOULDER STREET
COLORADO SPRINGS, CO. 80909
PHONE: 303-578-4576

Appendix III

BY-LAWS OF THE INTERNATIONAL BOWHUNTING ORGANIZATION OF THE U.S.A.

PREAMBLE

To unify Bowhunters and Bowhunter organizations at an international level for purposes designed to:

Promote, encourage and foster the sport of Bowhunting; Bowhunters' education; act as a liaison for the betterment of Bowhunters; to function as a clearing house for essential Bowhunter information; to assist and foster the conservation and preservation of wildlife; and to adhere to the basic ideal of the International Bowhunting Organization of the U.S.A. which is the UNIFICATION of BOW-HUNTERS.

ARTICLE I. NAME

The name of this organization shall be the International Bowhunting Organization of the U.S.A.

ARTICLE II. PURPOSES DEFINED

1. The corporation is organized exclusively for charitable, educational, religious, or scientific purposes within the meaning of section 501 (c) (3) of the Internal Revenue Code.

2. To unify bowhunter shoots, and bowhunter shoot scheduling; to assist youth organizations for the promotion and encouragement of the sport of bowhunting; to schedule seminars; promote and endorse bowhunting education; National Bowhunters Education Program (NBEP) and International Bowhunters Education Program (IBEP) projects.

3. Promote and participate in state and local bowhunter and hunter safety programs and provide seminars upon request pertaining to all aspects of bowhunter education.

4. To promote and encourage appointment of instructors in all levels of participation.

5. To endorse and lend assistance to "Bowhunters Who Care" and similar organizations for the purpose of fostering bowhunting.

6. To coordinate issues of Bowhunting concerns; aid and assist in the scheduling of shoots to prevent possible over scheduling; act as an information center for the purposes of providing a list of topics and possible speakers.

7. Provide coordination of activities on a voluntary basis for all bowhunter clubs—local, state, national and international—according to the purposes herein stated.

8. To lend assistance and the name of the IBO/USA to shoots and activities subject to the ideals and guidelines of the IBO/USA.

9. To lend assistance and promote the conservation and preservation of all forms of wildlife for the benefit of the environment and the sport of bowhunting.

ARTICLE III. BOARD OF DIRECTORS OF THE INTERNATIONAL BOWHUNTING ORGANIZATION OF THE U.S.A.

1. The International Bowhunting Organization of the U.S.A. shall at all times have a board of directors consisting of 13, but not less than 11, members in number. The board shall determine and elect its own board members and officers consisting of a president, vice president, and recording secretary/treasurer from its own ranks by nomination from the ranks of the board by a taking of a vote by secret ballot. The majority of all votes cast among the total board in existence shall constitute an election to the office to which nominated. Each officer shall serve for a term of two (2) years. The initial directors shall be elected to office by the delegates from the following-named clubs: Auroraland Archery Club of Aurora, Illinois; Dogwood Archery Club of Loogootee, Indiana; The Triangle Lakes Archery Club of Middletown, Ohio. Each member of the board shall serve as a member until removed for cause, he/she resigns or is deceased.

2. The board of directors shall meet on the call of the president who shall schedule no less than two meetings per year. With the annual meeting during the month of March at which time the board of directors shall nominate and elect the IBO/USA officers for the following term.

3. The president, vice president or any three board members may call a special meeting on any occasion other than the regularly scheduled board meetings by notifying each of the board members at least ten days prior to such a meeting setting forth the purpose of the meeting, the date, time and place of such meeting.

4. A special meeting may be called by the president or vice president, by phone or teleconferencing, establishing a contact with each of the members of the board provided that the vote of the board be verified by mail or at the next meeting of the board.

5. Each board member must attend two regular meetings per year. Any director or officer who fails to attend two meetings per year may be dismissed by the board of directors, for cause.

6. Except as otherwise stated herein, each director and officer shall have one vote on any matter before the board.

ARTICLE IV. POWERS AND DUTIES
OF THE BOARD OF DIRECTORS

1. The board of directors shall direct all of the activities, policies and properties of the IBO/USA.

2. The board of directors shall determine all policies and matters as to membership and dues.

3. All matters not provided for in the bylaws shall be determined by the board of directors by an appropriate working or operating rule.

4. The board shall pass its own operating or working rules and such rules shall have the same force and effect as if it were part of the bylaws. Quorum shall consist of a majority of all existing board members. A majority vote shall be required to enact, amend, or rescind a working rule.

5. The board of directors shall determine the rules, regulations, and the site of each of the National Bowhunter Shoots comprising the "TRIPLE CROWN" National Championship shoot. These shoots shall be protected with a 400 mile radius.

6. The board shall conduct such other business which shall properly come before it.

7. Any board member or officer may request that the "ROBERTS RULES OF ORDER" be applicable in any matter which is not governed by these bylaws or any working or operating rule duly passed by the board of directors. The matter before the board shall then be handled in accordance with "ROBERTS RULES OF ORDER".

8. Except as otherwise set forth herein, majority of the members of the board of directors shall constitute a quorum for the transaction of business at any meeting of the board, provided that if less than a quorum of the directors are present at said meeting, a majority of the directors present may adjourn the meeting to another time without further notice.

9. A quorum of the Board of Directors in all instances shall be determined from the Directors duly elected or appointed of record.

10. The act of a majority of the directors present at a meeting at which a quorum is present shall be the act of the board of directors, unless the act of a greater number is required by statute, these bylaws or the articles of incorporation.

11. Any vacancy occurring in the board of directors and any directorship to be filled by reason of an increase in the number of directors may be filled by the board of directors.

12. The board of directors may designate any place as the place of meeting for any annual meeting or for any special or regular meeting called by the board of directors.

13. Any officer elected or appointed by the board of directors may be removed by the board of directors whenever, in its judgment, the best interest of the IBO/USA would be served thereby.

14. Directors shall not receive any stated salaries for their services, but by resolution of the board of directors, expenses for attendance, if any, may be allowed for each regular or special meeting of the board, provided that nothing herein contained shall be construed to preclude any director from serving the IBO/USA in any other capacity and receiving reasonable compensation thereof.

15. The board of directors may retain an accountant, a public relations consultant, and legal counsel to assist in the operation of the IBO/USA. The board of directors may appoint, retain or hire such personnel as are deemed necessary by the board to aid in the operation of the IBO/USA.

16. The directors shall be authorized and empowered to pay reasonable compensation for services rendered and to make payments and distribution in furtherance of the purposes set forth above.

17. None of the directors shall be required to furnish any bond or surety. None of them shall be responsible or liable for the acts or omissions of any other of the directors or of a predecessor or of a custodian, agent, depositary or councel selected with reasonable care.

18. A written resignation from the board may be accepted in behalf of the Board by any officer who shall then report of such resignation at the next scheduled Board Meeting. Acceptance shall be in writing and the resignation shall be effective as of the date of that letter. Nothing here in shall bind any officer to accept a resignation prior to its presentation to the full board for consideration.

ARTICLE V. DUTIES OF OFFICERS/ BUSINESS OFFICE MANAGER

1. The president shall be the chief executive officer whose duty is to preside at all meetings and to perform such other duties as ordinarily pertain to this office.

2. The vice president shall assume the duties of the president, when absent, and shall serve as the assistant executive officer performing such duties as ordinarily pertain to the office of vice president.

3. The recording secretary shall keep the minutes of each meeting and shall perform such duties as assigned by the president, vice-president or as required by the board of directors.

4. The Business Office Manager (appointed position) shall be responsible for all correspondence as required by the board and shall keep a list of officers, board members and general membership and in the absence of the recording secretary shall assume his/her duties. The Business Office Manager shall also keep an accurate record of monies received and receipts payable. The Business Office Manager shall also perform such duties as shall be assigned by the president or are required by the board of directors.

ARTICLE VI. REMOVAL OF BOARD MEMBERS AND OFFICERS

No board member or officer can be removed unless there be a quorum of two-thirds board members and there be an affirmative two-thirds vote for removal. A vote to remove an officer from his office shall not constitute his removal as a director unless specifically raised, in which event a separate vote shall be taken on both the removal as officer and as a director, except a removal of any director shall constitute an automatic removal of each such director as an officer if serving in the capacity of an officer without any additional vote.

The removal of any appointed position is done by a two-thirds vote for removal by a quorum of the board of directors.

ARTICLE VII. MEMBERSHIP
Generally

A. The board of directors may determine from time to time the amount of the initiation fee, if any, and annual dues payable to the IBO/USA by members of each class; the nature, extent, suitability, and content of any advertising sponsored or provided by the IBO/USA or in any periodical, magazine, newsletter or other papers sponsored by or under the control of the IBO/USA for the benefit of any member.

B. There shall be six classes of membership: individual, club, associations, Manufacture-sponsor, Dealer-sponsor and charter/founding sponsor.

C. Each club accepted into membership will receive a membership certificate and a copy of the bylaws.

D. Each sustaining sponsor will receive a certificate of support and a copy of the bylaws.

E. Each charter/founding sponsor will receive a certificate for framing, copy of the bylaws, and advertising with the IBO/USA during the existence if the IBO/USA in accordance with their agreement.

F. All memberships shall be for a term of one year subject to renewal upon payment of dues except the charter/founding sponsor membership.

G. The board may provide any additional membership benefits as it deems appropriate.

H. Membership in the IBO/USA is not transferable or assignable.

I. No member shall have any voting rights. All voting rights are vested solely in the directors.

Causes for Suspension

A. Game law violations (with suspension of hunting license).

B. Any conviction of a game law offense.

C. Unsportsman like conduct, whether such conduct is actionable at law or not. All members must adhere to the rules of fair chase and in the agreement with the ideals of the International Bowhunting Organization of the U.S.A.

Penalties

A. Violator or offender will be suspended or expelled from the IBO/USA membership for a period up to five years upon finding of proper cause for suspension by the board.

B. Any reoccurrence of violations shall be grounds for permanent expulsion.

C. Any penalties, suspensions or expulsions for cause shall be by a majority vote of the board at any regular or special meeting after an appropriate hearing which shall be scheduled at any regular or special meeting at which time the member subject to the penalty may appear on his own behalf.

ARTICLE VIII. CHANGES AND AMENDMENTS TO THE BYLAWS

The power to alter, amend, or repeal the bylaws or adopt a new bylaw shall be vested in the board of directors unless otherwise provided in the articles of incorporation or the bylaws. Such action may be taken at a regular or special meeting for which written notice shall be given. The bylaws may contain any provisions for the regular and management of the affairs of the IBO/USA not inconsistent with law or the IBO/USA bylaws.

The bylaws may be amended by a resolution from any board member setting forth such amendment at any meeting of the board. The presiding officer thereafter shall set the matter for a vote at a subsequent board meeting which shall not be less than two weeks from the date that the resolution is made.

The Business Office Manager shall send a copy of the resolution to each board member at least one week prior to the date on which the amendment shall be presented to the board for a vote. The quorum and vote on any resolution to amend the bylaws shall be the same as set forth herein at Article IV., paragraph 4.

ARTICLE IX. COMMITTEES

1. One or more committees may be designated by the president by a resolution to the board. The resolution to form a committee shall be adopted by a majority of the directors present at a meeting at which a quorum is present.

2. The president shall appoint the chairman of any committee from the members of the board. The president may request that any member of someone from the duly constituted advisory staff to the board serve as a committee member.

3. Each committee may adopt rules for its own government not inconsistent with these bylaws or with rules adopted by the board of directors.

ARTICLE X. INDEMNIFICATION OF OFFICERS, EMPLOYEES AND AGENTS – INSURANCE

The IBO/USA may indemnify any person who was or is a party or is threatened to be made a party, to any threatened, pending or completed action, suit or proceeding, whether civil, criminal, administrative or investigative (other than an action by or in the right of the IBO/USA) by reason of the fact that he is or was a director, officer, employee or agent of the IBO/USA, against expenses (including attorneys fees), judgements, fines and amounts paid in settlement actually and reasonably incurred by him in connection with such action, suit or proceeding, if he acted in good faith and in a manner he reasonably believed to be in, or not opposed to, the best interests of the IBO/USA, and, with respect to any criminal action or proceeding, had no reasonable cause to believe his conduct unlawful. The termination of any action, suit or proceeding by judgement, order, settlement, conviction, or upon a plea of nolo contendere or its equivalent, shall not, of itself, create a presumption that the person did not act in good faith and in a matter which he reasonably believed to be in or not opposed to the best interests of the IBO/USA, and, with respect to any criminal action or proceeding, had reasonable cause to believe that his conduct was unlawful.

The IBO/USA may indemnify any person who was or is a party or is threatened to be made a party, to any threatened, pending or completed action or suit by or in the right of the IBO/USA to procure a judgement in its favor by reason of the fact that he is or was a director, officer, employee or agent of the IBO/USA against expenses (including attorney's fees) actually and reasonably incurred by him in connection with the defense or settlement of such action or suit, if he acted in good faith and in a manner he reasonably believed to be in or not opposed to the best interest of the IBO/USA, and except that no indemnification shall be made in respect of any claim, issue or matter as to which such person shall have been adjudged to be liable for negligence or misconduct in the performance of his/her duty to the IBO/USA, unless, and only to the extent that the court in which such action or suit was brought shall determine upon application that, despite the adjudication of liability, but in the view of all the circumstances of the case, such person is fairly and reasonably entitled to indemnity for such expense as the court shall deem proper.

Any indemnification pursuant to the above (unless ordered by a court) shall be made by the IBO/USA only as authorized in the specific case, upon a determination that indemnification of the director, officer, employee or agent is proper in the circumstances because he has met the applicable standard of conduct set forth in above. Such determination shall be made (1) by the board of directors by a majority vote of a quorum consisting of directors who were not parties to such action, suit or proceeding, or (2) if such a quorum is not obtainable or, even if obtainable, a quorum of disinterested directors so directs, by legal council in a written opinion.

Expenses incurred in defending a civil or criminal action, suit or proceeding may be paid to the IBO/USA in advance of the final disposition of such action, suit or proceeding, as authorized by the board of directors in the specific case, upon receipt of an undertaking by or on behalf of the director, officer, employee or agent to repay such amount, unless it shall ultimately be determined that he is entitled to be indemnified by the IBO/USA as authorized in this section.

Any indemnification provided by this Section shall not be deemed exclusive of any other rights to which those seeking indemnification may be entitled under any bylaw, agreement, vote of members or disinterested directors, or otherwise, both as to action in his official capacity and as to action in another capacity while holding such office, and shall continue as to a person who has ceased to be a director, officer, employee or agent, and shall inure to the benefit of the heirs, executors and administrators of such a person.

The IBO/USA may purchase and maintain insurance on behalf of any person who is or was a director, officer, employee or agent of the IBO/USA, against any liability asserted against him and incurred by him in any such capacity or arising out of his status as such, whether or not the IBO/USA would have the power to indemnify him against such liability under the provisions of the section.

ARTICLE XI. DISSOLUTION CLAUSE

Upon the dissolution of the corporation, the Board of Directors shall, after paying or making provisions for the payment of all the liabilities of the corporation, dispose of all the assets of the corporation exclusively for the purposes of the corporation in such manner, or to such organization or organizations organized and operated exclusively for charitable, educational, religious, or scientific purposes as shall at the time qualify as an exempt organization or organizations under section 501 (c) (3) of the Internal Revenue code of 1986 (or the corresponding provision of any future United States Internal Revenue Law), as the Board of Directors shall determine. Any such assets not so disposed of shall be disposed of by the Court of Common Pleas of the county in which the principle office of the corporation is then located, exclusively for such purposes or to such organization or organizations, as said court shall determine, which are organized exclusively for such purposes.

ARTICLE XII. CONSTITUTION OF THE INTERNATIONAL BOWHUNTING ORGANIZATION OF THE U.S.A.

The Articles of Incorporation are hereby included and made a part of the Bylaws. The Bylaws and the Articles of Incorporation shall constitute the Constitution of the International Bowhunting Organization of the U.S.A. and will be the governing document of the International Bowhunting Organization of the U.S.A.

IBO/USA CLASSES DEFINED

ALL MALE, FEMALE AND YOUTH SHOOTERS

MAXIMUM OF 80 POUND PEAK BOW WEIGHT IN ALL MALE CLASSES, 60 POUNDS IN ALL YOUTH & FEMALE CLASSES, 40 POUNDS IN CUB CLASS. Must shoot an arrow weighing at least 5 grains per pound of bow peak weight. Sights, stabilizers and V-Bars, if used, must not extend more than 12″ from the forward edge of the bow nearest the point of attachment. Overdraws are legal in all classes. There is no limit to the number of pins on the sight.

Male Compound Aided

A Compound Bow with fixed pins. Must be shot with glove, finger tab or bare fingers.

Female Aided

A Compound, recurve or long bow with fixed pins. Must be shot with glove, finger or tab or bare fingers.

Male Compound Unaided

A Compound Bow with no sighting device. A rest and plunger are all that may reside within the sight window. There will be NO markings on the bow or on the Bow String that could be construed as sighting marks. Must be shot with glove, finger tab or bare fingers.

Female Unaided

A Compound, recurve or long bow with no sighting device. A rest and plunger are all that may reside within the sight window. There will be NO markings on the bow or on the Bow String that could be construed as sighting marks. Must be shot with glove, finger tab or bare fingers.

Male and Female Bowhunter Release

A Compound, recurve or long bow with or without a sight. If a sight is used, it will have fixed pins. Must be shot with some type of release aid.

Male and Female Bowhunter Open

A Compound, recurve or long bow with a movable sight, scope or laser sight. Any type of release aid, glove, finger tab or bare fingers may be used.

Male Recurve Aided

A recurve or long bow with fixed pins. Must be shot with glove, finger tab or bare fingers.

MALE RECURVE UNAIDED

A recurve or long bow with no sighting device. A rest and plunger are all that may reside within the sight window. There will be NO markings on the bow or on the bow string that could be construed as sighting marks. Must be shot with glove, finger tab or bare fingers.

YOUTH AIDED – AGES 13 THROUGH 17 YEARS OF AGE

A bow with fixed pins, movable sight or scope. Must be shot with a glove, finger tab or bare fingers.

YOUTH RELEASE – AGES 13 THROUGH 17 YEARS OF AGE

A bow with fixed pins, moveable sight or scope. Must be shot with some type of release aid.

YOUTH UNAIDED – AGES 13 THROUGH 17 YEARS OF AGE

A bow with no sighting device. A rest and plunger are all that may reside within the sight window. There will be NO markings on the bow or on the bow string that could be construed as sighting marks. Must be shot with glove, finger tab or bare fingers.

CUBS – THROUGH 12 YEARS OF AGE

May shoot any type of equipment or styles described above.

ADDITIONAL INFORMATION

Clickers – fine line type sights – and levels are permissible.

Fixed pins are defined as pins which are set at a predetermined distance and are NOT ALLOWED to be moved while on the range.

String walkers with marks on the string will be considered as aided. NO marking on tab or glove.

All unaided classes will be additionally defined as a string with nothing other than a knocking point.

If you have any questions on your equipment, ask before you register and start out on the range.

CHECK RULES FOR POSSIBLE CHANGES
Protests

ALL protests to the PROTEST COMMITTEE must be in writing on the form provided with a $50.00 fee which will be returned if the protest is upheld. The PROTEST COMMITTEE may rule on any problems or items not specifically covered. All protests are to be filed with REGISTRATION.

ALL DECISIONS WILL BE FINAL UNLESS A WRITTEN APPEAL IS RECEIVED BY THE IBO/USA AT THEIR BUSINESS OFFICE WITHIN FIVE DAYS.

INTERNATIONAL BOWHUNTING ORGANIZATION of the USA
P.O. BOX 1349
MADISONVILLE, KY. 42431